MEDICINE RIVER

MEDICINE RIVER

A STORY OF SURVIVAL
AND THE LEGACY OF INDIAN
BOARDING SCHOOLS

MARY ANNETTE PEMBER

PANTHEON BOOKS

NEW YORK

FIRST HARDCOVER EDITION PUBLISHED BY PANTHEON BOOKS 2025

Published by Pantheon Books, a division of Penguin Random House LLC, 1745 Broadway, New York, NY 10019.

Pantheon Books and the colophon are registered trademarks of Penguin Random House LLC.

Library of Congress Cataloging-in-Publication Data
Names: Pember, Mary Annette, author.
Title: Medicine River : a story of survival and the legacy of Indian boarding schools / Mary Annette Pember.
Description: First edition. | New York : Pantheon Books, 2025. | Includes bibliographical references and index. | Identifiers: LCCN 2024031654 (print) | LCCN 2024031655 (ebook) | ISBN 9780553387315 (hardcover) | ISBN 9780593470466 (trade paperback) | ISBN 9780553387322 (ebook)
Subjects: LCSH: Pember, Bernice Rabideaux, 1925–2011. | Pember, Mary Annette—Family. | Robidou family. | St. Mary's Indian Boarding School (Odanah, Wis.)—Biography. | Ojibwa women—Biography. | Off-reservation boarding schools—Social aspects—United States. | Indian children—Abuse of—United States. | Ojibwa Indians—Social conditions— 20th century. | Bad River Reservation (Wis.)—Biography. | Odanah (Wis.)—Biography.
Classification: LCC E99.C6 P463 2025 (print) | LCC E99.C6 (ebook) | DDC 977.004/97333092 [B]—dc23/eng/20240802
LC record available at https://lccn.loc.gov/2024031654
LC ebook record available at https://lccn.loc.gov/2024031655

penguinrandomhouse.com | pantheonbooks.com

Printed in the United States of America

2 4 6 8 9 7 5 3

The authorized representative in the EU for product safety and compliance is Penguin Random House Ireland, Morrison Chambers, 32 Nassau Street, Dublin D02 YH68, Ireland, https://eu-contact.penguin.ie.

To Zagima, Cele, and John

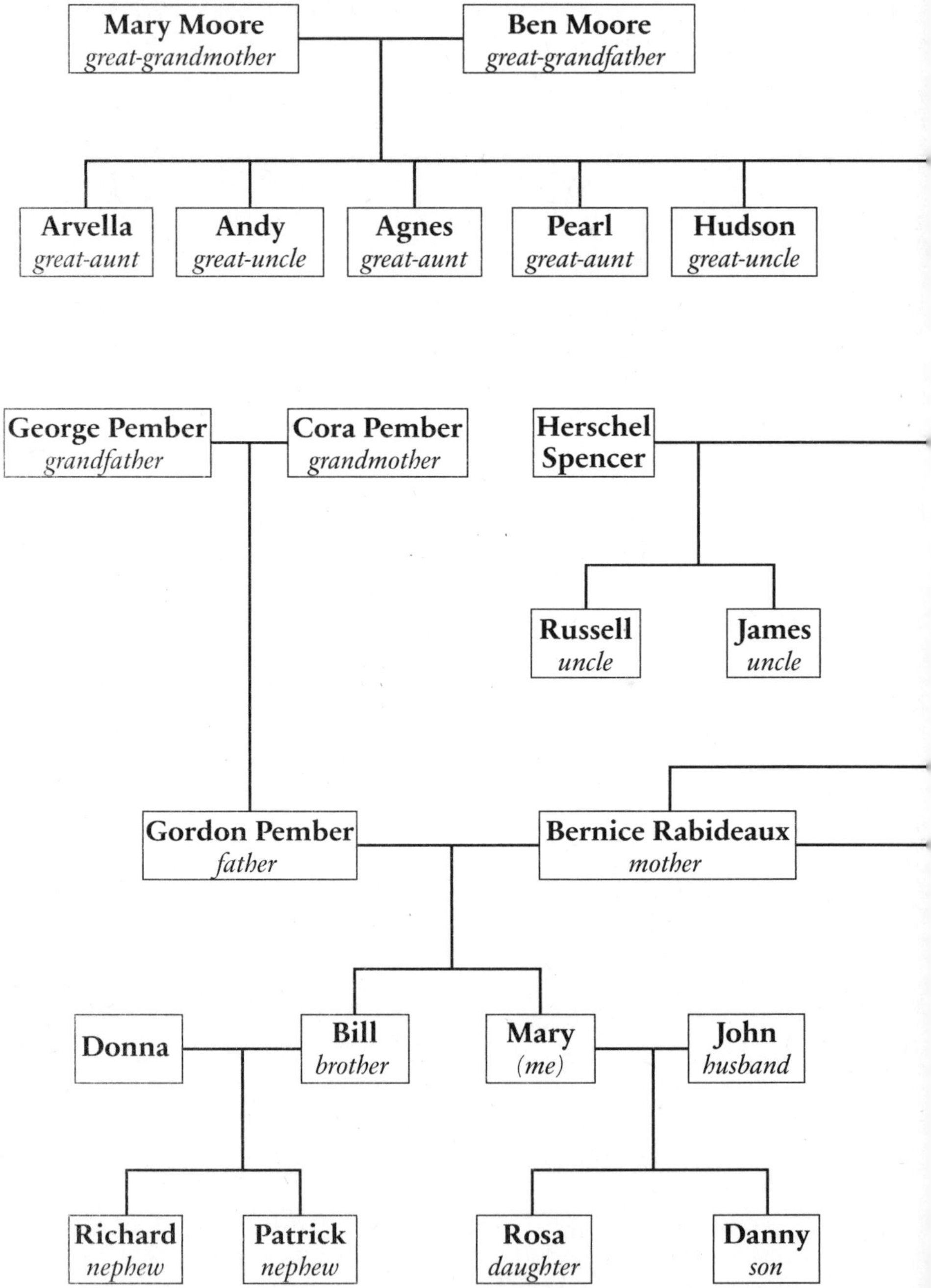

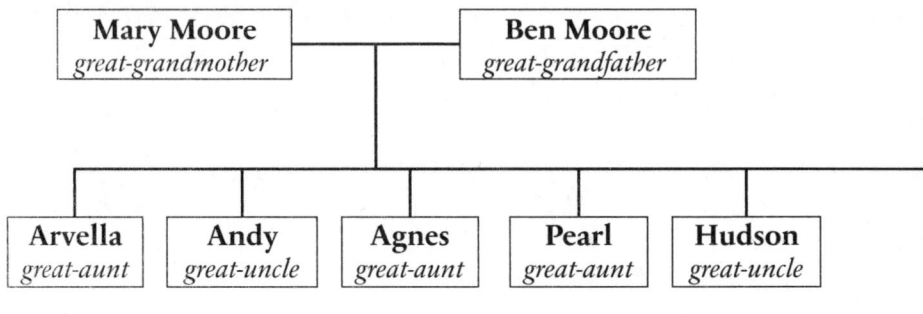

| Mary Moore | | Ben Moore |
| *great-grandmother* | | *great-grandfather* |

| Arvella | Andy | Agnes | Pearl | Hudson |
| *great-aunt* | *great-uncle* | *great-aunt* | *great-aunt* | *great-uncle* |

| George Pember | Cora Pember | Herschel Spencer |
| *grandfather* | *grandmother* | |

| Russell | James |
| *uncle* | *uncle* |

| Gordon Pember | Bernice Rabideaux |
| *father* | *mother* |

| Donna | Bill | Mary | John |
| | *brother* | *(me)* | *husband* |

| Richard | Patrick | Rosa | Danny |
| *nephew* | *nephew* | *daughter* | *son* |

Family Tree

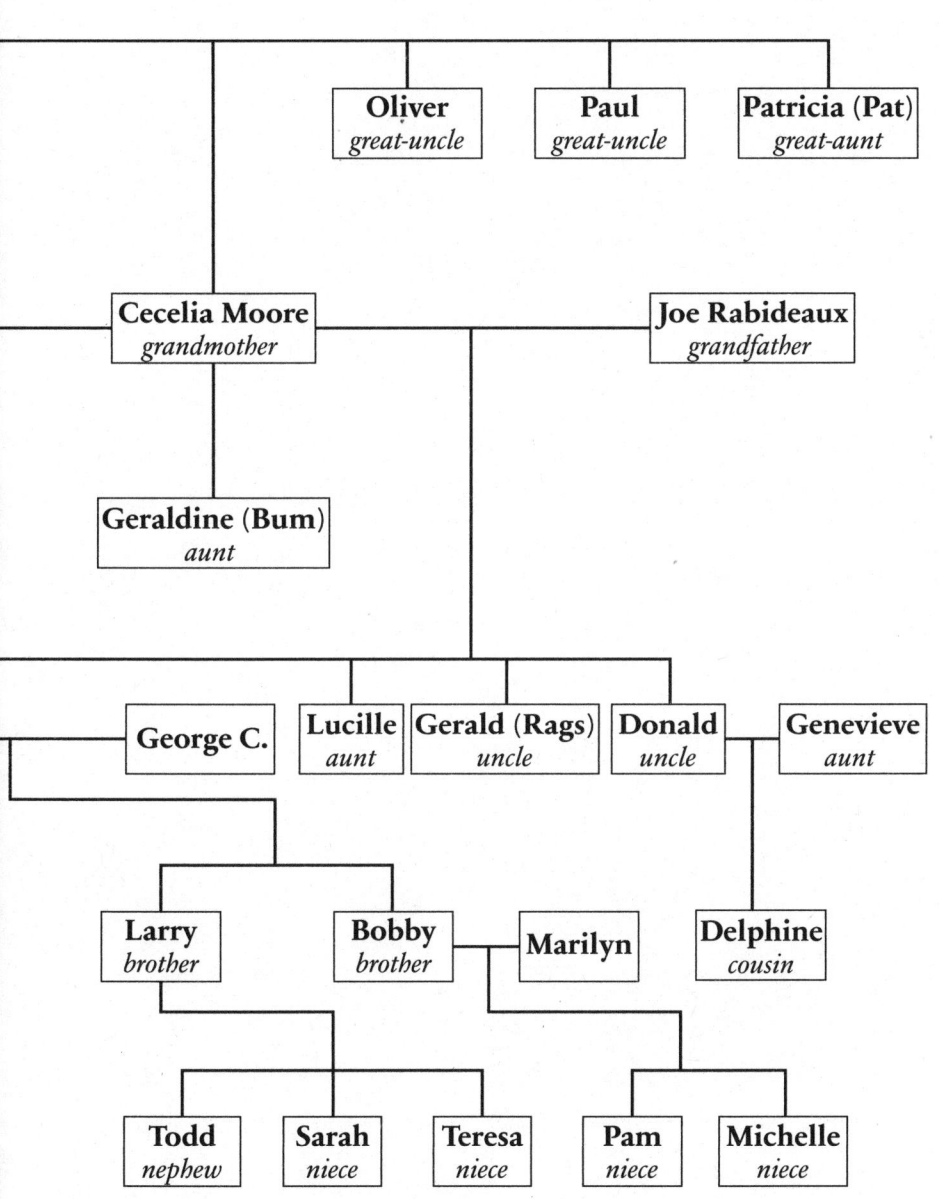

Oliver *great-uncle*	**Paul** *great-uncle*	**Patricia (Pat)** *great-aunt*

Cecelia Moore
grandmother

Joe Rabideaux
grandfather

Geraldine (Bum)
aunt

George C.

Lucille
aunt

Gerald (Rags)
uncle

Donald
uncle

Genevieve
aunt

Larry
brother

Bobby
brother

Marilyn

Delphine
cousin

Todd
nephew

Sarah
niece

Teresa
niece

Pam
niece

Michelle
niece

CONTENTS

MEDICINE RIVER

My mother's migraines hold me prisoner for much of my childhood.

It's early summer and the air is torpid and hot. Janesville, Wisconsin, hot. The days of my youth predated home air-conditioning in the Midwest, especially for working-class families like mine. Our little frame house, however, is dark and cool, shaded by elms, ringed with gardens of shadow-loving lilies of the valley. My mother's favorite flower.

It is 1961 and I am four years old. My mother and I are alone in the house, as we often are during the day. My father, Gordon, is at work and my elder brothers, Larry and Bill, are at school. I am the youngest; a ten-year gap separates me from my brothers, setting me apart from the family somehow. I am in my usual spot under the kitchen table, where I can safely watch and listen to my mother. I press my black crayon on the underside of the table and draw. My way of ordering the chaos. My black and russet dachshund, Hansy, keeps watch with me as we try to think of what to do. Above all we must be quiet. Hansy's long toenails click as he walks across the linoleum floor. *Be quiet. Mama doesn't feel good,* I hiss at him. He sits down next to me again, his dog brows knit in embarrassment.

I crawl from under the table and find my red wooden step stool and use it to reach the kitchen countertop. I make toast, find the aspirin bottle, and fill a glass with water. I am very careful; I bring it all into her dark bedroom without spilling anything.

I creep to the living room quietly and climb up on the back of the sofa, gathering up all my mother's glass and porcelain figurines, and retreat into the forest of chrome kitchen table legs. I line up the Elf, the Santa, the Blond Girl in the Pink Hoop Skirt, and the Deer Mother with her twin fawns attached to her throat by a golden chain. The twin fawns' bodies are badly chipped: victims of my kitchen theater.

I whisper detailed instructions to my little actors. After a while Mama calls out for me in a low voice, *Mary.*

I go to the darkened bedroom where Mama lies on the bed. The bedspread, stiff from the clothesline, is fragrant with fresh air and my mother's scent. She spends hours washing the laundry—*White! White!*—as the sisters taught her, rushing up and down the cellar steps with baskets of heavy, wet sheets. Lying on the bed next to her in the dim light, I secretly look at her face. Normally her facial muscles are constantly at work arranging her face in an effort to guard against scrutiny. Mama hates being looked at, especially by me, and angrily shakes her head when she catches my eyes. She is pretty, but her dark skin has an unhealthy muddy cast caused by childhood years of anemia. But I love her, and I think she is beautiful. The well created by her clavicle, womanly, dark, mysterious. She allows me to freely examine her hands, which are seldom at rest. But here in bed she submits limply as I gaze at her long, graceful fingers and nails. Turning them over, I inspect her tiny wedding band with the orange blossom pattern now nearly worn away.

I am four. I am her helper. Her crutch. Her whipping post. I am her secret confessor and her most trusted coconspirator. I love her terribly. But I am wary of her. Constantly on guard against her fickle moods, I am hungry for her attention and delighted by her trust; her stories thrill me and fill me with fear and dread. She pours the Sister School stories into me as I lie next to her, afraid to move.

We were always hungry, she says.

Sister Catherine beat her for stealing an apple from the cellar where the nuns stored food for themselves and the students. Hunger is a constant theme of the stories she tells. A stolen apple or gulp of cream from the milking parlor earned a brutal beating. Although she knew she'd be punished, my mother couldn't resist the apple. Or the cream. She savored both the apple's taste and the retelling of her beating, during which she refused to shed a tear.

But it was Sister Catherine's shaming words, delivered as though from God himself, that seem to have cut deeper than any strap. According to Sister Catherine's God, Indians were dirty, lazy, barely human creatures unfit to raise their own children. She believed her God had sent her to save those children—soul by soul, brick by civilized brick—and make them into his servants, whether they liked it or not.

Sister Catherine's belittling phrase "dirty Indian" lingered in my mother's ears, which she eventually poured into mine: a stain that never yielded completely to her lifetime of obsessive scrubbing and cleaning. It was ingrained too deeply.

How I loved her terrible stories. I grew to thrive on the trauma of it all. They were fairy tales in which good always triumphed over evil. Like Cinderella, who escaped an evil stepmother and her daughters, my mother escaped a jealous mother and evil nuns of her youth. In my mother's stories, she was the fearless heroine who battled people and nameless forces that wanted to keep her poor and undeserving of a happy life. And as in all fairy tales, the happy endings were leavened with horror. Fairy tales require both. They also require a teller and a listener.

Somehow I knew these stories were fantasies—with only shreds of truth—invented to protect not only me but also her own mind. Her job was to tell them. Mine was to listen and believe.

Like thousands of other Native American children, my mother, Bernice Rabideaux, was sent to an Indian boarding school. For 150 years, tens of thousands of Native children were forced or coerced to attend a vast network of nearly five hundred boarding schools in the United States. Some of the schools were operated by the federal government, some by Christian missionaries. The federal government also supported more than a thousand additional day schools, stand-alone dormitories, orphanages, and asylums dedicated to the "education" of Native children. These schools and institutions were located across thirty-seven states or territories, including Alaska and Hawaii.

Although a few schools, such as the Carlisle Indian Industrial School in Pennsylvania, one of the first federal schools, were located in eastern and southern states, the majority were built in the Great Lakes region and areas west of the Mississippi. Oklahoma contained seventy-six, the highest number, followed by Arizona with forty-seven and New Mexico with forty-three schools. A large proportion of the cost for both federal and Christian schools came from Indian trust and treaty funds in addition to federal appropriations. We were forced into schools and, adding to that injury, forced to pay for them. We literally funded our own abuse. The government directly provided allotted Indian lands to many Christian denominations for schools, some of which are still held by churches today. From the first European contact in the Americas, Christian missionaries played a foundational role in tying Indigenous conversion to Christianity as an essential element of "civilization by assimilation" through the use of violent education. Missionaries went on to play essential roles in creating federal Indian policies.

From the very beginning, missionaries, fueled and validated by the doctrine of discovery, the Great Commission, and the desire for power, were agents of empire. In 1493, Pope Alexander VI issued one of several papal bulls or laws setting forth the doctrine, assigning Spain the exclusive right to acquire lands in the New World. According to the bulls, any land not inhabited by Christians was available for discovery, occupation, and exploitation by Christians.

Indigenous or pagan people living on the land could be forced to convert to Christianity under penalty of death. Christian missionaries became agents of empire intentionally or by using God-speak to sanction the taking of lands and then in the name of Christian education by championing the practice of separating kids from parents, targeting and demonizing Indigenous families and culture as barriers to civilization. "Many [families] refuse all aid towards Christianizing and civilizing their children," wrote the Catholic priest Martin Marty in 1889. "Enforced attendance at school can alone exempt the children from these debasing influences."

Not only Catholics but other denominations joined the efforts, seizing an opportunity to gain power and influence, both materially and spiritually, by carrying out God's and the church's directives as means to further one's path to heaven by separating Native people from the land and from themselves and from their children. A divine and temporal mission, Christian humanitarianism and spirituality merged with capitalism, carrying saving the Indians into the future, one dominated by a distinctly European worldview: individualism over community, personal growth and enrichment over the family and community. To those ends, eventually boarding school curricula focused primarily on manual labor and vocational skills related to agriculture, construction, housekeeping, and other labor-intensive pursuits. Rules were strict and often enforced through physical punishment including flogging, whipping, confinement, and starvation. Today, approximately ninety of the more than four hundred original schools still operate as educational facilities for Native Americans. Some still board Indians, but not all receive federal funding. In a substantial change to past policies, tribal leaders are directly involved in the administration of most of these facilities. But in many ways, boarding schools are still the child-care option of last choice for Indian families. The messaging that we are incapable of raising our own children in the modern world lives on.

Compelling Indian families to send their children to boarding schools has long been part of the federal government's systematic assimilation and civilization policies intended to dispossess Indigenous peoples of their lands and resources so white people can settle and acquire our lands. And while that may sound like an oversimplification, it's really not. Beginning with President George Washington in the 1780s and 1790s, federal Indian education policy was part of federal land policy. In his 1792 speech to the Five Nations delegation at Philadelphia, Washington promised an annual sum of $1,500 to pay for livestock, agricultural implements, and education to "impart such blessings of civilization as may at present suit your condition and give you further desires to improve your happiness," he said. "Let it be spread abroad among all your villages and throughout your land that the United States are desirous, not only of a general peace with all the Indian tribes, but of being their friends and protectors." The Indian's "lack of civilization" was the justification used for taking his lands. Benjamin Franklin observed that it was necessary to "extirpate the savage in order to make room for cultivators of the earth." Education, it was reasoned, would lead to civilization and a change in Indian land economy from hunters and gatherers who required large swaths of land into farmers who relied on far smaller pieces of land to feed themselves.

Much later, Senator Henry Dawes mused that the goal of civilization and of the act of Congress he authored was for Indians to "wear civilized clothes ... cultivate the ground, live in houses, ride in Studebaker wagons, send children to school, drink whiskey [and] own property." Not necessarily in that order. Thomas Hart Benton, a well-known attorney and political leader in the early nineteenth century and later senator from Missouri, claimed that whites must usurp Indians because "whites used the land according to the intentions of the Creator." Thomas Jefferson described the settlement of America by whites as inevitable progress and divine fate:

> Let a philosophic observer commence a journey from the savages of the Rocky Mountains eastwardly towards our seacoast. These he would observe in the earliest stage of association living under no law but that of nature, subsisting and covering themselves with the flesh and the skins of beasts. He would next find those [white settlers] on our frontiers in the pastoral state, raising domestic animals to supply the defects of hunting. And so, in his progress he would meet the gradual shades of improving man until he would reach his, as yet, most improved state in our seacoast towns. This, in fact, is equivalent to a survey, in time, of the progress of man from the infancy of creation to the present day.

In 1819, Congress enacted the Civilization Fund Act to create schools whose mandate was to instruct Indians in the habits of civilized life, including abandoning nomadic hunting and gathering ways in favor of sedentary farming or wage labor. This was a deep irony: by the turn of the nineteenth century nearly all Native peoples east of the Mississippi (including tribes such as the Cherokee, Delaware, Seneca, and Mohawk) were sedentary, village-dwelling, agrarian communities. Families were coerced into sending their children to schools under threat of incarceration, starvation, and the withholding of treaty annuities. In 1891, Congress authorized the Commissioner of Indian Affairs "to make and enforce by proper means such rules and regulations as will secure the attendance of Indian children of suitable age and health at schools established and maintained for their benefit." It was understood that Indian agents were justified in using force to ensure families obeyed. Later, in 1893, the Fifty-Second Congress added additional incentives: "The Secretary of the Interior, may in his discretion, establish such regulations as will prevent the issuing of rations or the furnishing of subsistence either in money or in kind to the head of any Indian family for or on account of any Indian child or children between the ages of eight and twenty-one years who shall not have attended school during the preceding year in accordance with such regulations."

As Indian lands dwindled, families could no longer count on traditional hunting and gathering ways to feed themselves. Many came to rely on distribution of government rations to stave off starvation. Children as young as four years old were sometimes transported thousands of miles away from their families to the schools, often for years at a time. Families resisted these policies, either through outright refusal or by hiding their children from government authorities. At nine years old the Métis writer D'Arcy McNickle ran away from the train station when he was scheduled to travel from his home on the Flathead Reservation in Montana to Chemawa Indian boarding school in Oregon. His parents were charged with kidnapping for failing to send McNickle to school. Charges against them were eventually dropped, and the boy was sent to Chemawa in 1914.

McNickle later described his boarding school experience as the government's effort to erase "all traits of Indian culture." Students were forbidden to speak their traditional languages at the schools and forced to learn English. Sometimes teachers would wash students' mouths out with lye soap or deprive them of food for speaking their Native languages. "The kids would end up with the inside of their mouths raw," reported a student at an Indian School in Oklahoma.

They were deprived of their cultural ways, spirituality, and dress while Christianity and white social and cultural norms were shoved into the vacuum. In a letter to a former student of Fort Mojave boarding school, the superintendent, Samuel M. McCowan, wrote, "I can remember when I first took you into the Ft. Mojave school and what a time I had in cutting your hair for the first time. I can see now all the old Mojave women standing around crying, while you covered your long hair with your arms and told me that I wouldn't dare to cut that hair off.... I compelled you to have your hair cut off, not because of any objections to the long hair in itself, but merely because the long hair was a symbol of savagery." One of the first orders of business at boarding school was exchanging children's traditional names for names in English. White teachers often claimed literal English translations were embarrassing or too difficult to pronounce. So they simply created new American names for the students. Initially students rebelled but soon grew embarrassed by their traditional Indian names. A student at Flandreau Indian School asked that her name, Lydia Blowsnake, be changed to Alice Carley. She received checks from the Indian agent at her reservation with the name Lydia Blowsnake, which she found embarrassing. She wrote to the agent, "I just hate to get the checks cause they make fun of my name and I don't want them to know that's my name." The intent of the Indian school program was to assimilate Native Americans into white mainstream culture through the disruption of family ties. Both children and their families suffered during the prolonged separation; children wrote letters to family and school leaders begging to return home. And families begged authorities to allow children to return home due to homesickness or to see a dying parent before it was too late. When a father wrote to Flandreau asking that his teenage daughter Mattie be allowed to return home because her mother was dying from tuberculosis, the superintendent denied the request. "It would be pretty bad for her school interests for Mattie to leave now." Mrs. Isabella Strong of the Red Lake Reservation in Minnesota also wrote a letter to the superintendent of Flandreau asking for her daughter Claudia's return. Claudia was "terribly homesick," according to Mrs. Strong. "It seems it would be easier to get her out of prison than out of your school," she wrote. Government and church leaders promoted this plan of family separation as a necessary, enlightened method to address the country's Indian problem. Because it was framed as a humane alternative to outright extermination, little thought was given to the generational fallout and trauma ignited by these policies. Quite simply: boarding schools were intended to destroy Indian families in order to destroy tribes to free up land for white settlement and exploitation.

Conditions at the schools were often substandard. Food was inadequate and poor; even very young children were dangerously overworked. The heyday of the off-reservation federal boarding school system, from approximately 1879 to the 1930s, was marked by draconian, unforgiving rules, brutal enforcement, and discipline such as whipping, beating, incarceration, and the withholding of food. Attendance, often forced, grew to be the unfortunate norm in Native life, a common experience to be endured. By the 1920s about 76 percent of Indian children, some as young as four years old, attended boarding schools. According to the Meriam Report, a 1928 congressional examination of conditions at boarding schools, "The labor of [Indian] children as carried on in Indian boarding schools would, it is believed, constitute a violation of child labor laws in most states." Many children died from communicable diseases such as tuberculosis in the schools' crowded dormitories; many also perished while trying to escape or from other dubious, undocumented causes.

To date, the Department of the Interior has identified approximately seventy-four burial sites associated with the schools, accounting for nearly one thousand student deaths. Since many school campuses included a cemetery, the number of burial sites and graves is expected to increase as investigations by the Department of the Interior continue. All Indian children were sent to boarding school to become "civilized." But many ended up dead. Canada, which launched an investigation and Truth and Reconciliation Commission (TRC) for Indian residential schools in 2007, has accumulated substantial data on the number of schools, children who attended, burial sites, and graves. Canada operated 139 federal schools with more than 150,000 Indigenous children attending between the 1870s and 1997. So far, Canadian authorities have detected over two thousand unmarked children's graves at residential school sites.

U.S. boarding school policies predate those in Canada by about fifty years; as such, they served as a model for that country's Indian residential school program and operated more than three times the number of schools. Yet the United States languishes behind its northern sister: the United States has only recently begun acknowledging and investigating its policies and its past vis-à-vis boarding schools. It wasn't until the discovery of student graves in Canada hit the news in May 2021 that the United States could no longer dodge its own boarding school history. In June 2021, Secretary of the Interior Deb Haaland of the Laguna Pueblo tribe issued a memorandum directing her agency to investigate U.S. Indian boarding school history. The agency issued a report in 2022, the *Federal Indian Boarding School Initiative Investigative Report,* sharing limited preliminary data regarding the number of schools, locations, children who attended, and those who died. It is the first effort of its kind in this country. Although the history of Indian boarding schools is new information for most Americans, it is a story well known to us. As Secretary Haaland noted, there are few Indigenous families who are untouched by the boarding school experience. "Indian boarding school policies have touched every Indigenous person I know. Some are survivors, some are descendants, but we all carry the trauma in our hearts," Haaland said on the first stop of her "Road to Healing" tour, in which survivors were heard on a national scale for the first time. "I'm determined to use my position for the good. I launched the boarding school initiative last year to undertake a comprehensive effort to recognize the legacy of boarding school policies with the goal of addressing their intergenerational impacts and to shed light on the traumas of the past." Quantitative research indicates that disparities in mental health, addiction, and increased chronic physical conditions such as diabetes and cancer are connected to boarding school attendance among Native Americans. According to the Department of the Interior report as well as research by health professionals, cultural and familial disruption as well as physical and mental trauma experienced by generations of Indian people at boarding schools has contributed to intergenerational trauma that continues to plague Indigenous communities today. My mother, an enrolled citizen of the Bad River Ojibwe tribe in northern Wisconsin, was five years old in 1930 when she and her siblings were separated from their parents and sent to St. Mary's Catholic Indian Mission School in the little town of Odanah on the Bad River reservation. The Indians called it the Sister School after the Franciscan order of nuns, the Sisters of Perpetual Adoration, who built the school near the banks of the Bad River in 1883. The school closed in 1969.

The Bad River reservation is located along the south shore of Lake Superior, not far from Duluth, Minnesota, and was described in a Franciscan history of the school as a vast wilderness that could only be reached from the railway station in Ashland fifteen miles away by foot, horseback, or bobsled in the winter. Bad River lands are on a continental divide, a geological line, where rivers here flow north rather than south, through sloughs and small lakes and wetlands into Lake Superior. Some have called the northern tier of Wisconsin the Everglades of the North. Jesuit missionaries accompanied French fur traders to the region in the mid-seventeenth century, establishing a mission at Chequamegon Bay in 1665. Ojibwe frequently traded with European traders beginning in those early days, but when the Franciscans arrived in 1883, northern Wisconsin was, for the most part, an untouched land rich in timber, game, and minerals. It was rich, too, as far as we were concerned, in wild rice, cranberry bogs, sugar maples, and fish—the traditional foods that have sustained us for centuries.

The Bad River reservation was established in 1854 by the Treaty of La Pointe, but Ojibwe lived in this area long before then. Indigenous peoples were present in the Great Lakes region thousands of years prior to European arrival. There is evidence dating from 11,000 BP of Paleo-Indians near Chequamegon Bay. Evidence of the Woodland tradition, affiliated with Ojibwe people, appeared around 2,100 BP. The Ojibwe bands first encountered by Europeans are descended from these people of the early Woodland tradition; according to ancestral teachings, Ojibwe first lived in the East on the shore of a great salt sea before migrating to the Great Lakes.

In those days, the forest was the cornerstone of Ojibwe economy. Their diet was based on seasonal hunting, fishing, gathering wild foods, and some agriculture. In addition to gathering wild plants for food and medicine, women planted small gardens of squash, corn, yams, and beans. Women also harvested white birch bark to make pails, dishes, and other containers.

Men hunted deer, elk, and other animals. People fished year-round. When the winter hunting season came to a close, families gathered together to make maple sugar in temporary camps. "There is one thing we always had, that is maple sugar. We had everything ready by the first run of the sap. We went on in the old Indian way of tapping maple trees," recalled Eliza Morrison, Bad River citizen.

Before Europeans arrived, Ojibwe occupied more than twenty-two million acres in the region, but their lands were reduced by more than 98 percent according to the terms of the 1854 treaty. The population of the seven bands of Ojibwe, including Bad River, in northern Wisconsin in the late nineteenth century was about five thousand.

Without access to lands to support traditional hunting and gathering, Ojibwe soon began settling on reservations, growing more dependent on government rations and wage labor to feed their families. The federal Dawes Act of 1887, which divided large tracts

of Indian land into small individual allotments, further reduced
their landholdings. By the early twentieth century, approximately
one thousand Indians lived on the Bad River reservation. Despite
timber company promises that tribal members would receive pref-
erential hiring over white workers, only around five hundred were
employed by the J. S. Stearns Lumber Company, the company that
dominated in Bad River, and were paid significantly less than their
white counterparts. More than a thousand of the jobs went to non-
Indian laborers who were rapidly moving to the area, drawn by work
at the timber companies. By 1930, however, the timber barons had
stripped the 125,000 acres of Bad River lands almost bare of the eastern white pine that had covered the area. As the tree harvest declined
and both Indian and white loggers organized a strike against the mill,
J. S. Stearns abruptly pulled up stakes and left Bad River in the early
1920s. Most of the white residents moved away. Shortly afterward,
the Great Depression set in. Without wage labor from the lumber
mill and amid a declining economy in the region, this was an especially bleak period not only on Bad River but across Indian country
as a whole. As unemployment rose, Indians began moving back to
Bad River, where the cost of living was cheaper, during the Depression; however, fully half of the population was destitute. Into this,
my mother was born.

Bernice, her sisters, Lucille and Geraldine, and brothers, Donald
and Gerald (known as Rags), were sent to the Sister School after their
parents' marriage fell apart. They attended this and other Indian
boarding schools from 1930 until about 1942. My mother was the
youngest girl in the family. I didn't know her as a little girl, of course.
And I've tried to imagine her childhood but struggle to do so. I did,
however, know her when she was older and saw the effects of the
schools on her character, emotional habits, and disastrous parenting
style.

I can still see her as she tried to outrun her invisible tormentors,
walking across the floor of our house, sometimes for hours, desperately shaking her head from side to side to keep the terrible memories at bay, flapping and wringing her hands over and over, as if trying

to rid them of something. She was lost to our family during these times. She could never speak of nor even allow herself to remember all that happened. Instead, she kept her little hands and stories clenched into fists. My childhood was filled with my mother's seemingly random declarations of defiance. *I made up my mind!* she'd say as she tossed her head, flipping the curl of her carefully styled short black hair. Proudly thrusting her chin upward and pulling her tiny frame to its tallest height, she'd twist her rear end down into the seat of her chair, gazing haughtily off into a distance at something only she could see. She seldom named the subject of her decision, but she really didn't have to. Even as a little girl, I knew my mother was referring to all that the sisters had done and said to her: the unfairness, the indignities, the shame. For all her anger and resentment over the nuns' humiliation, however, was the niggling, inescapable belief that they were right. That they were right about her. That they were right about all of us. When they were little, the nuns took the Indian children to town to beg for money for the reservation school, and pointed to the little ragged group. *Help these poor, dirty Indians,* they said. Those words, and the sentiment behind them, continued to ring out in my mother's ears throughout her life. The sentiment—we were dirty, savage, backward, uncivilized—took root in her behaviors, too.

My mother filled my childhood with constant cleaning and scrubbing. *Get down on those prayer bones, girl,* she'd say as she instructed me on how to clean the floor. Often she muttered, *We may be Indian, but by God we ain't dirty!* Ever vigilant against the enemies of dirt and disorder, she made our home her great point of pride. But the pride was forever sullied by suspicion that others knew her secret: that she was Indian and thus that she was less, tainted, spotted, stained; an impostor in the white man's world. I am an observer, often an annoyance, who tears her away from tending her obsessions—her ghosts and her secrets—with my needs. But on this afternoon in the 1960s, when I was four, we sit together quietly for a time.

A few days later, standing silently by the heavy trapdoor that leads to our basement, I wait for her to rush up the steep steps with a basket of wet clothes. As she stomps up the steps, I push the trapdoor shut; it hits her squarely on the head. There is no sound as she falls back down the steps. Later I watch from my place under the kitchen table as she lies on the couch, surrounded by my father and the doctor. *Mama has a tummy ache; we need to let her rest,* they say. Later, I learn that she was pregnant and lost the child from the accident. I felt no remorse over, nor connection between, my actions and the violence of her miscarriage.

Her angst, mysterious headaches, nameless fear, shame, cruelty, and hypervigilance dominated our home life. It was our job to defend her from unnamed enemies. We could unwittingly trigger something for her at any moment. The mysterious nature of what plagued her made it all the more terrifying. She could be cruel and unloving. Often irritable and quick-tempered, she grew enraged without warning. She screamed at us, slapping me or my brother Bill across our faces, called us thoughtless, selfish, blamed us for this or that. She described herself as nervous, which meant she chain-smoked Camel straights while drinking cup after cup of black coffee. I wondered what nervous felt like as I watched her flit from one activity to another. Magically, she worked herself into a rage-filled defense against *those goddamned white hypocrites,* responding to accusations only she could hear. Abruptly, she would get quiet again, crying the way a lost child cries. I stood by helplessly; I said nothing. I knew she could never hear me. I learned to be quiet. From my place under the table, I secretly began constructing my own armor and defiance. Under that table I began constructing my self—my faults, my ambition, my heart.

She was intolerant of weakness or mistakes. Quick to deliver a well-aimed dagger, she once quipped, *He just used you, anyway!* when she caught me weeping over an unrequited teenage love. Learning that my periods ceased a few months after they began, she shrieked at me, *What have you been doing?!* I was innocent of sexual knowledge and had no idea why she was angry with me. It turned out to simply be the random nature of adolescent menstrual cycles.

Sometimes grown-ups, relatives and friends, came to our house and drank beer and played cards at the kitchen table late into the night. Mama got drunk quickly and easily. We were all helpless against it. I stayed under the table, where they forgot about me and I was free to draw my secret symbols on the underside with my black crayon. I pressed hard when they began to weep and fight, but my medicine didn't work, and they ran out of the house, slamming the door behind them.

She often spoke of her childhood dream of having a family. As I uncovered her secrets and history, I discovered that creating our family was part of her master plan to reinvent herself, to become worthy of respect. To become white. In many ways, she achieved her goal, but at the same time the scheme choked her. In the end, she pitied and despised us and pitied and despised herself in equal measure. But the Sister School stories created a coded, unbreakable bond between the two of us. As an adult, I learned she kept the stories and Ojibwe teachings from my brothers. I was, for better and worse, her secret comrade. I don't know why. She threw her stories down before me like a gauntlet, a challenge. Daring me and yet begging me to validate and avenge her life. And there it sat, for decades: her life. And mine. And the awful history between us.

ONE

POKING

n August 2015, four years after my mother's death, I found myself
alone in the vast reading room of the special collections library
at Marquette University, in Milwaukee. I was there to find and
read archived records of the Sister School: to marry the mother's
milk of the stories on which I had been raised to the facts (obdurate,
conclusive) of the historical record. There was the faintest scent of
frankincense and wax in the spacious reading room. A receptionist
gazed down at me from her perch at the reference desk from behind
thick, black-framed glasses. I had traveled from my home in Cincinnati on a sweltering summer day to sift through the university's trove
of records from the Bureau of Catholic Indian Missions, stored and
preserved in climate-controlled luxury. The bureau was founded in
1874 by the Catholic Church and was charged with disseminating
federal and charitable money to these schools. The organization
served to centralize the Catholic Church's administration of what
would become around a hundred boarding schools for Native American children, far more than any other Christian denomination.
Although some duplicates of these records are kept by the National
Archives, the documents held by the Raynor Library at Marquette
are a trove of minutiae, shedding light on the forces that drove Catholic leadership in their extensive work in Indian education. Letters.

Receipts. Purchase orders. Administrative addenda. As a professional journalist, I have been researching boarding school history in the United States and Canada for more than twenty years. As the child of a boarding school survivor, there wasn't a time when I wasn't, in one way or another, investigating this history. My mother—caught her whole life in the terrible tension of vouchsafing and withholding the details of her experience—had always hated my interrogations. *Why do you always have to go poking?* she demanded. Poking is what journalists do. It's also what children do. I hoped to find my mother's records, details left out of her stories. Although the day is hot and sticky, the temperature in the inner rooms of the Bureau of Catholic Indian Missions archives was icy cold. I sat at the end of a long oak table and opened the first of many boxes I had requested from the bureau's archivist. In advance of my trip he had grilled me about my research intentions, and ultimately agreed to my visit and promised to meet with me at the library. But when I arrived that morning, the receptionist explained he'd been called away on a personal matter and wouldn't be there. He'd arranged to have several boxes of photocopied records available, but, disappointingly, they contained only basic, colorless information: lists of former students who had attended the various schools that once dotted Indian country. The only personal details were check marks in columns indicating whether the students had graduated, run away, or died. I'd hoped to see the original documents, rather than photocopies, and to find students' report cards or evaluations—really anything that might offer a hint of insight into their lived experiences at the schools.

After I had spent what felt like hours searching through faint, photocopied lists of names, the archivist suddenly arrived, flushed and out of breath. A white man in his mid-sixties, he was a lay employee of the university and helped establish and organize the bureau's collection there. I sensed my presence amounted to a mild emergency. His hands flapped nervously as he told me repeatedly that many Native people loved their Catholic boarding school experiences, and he informed me that he was an adopted member of the

Ho-Chunk Nation of Wisconsin. He described the education style at the schools as examples of "tough love." Thankfully, my inner journalist silenced my shock; I needed to hear all this man had to say. I'd brought my and my mother's proof of tribal enrollment, as well as her birth and baptismal and death certificates. He examined the documents closely. Unlike the National Archives, the holdings here are considered a private collection and access is discretionary. Once it became clear I wasn't going away, he finally explained that even the original collection—its documents yellowed with age—held very little personal information about any of the students who had attended the Native American boarding schools so long ago. The documents were largely administrative, related to ensuring funding from Indian trust and treaty funds continued to flow to the schools and the bureau. They focused primarily on bureaucratic exchanges between the men and women who ran the schools, offering little insight into the lives of the students themselves. *But I'd be happy to share them with you,* he said halfheartedly.

I could see he hoped I'd decline and leave, but I'd come all this way and felt I might as well take a look at what they had. *Why not?* I asked with a polite smile. He soon brought out another cartload of cardboard file boxes, which, as promised, contained mostly bureaucratic reports and correspondence between generations of boarding school principals and the Bureau of Catholic Indian Missions in Washington, D.C. There was nothing in the dry letters and reports concerning the people I most wanted to learn about, the students. Just as I was about to give up, twenty minutes before the library was set to close, I pulled out a folder that was marked "Saint Mary's School." My breath caught in my throat. This was a name that haunted my childhood, the setting of my mother's most disturbing bedtime stories. Slowly opening the folder, I found a yellowed, typewritten letter dated January 3, 1934. It was addressed to the Right Reverend Monsignor William Hughes, the director of the Bureau of Catholic Indian Missions, from Sister Mary Macaria Murphy, the sister secretary of St. Mary's. My eyes scanned down the page:

By the time these lines reach you, our dear Mother Superior Sister Catherine will, no doubt, have been called to her eternal reward. On December 19, she fell off the second last step leading down to the kitchen entry.

She must have pitched forward with great force, for in striking her head against a windowsill; a gash was cut in her forehead by the temple of her glasses. On Friday Dec. 29, the Sister nurse noticed a change in Sister's condition and told us she feared a stroke.

Our dear sister had convulsions, was anointed and has been speechless since. The doctor says it can hardly be but a matter of a day or so at most if she does linger even that long.

We know you will pray earnestly for her eternal repose and for a speedy relief from her sufferings. Sorrowfully yours in the agonizing Heart of Jesus.

Sister Macaria

When I reached the end of the letter, I stood straight up out of my chair. Startled, the receptionist widened her eyes; she seemed to consider calling for help. I smiled at her weakly. Reassured but on alert, she returned her gaze to her computer. Once I recovered myself, I quickly went through the contents of the box again. I found an original photo of Sister Catherine. Covered from head to toe in her black-and-white nun's habit, she gazed sternly into the distance through thick, wire-rimmed glasses. The air-conditioned room was icy, but I was sweating as I read the remaining documents in the St. Mary's file.

I knew Sister Catherine long before I saw her photograph in the archives that day. When my mother's migraines eased during those claustrophobic afternoons of my childhood, she called to me. Crawling out from my place under the kitchen table, I'd find her lying in the dark, with one arm thrown over her eyes; the other arm open for me. Silently, I'd climb onto the bed, fitting myself into her armpit and gazing at the tiny blue Virgin Mary medal pinned to her brassiere, a remnant of her boarding school days. Her deep voice slid over me in the bedroom on those late summer afternoons as she, as she

had done hundreds of times before, told me her "Sister School" stories. They almost always included stories about the evil nun Mother
Superior Sister Catherine of the Franciscan Sisters of Perpetual Adoration, who was the principal of St. Mary's Indian boarding school.
She described the nun's inexplicable cruelty—the beatings, the
shaming, and the withholding of food. She told of the harsh work
schedule and how, obsessed with cleanliness, Sister Catherine forced
the children to refinish the huge dining room hall by using shards
of glass to remove the old finish from the wood. On their hands and
knees, the children formed a line, working backward as they scraped
away the old varnish into heaps of dust. When I listened to this familiar litany of the nun's harsh ways, I snuggled closer to her in anticipation. At last, the mood of her story lifted, and her voice took on the
conspiratorial tone that I loved. *One year during the Christmas season,
Sister was marching down the cellar steps to check if we stole any food,* she
said. *She fell on the bottom step—crash! She hit her head bad! Not long
after, she died.*

What a silent cheer us kids made! she continued. *Maybe it was terrible, but it was the best Christmas present we ever got!* She clasped her
hands together and laughed. Reading the letter, I finally knew that
Sister Catherine's death had occurred exactly as she had described
it to me. I had understood that story, and the others, as real-life terrible fairy tales. Later they became part of some nameless ongoing
ceremony as she tried to work through and make sense of the senseless past at St. Mary's. But she could never diminish their control
over her; so instead she passed them on to me. Padded, as they were
passed down, with imagined moral lessons, for my benefit as much
as her own. Surely the tale, with its juicy moral reward, I thought,
couldn't be true. But what had always been a kind of fairy tale when
told by my mother had merged, with the help of archives, into fact. If
I sometimes had doubts about my quest, events such as verifying the
Sister Catherine story drove me onward.

I didn't understand my mother while she was alive. I'm not sure
I understand her now. I'm not even sure I understand my obsessive
drive to uncover her past. But I need to understand all of it in order

to live; in order to move forward as an Indian woman in the world and as a mother to my own children. In order to do that—to continue—I need to go back into the history of the Sister School, back even further into the history of Indian education, and into my mother's life and my own and our relationship with each other. I need to know her, to understand all that happened. This book is, I suppose, above all, a quest. To understand myself, our family's collective disease, Indian people's unparalleled ability to survive, and the history of Indian boarding schools.

T W O

LIFE AT THE
SISTER SCHOOL

Bernice remembered the bewildering day in 1930 when a large black car arrived at Nookomis's house to take her and her siblings to the Sister School. It was early fall and the weather was still warm as Bernice and her siblings tumbled with the great crowd of children who, in Ojibwe tradition, were more like brothers and sisters than distant cousins. At Nookomis's house she slept between the cousins, crowded snuggly into one bed, sleeping in a friendly tangle. In those days Ojibwe lived in small wooden frame houses, chaotic with children, spilling over with washing, cooking, and visiting relatives.

Sometimes Nookomis hollered good-naturedly at the children, but discipline in Ojibwe households was mostly a matter of suggestion or withholding of approval. When the children grew too loud and unruly, Nookomis or an older cousin would sneak outside and slowly slide a stick with an old moccasin tied to the end, called a ghost leg, into the slightly opened door while making a low moaning sound. Startled and frightened, the children would fall silent.

Nookomis told my mother and her siblings that soon they'd go to stay with the sisters because there weren't enough "eats" at her house to go around. When Bernice asked why, Nookomis said, *Your*

folks busted up. She muttered under her breath to no one in particular, *And your goddamned father won't give me any money.*

Bernice didn't understand; she had just turned five years old in
May. Wearing a long homemade dress and leggings, barefoot, her
long hair gathered in a careless ponytail like the other girls, she went
back to playing and forgot about what her grandmother had told
her. She missed Ma and Pa, but Nookomis's house, so full of cousins, felt like home. But now, suddenly, the time had come. Bernice
and her siblings were herded into the car and were driven the few
miles to the school. Nookomis stood by watching, her mouth in
a straight line, saying nothing as the car retreated from sight. The
five children—Bernice, Lucille, Donald, Rags, and Geraldine—were
silent. *Don't cry,* Donald, the eldest, whispered to them. At her first
glimpse of the nun, clad in her long black habit, Bernice wanted to.
She'd seen the sisters when Ma took them to church, but up close
the sister's stern white face pinched tightly by the starched head-
piece was frightening. The nun seemed annoyed by the children's
arrival. *Hurry up,* she said impatiently as she hustled them into the
dormitory.

Rags, three years old, was the first to break down. He whimpered
as the nun undressed him and put him in the metal bathtub. She
jerked him roughly and slapped his face when he tried to wiggle
away from her. *You Indians are always so dirty,* the nuns often said.
The girls' hair was cut into a short bowl style while the boys' hair was
shaved almost to the scalp. They were given clean oversized worn
dresses and old shirts and pants to wear after being treated for lice
with strong-smelling chemicals. The sisters were quick-tempered and
impatient, ready to hand out a sound slapping or a painful pinch.
Bernice soon found that these slaps and pinches were part of everyday life at the school. In addition to the constant complaints about
the children being dirty Indians, sometimes the nuns handed out
harsher punishments with wooden switches or leather belts for
more egregious infractions such as stealing food. Unlike the culture
at Nookomis's house, the Sister School was austere and somber. The
scrubbed floors smelled of soap and submission. The high ceilings

seemed to swallow the children's voices before they even thought of laughing. Bernice was smaller than the other girls, and the oversized threadbare dress issued by the nuns nearly fell from her shoulders. At last, she was assigned a narrow iron bed in the girls' dormitory, packed together with identical beds. Alone in the vast array of sleeping girls, she began to cry for Ma. She joined many others who cried for their parents night after night. But no one came.

Her days at the Sister School were filled with hard labor. She began to learn her letters during the half day of school, but the nuns were strict and impatient with her progress. They frequently scolded her for having no-good parents, who forced the church to care for her and her siblings. She was unaccustomed to the routine slaps and pinches handed out by the nuns and was terrified by the whippings. But the days rolled on, one into the next, and an endless routine of scrubbing and washing, grief and fear, fear and shame, supplanted the rough love my mother experienced in her first five years of life.

Although it was new and frightening for my mother and her siblings, by 1930 being taken away to boarding school had been part of the Indian experience in the United States for more than a hundred years. Through force or poverty-fueled necessity, so many Indian children were taken to boarding schools through the 1970s that virtually no Indian family remains untouched by the experience today. The act of taking Indians, especially their children, away from their families and communities has deep roots in America, reaching far beyond boarding school history.

The use of education as the path to civilization through assimilation far predates the American Revolution and lies at the heart of the worldview permitting the conquest, murder, and enslavement of America's Indigenous population. Initially, if the first European explorers didn't kill us, they took us as slaves or used us as vessels to further their path to heaven by fulfilling their goals as Christians through our conversion. For instance, Pope Nicholas V issued one of the central papal bulls, or laws, in the mid-fifteenth century authorizing European agents to "invade, search out, capture, vanquish and subdue all Saracens and pagans whatsoever and other enemies of

Christ wheresoever placed, and the kingdoms, dukedoms, principalities, dominions, possessions and all movable and immovable goods whatsoever held and possessed by them and to reduce their persons to perpetual slavery."

Thus land and resources held and inhabited by Indigenous peoples viewed as pagans were up for grabs. Pagans, however, could be spared if they converted to Christianity. If not, they could be legally killed or enslaved. In a stunning example of collaboration between the Spanish crown and the Catholic Church in conquering the New World, the church granted a papal bull in 1508 to the king of Spain bestowing the privileges of *patronato real*. Under *patronato real*, the church granted Spain the right to exact patronage and fees and subject the Indigenous population to forced labor in the Americas in exchange for political and financial support for the church's efforts there. Spain in the fifteenth century was a land torn by generations of racial and religious intolerance; the Catholic monarchs Ferdinand and Isabella signed the Alhambra Decree in 1492, giving Jews four months to leave or convert to Catholicism even though Spanish Jews had lived in the country for more than a thousand years. Long before 1492, Jews and Muslims were subjected to forced religious conversions. Ferdinand and Isabella established the notorious Spanish Inquisition in 1478 to enforce conversion laws.

Racial and religious views of early explorers like Christopher Columbus and his crew were formed under this repressive, intolerant regime. Unsurprisingly, they viewed America's Indigenous inhabitants as resources to be harvested, equivalent to the lands, gold, and other riches they sought in the New World. Indigenous people were there for the taking, as slaves and forced converts to Christianity.

The first wave of Spanish explorers claimed lands and enslaved the Indigenous population as part of the Spanish encomienda system. Under this system, Spanish settlers and explorers had the legal right to enslave Indigenous peoples for forced labor. On October 14, 1492, Columbus wrote in his journal about encountering the Lucayan people on an island that would later be known as part of the Bahamas. According to Columbus, the people greeted him and his crew warmly, bringing them food and water. "These people are very simple as regards the use of arms [and could] be kept as captives [here on the island]; for with fifty men they can all be subjugated and made to do what is required of them." Columbus and his men kidnapped several of the inhabitants before sailing on to Hispaniola, now known as Haiti and the Dominican Republic, where he kidnapped five hundred members of the Taíno tribe to be taken to Spain as slaves. Only two hundred survived the journey; many of them died after being sold into slavery in Spain. Columbus established a fort in Hispaniola where Spanish settlers brutalized and enslaved the Taíno population, forcing them to grow crops and work in mines.

Bartolomé de las Casas, a Dominican friar, wrote graphic descriptions of Spanish brutality against the Taíno in his book *A Short Account of the Destruction of the Indies.* He wrote, "They slaughtered anyone and everyone in their path, on occasion running through a mother and her baby with a single thrust of their swords. They spared no one, erecting especially wide gibbets on which they could string their victims up with their feet just off the ground and then burn them alive thirteen at a time, in honour of our Saviour and the twelve Apostles, or tie dry straw to their bodies and set fire to it. . . . The islanders, previously so numerous, began to die out as would any nation subjected to such appalling treatment."

Casas traveled to Hispaniola in 1502, where he participated in enslaving the Taíno, but later, overwhelmed by his conscience, gave up his landholdings, took clerical vows as a Catholic Dominican friar, and returned to Spain. He advocated against enslaving and brutalizing Indigenous people until his death in 1566. Casas estimated that of the three million Taíno people living on Hispaniola in 1502, only two hundred remained by 1542. Casas won limited support in Spain from the crown for better treatment of Indians in the Americas and reform of the encomienda system, but ultimately his victory had no impact on the behavior of the colonizers half a world away.

The taking of Indigenous peoples was not confined to the Spanish. Before Squanto of the Wampanoag tribe famously taught the Pilgrims how to survive in the New World, he and several other tribal citizens were kidnapped by the English explorer Thomas Hunt in 1614 and taken to Europe, where they were sold as slaves. Remarkably, Squanto made his way to London, signed on as a guide on a ship to Newfoundland, and returned to his homelands in 1619 near what is now known as Plymouth. Thus he was able to say, "Welcome, Englishmen," to the Pilgrims, who never inquired how he came to learn English. Squanto's kidnapping is seldom included in popular renditions of the American Thanksgiving story. And the taking went beyond the physical. It included a spiritual harvest of Indigenous souls.

Catholic missionaries accompanied Spanish and French explorers to the New World, adding an essential spiritual dimension to European relationships with America's Indigenous peoples. Their mandate, drawn from biblical passages in the Gospel of Matthew, directs Christ's apostles to make disciples of all nations and baptize them. Baron Justinian von Welz, a seventeenth-century Austrian nobleman, later coined the term "the Great Commission" to describe this work. Pope Paul III's 1537 declaration finding that Indigenous peoples did indeed possess souls fueled Catholic and later Protestant missionary efforts or Great Commission work in the New World. Thus Christian missionaries functioned as agents of empire, imbuing European expansion and acquisition with divine right and Christian duty, excusing and invalidating any pain or suffering experienced by Indians along the way. Pope Paul's declaration further fueled the notion that Indigenous peoples also had the capacity to acquire the benefits of both Christian conversion and civilization. From the sixteenth-century European perspective, civilized people were Christian, lived settled lives in villages or cities, and adhered to European social and economic mores and norms. This variety of so-called civilization was seen as the pinnacle of human development. For Europeans, the Indigenous peoples of the New World were the zero point of human society. Thus, Christian conversion, civilization, and assimilation were inextricably intertwined with European Christian duty, all of it wrapped up in the skin of empire.

Early Spanish, French, and English Christian missionaries competed among themselves in an ecclesiastical game of "saving pagan souls" in the New World. Starting in 1540, Spanish Franciscans, an order of Catholic priests, joined conquistadors in what is now known as the U.S. southwestern states of California, Texas, Arizona, and New Mexico, where they created missions and schools among tribes, forcing them into agricultural labor and often brutally subjugating them in the process. Children were forcibly educated in Spanish lifeways over tribal traditions and converted to Christianity. Friar Junípero Serra's founding of nine California missions between 1769 and 1782 was a high point of these efforts. In 2015, Serra was canonized as a saint by the Catholic Church, which described him as a defender of Indian rights. Indigenous protesters, however, toppled his statues, complaining that Serra advocated imprisoning and enslaving Indians at California's missions in service to European conquest.

In what is now Canada, the Jesuits, a Catholic order of priests, joined French expeditions in the early seventeenth century in order to proselytize among the Indigenous peoples there. Unlike other Christian missionaries, the Jesuits often learned Indigenous languages in order to further their goals, sometimes traveling with tribes on hunting and gathering expeditions. The missionaries noted that Indians were keen observers and talented at creating tools from all aspects of their environment. Algonquian-speaking tribes—including Mohegan, Pequot, Narragansett, Abenaki, Ojibwe, and Ottawa—impressed the Jesuits with their resourcefulness and inventiveness, creating cooking vessels from birch bark, placing hot rocks in the pots to cook food rather than suspend them over fire. We were avid traders, long before the appearance of Europeans, constantly on the lookout for new technology. For instance, Indians quickly embraced the metal kettles brought by Europeans. Although very interested in metal manufactured goods, however, they were resistant to Christian conversion. Priests complained that although Indians often listened patiently to gospel teachings, they demurred when pressed to embrace Christianity. Instead, they expressed preference for their own beliefs, claiming it was as impossible for them to change their beliefs as it was for the priests to take up Indian spirituality. The missionaries were unable to grasp the nuanced Indigenous relationship with the divine since it was so unlike the structured, institutional nature of Christianity. Native spirituality, embedded in everyday life, didn't represent an authentic religion to the Jesuits. The missionaries and other Christians dismissed tribes' spiritual ways as meritless or, worse, as products of the devil. "Their religion consists only in superstitions. There is among them no system of religion, or care for it. They honor a deity who has no definite character or regular code of worship. They have no temples, sacred edifices, rites, ceremonies, or religious teachings, just as they have no laws, arts, or government, save certain customs and traditions of which they are very tenacious." But Indians did have shared religious teachings and ceremonies. Ojibwe kept extensive accounts of history and spirituality using mnemonic markings on birch-bark scrolls, some of which survive today. And although missionaries complained about Indians' disdain of agriculture and settled lives, many planted gardens throughout their territory that they harvested regularly.

Since the Jesuits found little success converting the adults, they chose to focus their efforts on the aged, sick, and young. Youth, they reasoned, were more impressionable, more amenable to conversion, especially if they were separated from their families. Jesuits began pressing the Indians to abandon their itinerant lives in favor of settling near missions and placing their children in boarding schools such as the newly built Notre-Dame-des-Anges in what is now Quebec City. Indian parents, however, began to object and often reclaimed their children. Jesuits and other Catholic orders later traveled throughout the Great Lakes region and other areas in the United States and Canada, establishing missions and boarding schools for Indigenous peoples, pushing conversion to Catholicism and civilization through assimilation and embrace of French lifeways. In 1634, Andrew White established the first Jesuit mission in the American colonies in Maryland, where he proselytized among the Indians. Christian missionaries, including the Jesuits, benefited both economically and politically from their cooperation with colonializing forces from the seventeenth century onward. Jesuits pledged loyalty to the French crown and worked to support French enterprises in agriculture and the fur trade. Their existence depended heavily on political and financial support from the French monarchy.

Jacques Marquette, for instance, legendary Jesuit missionary and explorer, was commissioned by the governor of New France in 1673 to find a possible passage from the Great Lakes region to the Pacific as a means to expand territory and trade for the French crown. Marquette teamed up with the fur trader Louis Joliet; together the men explored and mapped the upper regions of the Mississippi River.

During the early years of their missionary work, 1632 to 1664, the Jesuits wrote extended letters describing, in minute detail, Indigenous customs and culture as well as the missionaries' struggles and suffering in the untamed New World. The letters, sent to church officials who shared them with members of the French monarchy, were wildly popular among the French elite. Later collected and published as *The Jesuit Relations,* the letters included descriptions of the marital and social habits of the "savages" in salacious detail, at least by seventeenth-century standards. The Jesuits' texts were among the first examples of travel writing. The popularity of the *Relations* helped fuel conflicted fascination with the savage as envisioned by Europeans, commodifying and othering Indigenous bodies and lands, legitimizing their exploitation. Conversely, they fit into a European philosophical tradition beginning with Michel de Montaigne that glorified what Jean-Jacques Rousseau would go on to label the "noble savage," those who Montaigne believed exhibited humanity's "most true and profitable virtues." In this vision of democracy, philosophers elevated the "savages" of North America as living in a pure, untouched state of nature that featured elements of social justice and equality, comparing them to traditional folk democracy in parts of Europe. Through the noble savage concept, Rousseau hoped to inspire Europeans to embrace more humanized, egalitarian forms of government and society. The scholar Frank Thilly summarized Rousseau's thought by writing, "If all men are created free and equal, he reasoned, with the same natural rights and capacities, then there is no rationale for rule or inheritance by the privileged classes." But

Rousseau's and Montaigne's noble savage concept was an impossible, ultimately racist, fantasy envisioning natives as devoid of the full spectrum of human attributes. Indeed, this fantasy endures even today in New Age spirituality, which often typecasts Indigenous peoples as dwelling in a spiritual world removed from negative human traits and drives such as greed or violence. The *Relations* also helped the Jesuits earn wide popular and financial support in France and inspired waves of immigration to America. Missionary efforts in the New World helped cement the concept of using Christian conversion and education as a means to assimilate and civilize Indigenous peoples, advancing the ultimate colonial goal of land and resource acquisition. This model came to be baked into both U.S. and Canadian Indian policies, the only legitimate alternative to outright extermination.

Although the *Relations* was written through an undeniable lens of European hegemony, it represents one of the few ethnographic sources of information about tribes from that period. *Relations* authors noted that "Indians treat their children with wonderful affection but they preserve no discipline, for they neither themselves correct them nor allow others to do so; when the child cries they begin to dance and sing, thus rocking their little one, and when it stops crying they go on with their work." Traditionally, for instance, Ojibwe seldom used corporal punishment to discipline children, relying instead on indirect coercion, humor, storytelling, or fear. Adults might place a scarecrow or other object to frighten children away from unsafe areas; misbehaving children might be frightened by an adult wearing a mask made from birch bark. Adults were careful not to shame or disrespect their children. Mothers kept infants with them constantly. Some ethnographers have described the relationships between Ojibwe and their children as closer than those among whites. Typically mothers placed babies in a cradleboard during the day, keeping them close as they went about their daily chores. Mothers took great care in decorating the cradleboards, sometimes stitching a design of

a butterfly, considered the spirit of childish play, on the cloth covering. Mothers also hung small playthings or charms from a hoop
attached above the child's head. Soon after a child was born, parents
chose a respected person to name the child, inviting several people
to a feast. In addition to a name, the child received spiritual power
from the namer, who often received the name in a dream. During the
feast, the namer described the nature of his dream or vision, speaking at length about the power of the name to bless and guide the
child throughout their lives. Children were encouraged to dream for
power and direction in their lives and as a means to develop their
own relationship with the divine. Ojibwe consider themselves one
element among nature, no greater or less than any other living being;
all are imbued with spirit and bear recognition. Grandparents played
a special role in raising children, soothing babies, amusing toddlers,
preparing feasts, and instructing them in everyday chores as well as
acting as models of behavior. Most childhood lessons were taught in
situ, rather than through lecturing. The word "family" as known in
English as referring to the nuclear unit of parents and their children
doesn't exist in the Ojibwe language. A better English word might
be "household" to denote the Ojibwe extended family unit, which
includes parents, siblings, aunts, uncles, grandparents, and cousins
and even extends to members of one's clan. Consequently, there were
no orphans among the Ojibwe; extended family stepped in to raise
children whose parents were no longer on the scene. Fathers taught
boys how to hunt at an early age, taking them along on hunting expeditions. Similarly, mothers involved daughters in all aspects of wom-
en's work, instructing them in making maple sugar, harvesting wild
rice, using birch bark, and so on. The relationship between mother
and daughter was especially close because they spent extended time
together. By European standards, however, Indigenous people were
lazy, indolent creatures too fond of socializing and engaging in activities that failed to produce tangible goods. Ojibwe men, for instance,
binge-worked when hunting, but once the hunt was successful, they
rested until the next action. Multiple historical accounts complain
about Indians gathering in wigwams, talking, smoking, and laughing

for hours at a time. "They squat upon their haunches like monkeys; this is their custom while eating, deliberating, or conversing. They greet approaching friends with silly laughter, more often exclaiming, 'Ho, hho, hho!'" And worse, at least according to the missionaries, Indians frequently burst out laughing at some of their gospel teachings. The Jesuits were clearly disgusted by Indians' beliefs in an afterlife as a place located in the direction of the setting sun where their spirits retired to enjoy endless feasting, hunting, and dancing. "When they first heard of the eternal fire and the burning decreed as a punishment for sin they were marvelously impressed; still, they obstinately withheld their belief because as they said there could be no fire where there was no wood; then what forests could sustain so many fires through such a long space of time? This absurd reasoning had so much influence over the minds of the savages that they could not be persuaded of the truth of the gospel."

The Jesuits also complained about the amount of work done by women, noting the women busied themselves with food preparation and preservation as well as maintaining the family's clothing and lodging. Unlike those of European women, however, Ojibwe women's contributions allowed them power that was valued and recognized by the extended family and tribe. In traditional Ojibwe society, men did not gain the right to direct a woman's life or resources after marriage. As Brenda Child of the Red Lake Ojibwe Nation notes, older women in our tribe are called *mindimooyenyag*, or "those who hold things together." "Women continuously worked and otherwise interacted with relatives, and the roles of daughter, sister, mother, and aunt were important mantles of responsibility," she writes. Ojibwe women played a crucial role in negotiating treaties and relationships with European settlers. "Ojibwe ideas about property were not invested in patriarchy as in European legal traditions." For instance, Child describes how collectives of women controlled the social organization of the wild rice harvest, an essential dietary and spiritual staple for Ojibwe, who used the food in ceremony as well as for sustenance. "When early travelers and settlers observed indigenous women working, it would have involved a paradigm shift for them to appreciate that for the Ojibwe, water was a gendered space where women held property rights."

As Ojibwe, we are still taught that it is our duty as women to care for the water. The most important and essential element of life, water encircles our young in the womb and influences all life on earth. In the end, Ojibwe women have survived European attempts to undermine our role as "those who hold things together." These fundamental differences between European and Indigenous ideology underscored early conflicts and in many ways continue to influence settler relationships with Indians.

Work, constant, mind-numbing, Western-style labor, represented an essential element of civilization and expression of a good Christian life to the European. Christian missionaries and other Europeans failed to recognize that Indian men were conducting important business during the hours they spent visiting, such as communal problem solving and storytelling, work that maintained the fabric of the culture. But the Christian missionaries also sometimes expressed a wistful envy of Indigenous life, so free from shame and guilt. In a passage from *The Jesuit Relations,* an author wrote, "They are never in a hurry. Quite different from us, who can never do anything without hurry and worry; worry, I say, because our desire tyrannizes over us and banishes peace from our actions." He went on, "As long as they have everything, they are always celebrating feasts and having songs, dances and speeches." Reading these words today, one is reminded of the Western world's current obsession with mental wellness and techniques to rescue us from the spiritual impoverishment of lives built on acquisition. Tragically, even the seemingly healthy pursuit of mental balance has been monetized.

For missionaries, the best work was that which enriched and supported European empires. From earliest contact, from Columbus on through the twentieth-century U.S. Indian policy, white people have been putting Indians to work, often disregarding the work's usefulness in helping them to successfully take part in the civilized world.

Work and menial labor became central aspects of civilization programs like boarding schools. In solving the country's Indian problem, education became the weapon of choice beginning in 1789. President George Washington persuaded Congress to fund a missionary school for Indians. The weapon was aimed almost exclusively at Indian children.

All the children at St. Mary's Catholic Indian Mission School were poor. But only the poorest families boarded their children full time. Inevitably, orphans or those from single-parent homes ended up living at the mission. According to my mother, the nuns treated these children as living proof of the inferiority of Indian culture and family. The shame and humiliation of relying on the sisters' charity was a daily lesson, an essential teaching of the school. And their poverty drove them apart physically as well. Watching the day scholars, several of whom were her cousins, leave the school at the end of every day was a constant reminder of that division. The cousins who lived with Nookomis ran down the road toward home as soon as the bell rang signaling the end of the school day. Bernice and Rags ran with them until the sister shouted sharply, *Bernice and Gerald, come back here!* The daily disappointment continued for several weeks during their first months at the school. *Why can't we come home?* Bernice demanded of her aunt Pat, who was one year older. *Ma says yous gotta stay here with the sisters and to stop crying around and begging to come home all the time,* Pat said. Bernice stopped abruptly. She stood in the middle of the dirt road and watched Pat walk away until her checked dress disappeared from view. Bernice pretended not to hear the dismissal bell after that, but her face burned red with hurt and shame each time it rang.

Her mother, Cecelia, known as Cele, pronounced like "Seal," visited the children only once during their eight years at St. Mary's. One morning, my mother was on her hands and knees washing the wooden floor of the large dining hall when a nun called to her. *Bernice, your mother's here!* Bernice, about seven years old, stopped mid-scrub; she hadn't seen her mother since she and her siblings were taken from their grandmother's house and driven to the Sister School two years earlier. Hearing the nun's words wiped out all she'd suffered: it was finally over; Ma had come at last. She wiped her hands on her dress and ran to the visiting area near the vestibule. *Walk!* the sister commanded.

Bernice threw her arms around her mother, inhaling her smell, burying her face in the folds of Cele's dress. *Oh, Ma!* She choked out the words, too relieved and grateful to remember her anger and bewilderment at being left at the school. Ma sat down and smoothed out her new skirt.

So are you behaving for the sisters? she asked. Bernice glanced at the nun seated nearby and nodded her head in affirmation.

The children crowded around Cele, clinging to her. Cele pulled Rags's small arms from around her neck and spoke to the children. *I got married again; I'm living near Michigan with my new husband, but we got no room for yous, so you're going to have to stay here with the sisters,* she said.

They looked outside. There was an unfamiliar white man waiting in a car parked in front of the school.

Here, I brought presents, she said as she gave Bernice a five-pound box of chocolates.

Woodenly, Bernice walked back to the vacant dormitory and sat on her bed. She opened the cheap flowered box and began shoving the candy into her mouth, barely stopping to chew. Soon she grew sick, vomiting the too-sweet chocolate back into the box. From that moment on, shame, the master emotion, dug its claws into Bernice's vitals, taking up permanent residence there. *I never did like chocolates after that, and I never did like my mother,* she told me later.

Her shame was absolute; it included shame over being Indian, shame over being abandoned by her mother, and, worse, shame that extended family, the traditional Ojibwe social welfare system, did not extend to her.

She didn't understand that she and her siblings stood at a powerful historical nexus of Indigenous impoverishment. Nationally, federal policies had drastically diminished tribal landholdings, the assimilationist mission at boarding schools was hammering away at Indian language and culture, the Great Depression was just beginning, and locally the timber industry, one of the only employers, had recently packed up and left Bad River after denuding its forest of white pine. Perversely, Bernice and her siblings became pariahs among their own kin. Always without, the children represented everything that had gone wrong. Even cousins joined in the belittling messaging from the sisters. As most children do, Bernice blamed herself. In my research as an adult, searching to explain her intractable rage, especially toward her mother, I learned that shame and self-blame are the close companions of trauma, especially in early childhood. Rage is one of the few emotions that can survive such an onslaught. Struggling to find a way to go on, Bernice decided to hate Cele. Blaming her mother became her tool for survival.

Chocolate candy and Ma were a sweetness she would never have.

THREE

THE SISTER SCHOOL
COMES TO ODANAH

The United States began paying missionaries to civilize, convert, and educate Indians in 1792 by recommendation of Secretary of War Henry Knox to President George Washington. Washington authorized an annual payment of $1,500 to Samuel Kirkland of the Society in Scotland for Propagating Christian Knowledge in order to establish the Hamilton-Oneida Academy, a boarding school for both Indian and white students in New York. Washington wrote that the school would be "teaching them the great duties of religion and morality, and ... inculcate a friendship and attachment to the United States."

The Second Great Awakening at the dawn of the nineteenth century fueled evangelical missionary work among Native peoples. Eager missionaries, supported by government policies and funding, descended upon Indian country to evangelize and civilize primarily through education. By the middle of the nineteenth century, Christian missionary education for Indians became "a thing." Although some denominations' efforts were sparse and short-lived—in 1886, Unitarians successfully created one school on the Crow reservation in Montana—nearly every Christian denomination tried its hand at converting and educating Indians.

One of the most enthusiastic early government officials appointed to expressly deal with tribes was Thomas Loraine McKenney, a Quaker who began his service in 1816 as superintendent of Indian trade. Later, as superintendent of Indian Affairs in 1824, McKenney's Quaker faith played a major role in his dealings with Indians; he is considered one of the key figures in the development of federal Indian policy. He advocated for policies in Indian education and civilization run by Christian missionary societies. McKenney's work laid the groundwork for the enactment of the Indian Civilization Fund Act of 1819, which he proposed would "encourage activities of Christian benevolent societies among Indians." Congress allocated $10,000 per year for the effort. The number of religious Indian boarding schools began to rise: 32 schools in 1824, 38 in 1825, 52 in 1830, and 48 boarding schools and 102 day schools by 1877.

One of McKenney's lasting contributions to the philosophies of Indian education was inculcating instruction with "the habit of labor." From earliest contact, missionaries were outraged by what they saw as periods of unproductive work, of time spent on socializing, ceremony, storytelling among Indians, whose determination to enjoy their lives seemed to utterly frost white people. "Labor is painful," McKenney wrote. "Education and habit alone can reconcile him to it. It is upon this basis the present school system rests." But McKenney later admitted that work, prayer, education, and strict discipline alone were ineffective in quashing Indian culture and language. He complained that once removed from the school environment, children quickly reverted to their former habits. Indian people were not necessarily averse to Western education for their children; more than one-third of the nearly four hundred treaties signed between tribes and the federal government included provisions for education. Always innovative and responsive to their environment both physically and socially, Indians realized that white settlers were here to stay. Many willingly sent their children to missionary schools to learn English and settler ways as a means to survive and navigate the country's new reality. They envisioned maintaining their culture, language, and families in the process and resisted missionaries' insistence that children board at the schools and frequently removed them. Surely, Indians could have never imagined the wholesale onslaught against their hearts and souls that would soon become central to the country's Indian policies.

Fast on the heels of the Civilization Act, the wheels of federal assimilationist policies moved swiftly, reducing the amount of lands and resources for subsistence hunting and gathering, further impoverishing Indians. The white settler population exploded in the nineteenth century, creating greater demands for land. According to the U.S. census, the U.S. population of 5.3 million (excluding Native peoples, who had yet to achieve suffrage) in 1800 increased to 23 million by 1850, driven primarily by Irish, British, and German immigrants. By 1900, the number increased to 76 million. In a savage kind of math, while immigration exploded, Congress tried to reduce Indian lands to make room for the newcomers. In 1830, Congress passed the Indian Removal Act, which provided for the removal of all Indians east of the Mississippi to what was then Indian Territory. The government failed in its mission, but thousands of Indians from various tribes were removed to lands west of the Mississippi River, sometimes forcibly, to what is now known as Oklahoma. In 1887, Congress passed the Dawes or Allotment Act, which authorized the government to break up communally held tribal lands into plots, usually between 40 and 160 acres, for individuals and families. Land considered excess, beyond the number of allotments, was sold to settlers. Indian lands decreased from 138 million acres in 1887 to 48 million acres by 1934, when allotment ended. From the American perspective, the future for the country's Indigenous population was clear. As the superintendent of an Indian school in Kansas summarized, "The only alternative left is civilization or annihilation, absorption or extermination."

There was never any consideration that nineteenth-century white settlers would not take land and resources away from Indians; the only question was how it would be done and how the actions would be framed. Rather than theft, settler acquisition and dominance came to be envisioned as divine providence or Manifest Destiny, a collective social decree coined by the journalist John Louis O'Sullivan in

1845 to consecrate western expansion. It was the destiny and duty of white people to settle and conquer the continent. Indian lands, resources, and even children were commodified in the process. Indians would benefit by being lifted out of paganism and barbarism, assimilated into a new white America. The era of extraction economics had begun. Ojibwe in the Great Lakes region soon felt the impact of these events.

In 1837, several bands of Ojibwe signed a treaty with the U.S. government ceding about thirteen million acres of land in the current states of Wisconsin and Minnesota. Nicknamed the Lumberman's Treaty, the agreement gave the timber industry rights to harvest abundant white pine in the region. Although Ojibwe understood that they would still have access to the lands for hunting and gathering, in 1850 President Zachary Taylor revoked these rights and ordered tribes to "remove from their unceded lands" to an area west of the Mississippi. In 1850 and 1851, several bands of Ojibwe were lured to Sandy Lake in Minnesota, three to five hundred miles away from villages in Wisconsin, where the government said they would receive their annuities. Payment was scheduled for October 25. Thousands traveled to the site but found that no rations or annuities arrived. The government subagent John Watrous didn't arrive until late November, without the cash annuities and without any plans to feed and shelter the Ojibwe while they waited. It's estimated that 170 Ojibwe died at Sandy Lake from starvation, illness, and exposure while waiting for annuities that never arrived; another 230 died on their way back home in December. The anthropologist James Clifton describes the Sandy Lake event as the "Wisconsin Death March." Angry Wisconsin band leaders grew determined to stand their ground against the government's removal orders. Some Ojibwe talked of war, but in 1852, Chief Buffalo, leader of the Red Cliff band, organized a remarkable journey along with other Ojibwe leaders to take their case to the president himself in Washington, D.C. Buffalo, in his early nineties, included the white interpreter Benjamin Armstrong on the long trip, stopping along the way to meet with local newspaper editors and prominent leaders in white communities, gathering their support and signatures on a petition. The delegation met with daunting setbacks along the way, sometimes forced to organize public exhibitions and sell trinkets for travel funds. Soon, however, newspapers were filled with reports about the unfair treatment of the Lake Superior Ojibwe who were being pushed off their traditional homelands. The delegation secured a meeting with President Millard Fillmore, who agreed with their demands, leading to the Treaty of 1854, which set aside four reservations in Wisconsin, Red Cliff, Bad River, Lac Courte Oreilles, and Lac du Flambeau, as well as a small portion of land on Madeline Island.

The Bad River reservation was established as part of that treaty, but Odanah, the Ojibwe word for town or village, had been a cultural center for the tribe for centuries. In the seventeenth century French explorers had great difficulty navigating the river flowing through the region, so they dubbed it Rivière Mauvaise, or Bad River. But Ojibwe have always called it Mashkiiziibii, Medicine River; it's said that everything needed for *mino-bimadizwin*, a good life—food, medicines, and spirit—is available in its coffee-colored waters and along its banks. Mashkiiziibii and its tributaries simultaneously drain and feed seventy-five miles of lush land, in the Bad River watershed and the Kakagon Slough. The slough is home to wild rice, manoomin, the sacred seed that has sustained Ojibwe bellies and spirits for generations. Finally, at the mouth of the Bad River, Mashkiiziibii adds its rich alluvial lode to the Lake swollen with fish. The river frequently floods, so the lands along its banks are especially fertile. The sisters say they taught the Indians at Odanah how to garden, but Ojibwe have planted gardens here for generations at Gitiganing, the gardens, an area not far from where St. Mary's Church still stands today. One can still see remnants of the large, cultivated rows of that ancient *gitigaan*. The great wealth of natural resources at Bad River—timber, fish, minerals—soon caught the attention of the growing white settler population. Before long the wilderness first described by the sisters began to swarm with timbermen and entrepreneurs. Railroad construction in nearby Ashland began around 1872, bringing hundreds of workers to the region. By 1877 the rail to Chicago was finished. Suddenly the little village of Odanah was no longer an isolated wilderness. Almost overnight it transformed into a boomtown with a bustling main street and housing for lumberjacks and workers. The Bad River reservation found itself at the center of one of the world's largest timber booms. The traditional Ojibwe economy was disrupted; many turned to wage labor and were forced to sell their land allotments to survive, no longer able to rely on a subsistence lifestyle alone. Assimilation in all its forms, including boarding schools, had come to Mashkiiziibii.

The events leading up to and surrounding the nuns' time in Bad River are a microcosm of what unfolded in much of Indian country during the nineteenth and early twentieth centuries. Indeed, the genesis of the Sisters of Perpetual Adoration's civilizing mission can be traced back to the earliest days of the republic, when political leaders turned to Christian missionaries, the de facto Indian experts of the day, as they sought to solve the country's Indian problem. That problem was the barrier Indians presented to white settlement and westward expansion.

The Sisters of Perpetual Adoration packed heavy on their first trip to the Bad River reservation in 1883. They reasoned, rightfully, that little from their world at the Franciscan order's motherhouse in La Crosse, about two hundred miles to the south, would be available in the wilderness of northern Wisconsin on the shores of Lake Superior. The bulk of their supplies, however, supported their celestial mission rather than physical survival. That mission focused on civilizing the pagan Ojibwe through conversion and education; theirs was also a race to secure Bad River as a Catholic mission school. Under President Grant's Peace Policy, authorization and funding to erect schools on reservations were being divided up among Christian denominations.

The government, despite promises to the contrary, reneged on some guarantees to designate certain reservations for Catholics. Indignant and determined to claim as many reservations as possible, Catholics launched a full-court press in Indian country. The dioceses of La Crosse and Milwaukee offered initial financial support to the sisters, confident they would best the small Protestant mission already established in Odanah. In addition to their meager belongings, the two nuns, Sister Cunigunda Urbany and Sister Emmanuela Klaus, brought two huge altar stones, a tabernacle, monstrance, chalices, and numbers of linens and vestments for the priest, Father John Gafron, who presided over a primitive church in the little village of Odanah. The railroad was not yet finished, and there were few roads in the region then; like most travelers the sisters arrived in Ashland via ship on the great lake, about fifteen miles northwest of the reservation. It was late March, but the waters of Chequamegon Bay, which borders Ashland, were still frozen. After loading a bobsled with their heavy luggage and other items, they and their guides headed to Odanah over the bay and on to a dirt road. The nuns worried that the bobsled, so weighted down with Catholic sacred gear for the Mass, might break through the ice. But they arrived safely in the wilderness where the only buildings in sight were the little chapel and a rough house for the sisters' lodging. Fortunately for the nuns, Ojibwe social customs include feeding guests, regardless of their race or religious affiliation. Seeing that the nuns had little food, one of the pagan Ojibwe women began bawling out the Christian Indians for failing to feed their guests properly. Soon the nuns were supplied with maple sugar, fish, wild rice, venison, and dried turnips. They immediately began offering day school on the main floor of their little house, focusing on the gospel and training their students in the habits of "industry, cleanliness and virtue." In addition to reading and writing, girls were taught needlework, cookery, and domestic work, and the boys were taught gardening, agriculture, and "other useful work." Occasionally, the nuns visited huts and wigwams in the village to baptize the sick during outbreaks of measles and smallpox, sometimes facing off with medicine people conducting demonstrations of rites known as the medicine dance. In one case, although frightened by the "hideous antics," the nuns managed to sprinkle holy water on a sick girl. The chief of the proceedings angrily threatened the nuns. He seized a kettle of boiling wild rice soup to hurl at them, but one of the nuns lifted the crucifix of her rosary and shouted, "My God is stronger than your God!" Likely concerned with endangering those seeking healing at the ceremony, the chief backed down, but for the nuns the event represented a spiritual triumph. By 1888, more sisters traveled to the mission, where they succeeded in building a boarding school with the help of a government contract; the fifty students that first year grew to about two hundred by the 1930s.

The sisters traveled to Bad River on the tide of the federal boarding school movement, which had its beginnings in the U.S. Peace Commission of 1867 and later in President Ulysses S. Grant's Peace Policy of 1869. The post–Civil War years were devastating for Indians, with federal policies focused on assimilating and infantilizing them. Reformers fresh off a win with abolishing slavery eagerly embraced the Indian problem, advocating for assimilation and civilization rather than outright extermination. Christian reformers and humanitarians created various "friends of the Indian" organizations such as the Indian Rights Association and the Women's National Indian Association (notable for their lack of Indian membership), which advocated for education as the road to civilization and removing Indian children from their homes as the best means to assimilate them into white society. The cheapest solution to the Indian problem, they reasoned, was erasure of Indian identity, the breakup of Indian families, not outright war. Congress agreed, citing the expense of warfare with tribes as well as the public's antipathy toward extermination of an entire race of people. Carl Schurz, secretary of the interior, estimated that the cost of killing a single Indian was nearly $1 million versus the cost of eight years of schooling in a boarding school at $1,200. "The greatest danger hanging over the Indian race arises from the fact that, with their large and valuable territorial possessions which are lying waste, they stand in the way of what is commonly called 'the development of the country,'" Schurz wrote. Reformers also called for an investigation into the Indian Bureau, long a haven of corruption and patronage. Agents on reservations, they said, should be tasked with educating, Christianizing, and assimilating Indians.

President Grant created the 1869 Peace Policy to carry out these recommendations, including allowing religious denominations to appoint Indian agents. Grant's legacy, however, regarding Indians is complicated and contradictory. Grant's administration featured some of the worst cases of violence and brutality against Indians by the U.S. military, including the Camp Grant and Marias Massacres, in which mostly women and children were killed, and the Modoc War, a bloody conflict in Oregon and California. Infamously, Grant violated the Treaty of Fort Laramie with the Lakota, Dakota, and Arapaho tribes by sending General George Armstrong Custer to establish a fort in the Black Hills after gold was discovered there. Custer was defeated in the Battle of the Little Bighorn in 1876. The treaty, signed in 1868, formed the Great Sioux Reservation and included the lands of the Black Hills. Many Lakota citizens went to war with the federal government over these illegal incursions onto their lands. Grant appointed two of his colleagues from his Civil War days, General William Tecumseh Sherman as general in chief of the army and General Philip Sheridan, who famously claimed, "The only good Indian is a dead Indian," to be responsible for enforcing peace among the Plains tribes. Together the men embarked on a scorched-earth strategy similar to those they'd used successfully in the Civil War. In addition to aggressive military actions against the Indians, they encouraged the near-wholesale destruction of the buffalo as a means to starve out the Plains tribes who depended on the animal for survival. The strategy was effective. In October 1876, more than two hundred chiefs and headmen of the various tribes were forced to sign a new agreement ceding the Black Hills to the U.S. government. (Although the Supreme Court ruled in 1980 that the Lakota were entitled to damages for the taking of their land, they have refused the settlement, which now exceeds $1 billion. The Lakota want the Black Hills back.)

Grant was also guided by reformist sentiments; he supported civilization programs and assimilation over extermination and appointed Ely Parker, a citizen of the Seneca Nation, commissioner of Indian Affairs, the first Indian to hold that position. Parker, a Baptist Indian boarding school alumnus, also helped pen the Peace Policy, a hallmark of Grant's administration. Parker served on Grant's staff in the army and came to be a trusted friend. Parker and Grant unsuccessfully campaigned for citizenship for Indians as part of the peace policy. Political leaders and their economic lobbyists, however, railed against the loss of influence and patronage under Grant's plan and engineered Parker's removal, charging him with corruption. Although later cleared during a congressional investigation, Parker resigned. Religious leaders stepped back from their administrative role on reservations and returned to education. Controversially, Parker supported the reservation system and agreed with Grant's willingness to use force against Indians in order to ensure the success of the Peace Policy, which historians have subsequently described as "peace by choice or force." Tribes were forced to remain on reservations, individual Indians became wards of the state, and in a significant erosion of tribal sovereignty the United States stopped making treaties with tribes. Thereafter, the federal government used only statutes, executive orders, and, later, congressional plenary power to regulate the government-to-government relationship between tribal nations and the U.S. government.

Article 7 of the 1868 Fort Laramie Treaty between the U.S. government and the Sioux Nation stipulated that Indians pledge to "compel their children, male and female, between the ages of six and sixteen years to attend school." Federal leadership was eager to enforce this article as a means to maintain control over the Lakota and other Plains tribes. Fortuitously, Lieutenant Richard Henry Pratt offered a solution. Pratt, a Civil War veteran and outspoken leader in the "friends of the Indian movement," believed that it was only through the complete destruction of Indian language and culture that Indians could have a hope of survival. As director of a prison for Indians in Fort Marion in St. Augustine, Florida, he introduced classes in the English language, art, and craftsmanship, which the prisoners embraced, according to Pratt. "Defeat, imprisonment and exile," according to historian Jacqueline Fear-Segal, were Pratt's prison assimilationist tools, convincing him that only complete isolation from community and forced education could save the Indian or, in his words, "kill the Indian to save the man." Building on a century of experience by Christian missionaries who came before him, Pratt supported removing Indian children from their homes for total immersion in white culture. "In Indian civilization I am a Baptist, because I believe in immersing the Indian in our civilization and when we get them under, holding them there until they are thoroughly soaked." For Pratt, educating Native Americans and other people of color was comparable to animal husbandry. "Even wild turkeys only need the environment and kind treatment of domestic civilized life to become a very part of it," he said while preparing Thanksgiving dinner with his family. Pratt was a tireless self-promoter, and soon reformers of the day lauded the effectiveness of his work at the Florida prison.

In 1879, Pratt founded the Carlisle Indian Industrial School in Pennsylvania on the historic Carlisle army barracks. Built in 1757, the barracks had been closed for eight years when the Indian school was founded. Pratt successfully lobbied Congress for support, but the War Department had stipulations; Commissioner of Indian Affairs Ezra Hayt ordered Pratt to recruit the first students from the Lakota, Dakota, and Nakota tribes who had just signed an agreement ceding the Black Hills. Pratt later wrote that Hayt's hope was that "The children would be hostages for the good behavior of their people." So Pratt made the trip to the Dakotas, meeting with Chiefs Spotted Tail, White Thunder, Milk, and Two Strike at the Rosebud Reservation and Red Cloud in Pine Ridge. Many of the tribal leaders were dismissive of his proposal to send their children so far away to be educated at a white man's school. Chief Spotted Tail told Pratt through an interpreter, "The white people are all thieves and liars. We do not want our children to learn such things."

Spotted Tail was among those who were forced into signing the agreement ceding the Black Hills in 1876. But Pratt presented a persuasive argument. Had the Lakota been able to read and understand the white language and culture, he pointed out, they might have fared better in treaty negotiations. The Lakota were over a barrel. They were now confined to reservation lands, far smaller than under the original Treaty of Fort Laramie, they'd just ceded the Black Hills, a longtime hunting ground, the bison were nearly gone, and the people were now dependent on government rations to survive. Refusing to send their children to Carlisle would anger the Indian agent and the federal government, which would be risky for everyone. "As your friend, Spotted Tail, I urge you to send your children with me to this Carlisle School and I will do everything I can to advance them in intelligence and industry in order that they may come back and help you," Pratt said.

At last, Spotted Tail agreed to send his children with Pratt. He and the other chiefs made a brave show of support, many giving away several ponies and goods to honor their children's departure. Pratt promised that the education at Carlisle would make the children "equals of white youth." But the school was more like a military training camp with inflexible rules and a hierarchical justice system where discipline was strictly enforced even for minor infractions.

Discipline at Carlisle included corporal punishment, withholding of food, forced labor, public shaming, and incarceration in the barracks guardhouse. Assimilation and indoctrination into the ideals and values of white culture while destroying Indian culture and family were clearly a means to destroy tribal sovereignty. The children's long hair was cut short, which in some tribes is a sign of mourning for a loved one. They were forced to abandon their traditional clothing and forbidden to speak their tribal languages. They were dressed in military uniforms and subjected to incessant marching and drilling. Furniture and supplies had not yet arrived when the first children came to the school; they slept on the bare floor in the blankets they'd brought from home. "How lonesome the big boys and girls were for their far-away Dakota homes where there was plenty to eat. . . . The big boys would sing brave songs, and that would start the girls to crying," recalled Luther Standing Bear, a boy from Rosebud. They would remain at the school year-round, separated from family and community for four long years. Pratt created the "outing" system, which also became widespread among other boarding schools. Students were sent to work for low wages with white families as domestics and farmhands and even in factories and other commercial industries. Pratt maintained that these outing placements in "good white homes" would advance the assimilation and civilization process. Many children died or ran away during their outings, and although they were supposed to receive a portion of their wages, many did not.

"This is the panopticon," said Barb Landis as she spread her arms grandly before a gazebo surrounded on three sides by buildings that once housed students and administration of the Carlisle Indian school. Landis is in her seventies, and despite the helping hand of her "stick" she moves with alacrity as she takes me on a tour of the old campus. Sooner or later, anyone conducting research into Carlisle's history meets Landis, sort of the grandmother guardian of the history here. It's a beautiful fall day for our tour, and Landis warms to her subject. "Pratt used the panopticon, a design created by Jeremy Bentham in 1791 as a method for maintaining order and reforming prisoners, in creating the campus," she said. During the Carlisle days, a bandstand stood where the gazebo is now. Located at the school's hub, the bandstand commanded a view of the entire campus and all its buildings. It was from this vantage point that the mysterious all-seeing eyes of the "man on the bandstand" offered his observations of students, praise as well as criticism, in the weekly school newspaper, *The Indian Helper.*

Although most assumed the man on the bandstand was Pratt, the man's identity remains an unsettling mystery. The man had spies among students and staff who sometimes "whispered in the ear of the man-on-the-bandstand," allowing him to publicly discuss details of the children's lives in *The Indian Helper.* The man on the bandstand was described as "not an Indian," heightening the aura of control and obedience surrounding him. Some historians compare the use of the panopticon architecture in combination with the mysterious all-seeing presence of the man on the bandstand at Carlisle to Michel Foucault's theories of society's use of discipline and punishment. The function of prison, Foucault writes, is primarily to create docile bodies in service to societal economics, politics, and warfare. Rather than learning useful skills for self-support, Indians were drilled in useless work, an empty economic form supporting submission.

The old Carlisle buildings today have a pleasing colonial air, freshly scrubbed, white, and airy against the green of the expansive lawn. But knowledge of the man on the bandstand imbues the strategically placed gazebo with a sinister aura, reminding me of the 1960s television spy show *The Prisoner,* in which the protagonist wages war against a Kafkaesque, unknown, all-seeing jailer seeking the inner workings of his soul.

The effect on students must have been unnerving.

Pratt also built a six-foot-high fence around the perimeter of the school. "He claimed it was needed to keep out curious onlookers, but it was as much or more to keep the students from running away," Landis said. Many of them did anyway, although only a few made it back to their home communities. Most ended up back at Carlisle, sentenced to a month or more in the lockup, in the old Hessian Powder Magazine, built in 1777 during the Revolutionary War and converted to the Hessian Guardhouse in the mid-nineteenth century. It still stands today. The foundation of its four dank cells sits several feet belowground, likely creating a cold, miserable experience for children incarcerated there.

Carlisle has been in Landis's bones since the 1980s, when she began working part time at the Cumberland County Historical Society while raising her young family and pursuing her bachelor's degree. She describes herself as an army brat whose family moved frequently until she and her husband settled rather randomly in Carlisle. Initially she was ignorant of the school's history and Indian people in general, but as descendants began contacting the society in search of information about former students, she grew intrigued, drawn into a mostly undocumented world that affected thousands of people and generations of families. Landis is among the scores of homegrown historians, mostly women, both white and Indian, whom I've met over the years who are compelled to document and preserve America's Indian boarding school history. They've all known that the day of reckoning would eventually arrive, and when it did, they'd be ready to help guide the way.

It has been the work of people like Landis, Louellyn White of the Mohawk Akwesasne Nation, Denise Lajimodiere, Turtle Mountain Chippewa, Eva Guggemos, and SuAnn Reddick who've mostly volunteered their time to ensure that data and documentation are available to researchers today. Landis helped fuel the will of Dickinson College, also located in Carlisle, to create the first public digital Indian boarding school archives, the Carlisle Indian School Digital Resource Center. White, associate professor of First Peoples studies at Concordia University, conducts research on children who died during Carlisle's outing program. Lajimodiere, retired associate professor in the School of Education at North Dakota State University, created the first list of federal and religious Indian boarding schools and has published several articles and books containing testimonies of boarding school survivors. She is also a cofounder of the National Native American Boarding School Healing Coalition. Guggemos is an archivist and associate professor at Pacific University; Reddick is a writer and historian for Chemawa Indian School in Oregon. Together they created a public digital archive, Deaths at Chemawa Indian School, documenting deaths at Chemawa using public records. The archive represents more than ten years of research. "Suddenly through the horrendous events in Canada, the work we've been doing all these years is relevant; the media is finally talking about boarding school cemeteries," Reddick said. The archive includes a short 1907 article from the *Weekly Chemawa American* student newspaper about Charlie Fiester, a citizen of the Klamath Tribes who was shot dead while trying to steal food from a store in Chemawa. Fiester was eleven years old when he and two friends, no longer able to tolerate the harsh discipline and conditions, ran away from the school where Charlie had lived since the age of six. The boys built a rustic camp in the woods nearby, surviving on stolen eggs and potatoes. Growing hunger, however, drove them to break into the store where the guard shot Charlie. Like many other boarding school students, Charlie was a habitual runaway, and like many others, he died while trying to escape. Others died of exposure, drowning while trying to swim across rivers, or from accidents. The story of Charlie's death is one of many, most forgotten or never recorded. The work of researchers like Guggemos and Reddick is finally shedding light on this history. What began as primarily an academic, intellectual project for Guggemos, a professional archivist, quickly grew personal, a sentiment shared by many non-Indians conducting this research.

"I have four children; it's hard to read these things about children that age dying and not reflect on what it would be like to have that happen to your own children," she says. "By documenting their deaths in this way perhaps we can show patterns of what happened and provide another avenue of evidence from the past."

In 2021, after learning about Charlie's death, Klamath tribal leaders began a search for living relatives of the boy to decide what to do with his remains, which languish, along with those of eleven other Klamath and Modoc children, in the school cemetery. The Klamath tribal researcher Gabriann Hall grew emotional when she shared the information about Charlie with tribal leadership. Hall has recounted the story widely and chokes up every time she tells it. "He's not a statistic. He's not a number. He's shá-amoks, is the word we use. He's family." Although tribal leadership has been unable yet to find any living relatives of Charlie's, they continue the search.

The Carlisle Barracks is still an army base today, home to the U.S. Army War College since 1951. Although many of the Carlisle Indian school buildings still stand and are used today, the school closed in 1918 after operating for thirty-nine years. A few plaques dot the grounds explaining the school's history; several paintings and sculptures commemorate one of Carlisle's most famous students, Jim Thorpe of the Sac and Fox Nation. In 1912, Thorpe was the first Indian Olympic gold medalist and was considered one of the most versatile athletes in modern sports. But the Carlisle Barracks is army space, and its story is framed accordingly; the Indian school is presented as simply one event, albeit inconvenient, in the location's history. In recent years, the army has rather unwillingly accepted the public's ongoing interest in the Indian school. This wasn't always the case. Back in 1927, when army officials moved the Indian school cemetery to make room for a parking lot, they moved it to the very rear of the barracks, far from the public's eye; it was described then as an "Indian burial ground," hinting that it was part of a prehistoric past. Today, the neat rows of nearly two hundred simple military-esque headstones mark the graves of some of the children who died at Carlisle. "In 1927, the U.S. literally tried to erase the cemetery when they moved it," said Landis. According to an inscription on a small plaque, this is an Indian cemetery. The inscription goes on to read, "Buried here are the Indians who died while attending the Carlisle Indian School (1879–1918). The original Indian Cemetery was located to the rear of the grandstand on Indian Field in 1931. The graves were transferred to this site." I learn later that it was segregationist policies of the day that separated the dead by race.

I was surprised to see that as of today the cemetery is located directly across the street from the barracks' busy main entrance where the dead children seem to silently shout a daily "J'accuse" to the federal forces that sought to erase them. I'm not the first Indian to marvel at this irony. Nick Estes of the Lower Brule Sioux Tribe, assistant professor of American studies at the University of Minnesota, wrote about it in *High Country News* in 2019. It turns out, however, that the irony was unintentional; the army relocated the main entrance to its current location due to security protocols enacted in response to 9/11. The little cemetery and the Carlisle Barracks have since attracted rapidly growing public attention as the United States began reckoning with its brutal assimilationist past and the certainty that the graves of children who perished at Indian boarding schools are strewn throughout the country. In 2017, after years of battle and negotiation that began in the twenty-first century, army leadership for Carlisle Barracks finally began allowing tribes to repatriate the remains of their dead relatives. To date, thirty-two children have returned, often a century overdue, to their homelands.

Individually, each headstone at Carlisle carries a heavy burden of individual suffering, innocence lost, and yearning for family. Ernest White Thunder is one of them; his Indian name was Knocks Off. He was among that first contingent of Carlisle students; his father, White Thunder, was a chief from the Rosebud Agency, one of those leaders Commissioner Hayt instructed Pratt to target first. It appears that Pratt formed a friendly relationship with Chief White Thunder. "White Thunder, let me have your boy and girl and take them to Carlisle; I will be a father to them and all the children while they are with me," he said. White Thunder sent his son Knocks Off, then aged seventeen, whom Pratt renamed Ernest. All the children were given English names after arriving at the school. Knocks Off arrived in Carlisle on October 6, 1879, and from all indications immediately disliked the school. He wrote to his father complaining, asking to return home. Ernest was intensely homesick and chafed against the harsh discipline, like having his mouth washed out with lye soap for speaking Lakota. The meager food and strange surroundings, so different from familiar camp life, made the experience oppressive. Pratt also wrote to Chief White Thunder reporting that Knocks Off was obstinate and uncooperative. White Thunder wrote a letter to Ernest in response expressing his disappointment to his son. It read in part, "When the children went to school, many of the people found fault with us for letting them go and now if what your letter says is true they will find more fault. I am ashamed to hear from Captain Pratt and others in the school that you act bad and do not try to learn. You had your way too much when you were here. I hope you will listen to your teachers for it makes me feel bad when I hear you do not. When I come to visit Carlisle in the spring I shall talk to you. Remember the words I told you: I said if it takes five or ten years, if you did not learn anything, you should not come back here." Pratt often screened incoming and outgoing student mail, so after reading White Thunder's letter, he published it in *The Indian Helper* to shame Ernest into behaving. When White Thunder and the other chiefs visited the school in the spring, he insisted his son remain at the school. Ernest tried to stow away in the train as it headed back to South Dakota but was discovered and returned to Carlisle. Chief Spotted

Tail, however, was horrified by conditions at Carlisle, especially the corporal punishment and constant drilling and marching; he took his children with him back to Rosebud. In December, Knocks Off fell ill. In a letter to White Thunder, Pratt wrote, "White Thunder's son is very sick and I doubt if he recovers. I consider that it is entirely his fault. He is still very obstinate and seems to rather want to die."

Later Pratt wrote again to White Thunder, informing him Knocks Off had died on December 14, 1880, at age eighteen. "Your son died quietly without suffering like a man. We have dressed him in his good clothes and tomorrow we bury him the way white people do," Pratt wrote. Pratt's greatest concern, however, was the effect Ernest's death might have on other parents' willingness to send their children to Carlisle, which he expressed to White Thunder in a subsequent letter, urging him not to speak against the school. "You, my friend, are a good man. For that reason you now have with you children of three of the chiefs. Therefore, my friend, take good care of those children," White Thunder wrote in response. Pratt curried a friendship with White Thunder as a means to facilitate the mission of bringing Lakota children to Carlisle. But once Knocks Off died, Pratt had no more use for the friendship.

White Thunder and Spotted Tail as well as other chiefs at Rosebud wrote letters to Pratt and the commissioner in Washington complaining about the high death rates and requested that a school be built closer to the reservation. White Thunder also wrote requesting that his and another chief's son's remains be sent back to Rosebud. "Our hearts will grieve too long if we don't have what is left of them back to our homes. . . . My dear friend, we want you to send us the remains of our dear children." There is no indication that Pratt responded to White Thunder. Knocks Off languished in the cemetery for nearly 150 years until members of the Sicangu Youth Council from Rosebud successfully lobbied for the repatriation of Knocks Off's and eight other students' remains from Carlisle. In 2015, several members of the youth council traveled to the school and were shocked at seeing the student cemetery with gravestones marking their ancestors still languishing so far away from their homelands.

After praying and leaving offerings on the graves, the students began lobbying the tribe and Carlisle for return of their ancestors' remains.

"We put candy on each of the gravesites and a couple of us sang a song. When we were walking away, it was really heavy," said Chris Eagle Bear of the Rosebud Sioux Tribe and member of the youth council. Those in attendance reported seeing fireflies emerge from the graves. Overcome with emotion, youth council members vowed to work to bring their ancestors' remains home. It was a huge undertaking, but with the support of the Rosebud tribal council nine sets of remains of students who died at Carlisle between 1879 and 1896 were returned and reburied in their homelands in July 2021. The students who died at Carlisle were Dennis Strikes First, Rose Long Face, Lucy Pretty Eagle, Warren Painter, Knocks Off or Ernest White Thunder, Alvan One That Kills Horse, Friend Hollow Horned Bear, Dora Her Pipe, and Maud Little Girl. The children's remains were wrapped in buffalo hides before reburial. They were feasted and honored with a wake and ceremony at Sinte Gleska University, where members of the community were allowed, at last, to pay their respects. The repatriation ceremonies and events made international news, covered by several media outlets. Secretary of the Interior Deb Haaland attended the ceremonies. "The experience of our people and boarding schools' legacy has been stifled for generations," she said. "So many families have wanted to know what became of their relatives. People have wanted answers for a very long time, and I think that we finally have an opportunity to get those answers." Tribes continue to work to bring home the approximately 180 remains of children who are still buried at Carlisle.

Not long after visiting Carlisle, I uncovered disturbing information showing that the graves of children buried there and at other school cemeteries only hint at the actual mortality rates associated with boarding school attendance.

For instance, George Little Wound was gravely ill when he was sent home to Pine Ridge from Carlisle in 1889, just three years after his arrival there. Little Wound, the son of Chief Little Wound, was among a group of three Pine Ridge students shipped home together with what the school physician described as "incipient consumption" and "scrofula," a disfiguring infection of the skin and lymph nodes caused by the same bacteria as tuberculosis, according to Carlisle records. All three appeared to survive their illness for some time after they returned to Pine Ridge, though Little Wound was never the same. Forever weakened by the disease, he struggled to support himself and expressed disgust with his school experience. "I went to [Carlisle] school to get a good education . . . but I was greatly mistaken when I went to school," he wrote in 1911, in a survey he sent to Carlisle more than twenty years after returning home. "I come home with sickness and do not know any thing . . . and believe I may never get well from the sickness which I brought from the school," he wrote. "I am in a miserable place and bad condition living in a one-room log home without floor where I am unable to help myself." Government-sanctioned policies amounting to mass murder extended far beyond the number of burials in school cemeteries, fueling the deaths of more than 100,000 Indians, about one-third of the population, in a period of less than forty years. In 1860, the Indian population was estimated to be 339,000; by 1900, it had dropped to about 237,000. This rapid reduction in population coincides with assimilation policy years including the Dawes Act and boarding schools. Although the federal government failed to keep accurate death records for either boarding schools or reservations, schools clearly played a key role in spreading disease in the Indian population. Not unlike the smallpox-infected blankets distributed to Indians in the eighteenth century by British forces during the French and Indian War, U.S. government leaders either intentionally or through informed inaction weaponized contagious disease during the boarding school era in an attempt to create a final solution to the country's Indian problem. The vector, however, was far more sinister than blankets; they used the Indians' own children to spread disease and death.

Pratt's early concern about deaths at Carlisle was well founded. Children attending Carlisle and all the Indian boarding schools, especially those located off reservations, began to sicken or die almost immediately from tuberculosis, diphtheria, measles, and other diseases shortly after their arrival. Their diminished immune systems were exacerbated by poor food, hard labor, and the emotional toll of homesickness. Pratt's great scheme to kill the Indian to save the man soon included killing the man as well. By confining large numbers of children from sparsely populated rural locations into close, unventilated, dirty quarters, Pratt inadvertently created an especially efficient vector for transmission of disease. The deadliest was tuberculosis; in the years following the beginning of the federal boarding school era, 1880 to the 1920s, the rates of tuberculosis infection and death skyrocketed at schools and on reservations. Between 1896 and 1906, nearly one-fifth of the population on Pine Ridge died from the disease. Pratt soon realized his folly, but rather than risk casting doubt on his grand scheme, he placed the blame on the Indians themselves, accusing them of sending sick children to the school, and railed against their unhygienic, primitive ways as the cause of death. He blamed one student's death on contagion from a letter from home. Pratt quietly began sending very sick children home to die rather than enlarge the school's cemetery. Other schools soon followed suit. In a letter to the commissioner of Indian Affairs requesting funding for children's travel, Pratt describes the process as "getting rid of weak timber." The school's physician agreed, noting that children with incurable diseases who are likely to die young should be sent home.

Given the poor access to health care on reservations, sending a child sick with tuberculosis home was a death sentence not only for the children but also for their families and communities. In 1904, Pratt wrote a letter to the commissioner of Indian Affairs: "Occasionally students recover who are sent home under these circumstances (sick with tuberculosis) recover, but in most cases they linger awhile then for lack of proper treatment and attention and from being surrounded by the degrading, impoverished and irregular conditions at their homes, pass away." Although a total of sixteen children reportedly died at Carlisle between 1880 and 1881, thirty-seven sick children were sent home. Their fate, however, is unknown. There was no reliable method of, or effort dedicated to, gathering vital statistics among Indians during this era. Indian agents relied on a series of district or boss farmers to record data on births and deaths. The white farmers were employed by the federal government as part of the directives under the Dawes Act, teaching Indians how to farm on their land allotments. The data gathered by the district farmers was often incomplete and seldom included information beyond name and date of birth or death. There are numerous references, however, in historical records and archives that describe the high rates of tuberculosis and resulting death. A missionary at the Wind River Reservation in Wyoming calculated that between 1881 and 1894, more than half of the seventy-three children sent to Carlisle died either at the school or shortly after returning home. In 1897 the superintendent at Crow Creek Indian boarding school in South Dakota reported to Washington that the entire school population was infected with tuberculosis. As a parent, one can imagine the initial flood of relief when a sick child returns home, the tearful homecoming, and the chance to embrace and soothe. The relief, however, was fleeting. Parents stood by helplessly, watching their children suffer and die, and then horrifically witnessed other family members and maybe even themselves sicken and die from the contagious disease.

Complaints from Indian parents and reservation agents in the form of letters to Pratt and officials in Washington about the high rates of death related to disease and attendance at boarding schools began to rise. The Indian agent at Pine Ridge wrote to the commissioner of Indian Affairs informing him that 20 percent of the population were infected with some form of tuberculosis; 60 percent of related deaths were among school-age children. "It is not sufficient to send children afflicted with tuberculosis home from the schools without making some adequate preparation for caring for them. It is equivalent to sending them home to die," he wrote. By 1925, when the overall tuberculosis mortality rate in the United States was 87 deaths per 100,000, the rate among American Indians and Alaska Natives was 603 per 100,000, nearly seven times greater than that of the general population. James Walker, a physician in the Indian

Service who served as doctor at the Pine Ridge reservation from 1896 to 1906, carefully collected data relating to tuberculosis there and found the death rate rose by 62 percent for each of the years he kept data. In an 1899 report to the commissioner of Indian Affairs, W. H. Clapp, who oversaw Pine Ridge as Indian agent, wrote, "The prevailing disease among the Oglala Sioux Indians is tuberculosis, almost one-half of whom appear to be affected by it. The larger percentage is among the children and it appears to be increasing." By the early twentieth century, tuberculosis had grown to epidemic proportions across Indian country. "Pulmonary tuberculosis is widespread," wrote the Indian Service inspector William McConnell in a 1904 report to the commissioner about tuberculosis among Native populations. "It is common. It is fatal. It is insidious. It is everywhere."

Conditions at the other boarding schools, according to archives, were often worse than those at Carlisle. Pratt's high profile in the public eye helped him gain more government support, such as access to additional food rations and clothing for his students, but other schools didn't fare as well. For instance, when the Haskell U.S. Indian Industrial Training School in Kansas opened to twenty-two students in 1884 and increased to more than four hundred within the year, it was not considered fit to be occupied, the former director of the Haskell Cultural Center Bobbi Rahder told me in a 2004 interview. During the first year, ten students died from causes such as starvation, exposure, and disease, according to Rahder.

The situation at religious schools was similar. In 2022, I found a house diary kept by the Sisters of St. Francis who served at Holy Rosary Mission on the Pine Ridge reservation from 1888 to 1929. There are many references to parents complaining to the local Indian agent as well as the officials at the Bureau of Indian Affairs (BIA) about conditions at the school. The chief complaint focused on deaths and illness as well as harsh discipline meted out by the nuns and priests. "The Indians complained to the government that the sisters gave their children consumption." Other entries detail several nuns teaching children while infected with tuberculosis, including one about a visiting government doctor who forbade one nun from continuing to teach, saying she should be sent to a sanitorium. The nuns seemed oblivious but agreed to place the women in quarantine. The nuns' diary is among one of the few written historical accounts containing details of the suffering endured by students sick with tuberculosis and other diseases at boarding schools. A 1915 entry describes the short life and death of Clara Condelario. It appears that Condelario was in her early twenties when she died.

She is described as an orphan who first came to the mission in 1890. Her Mexican father and Indian mother were both deceased. She asked to remain at the mission (after her schooling was completed) and live like the sisters. The nuns allowed Clara to remain. "One day," the sister secretary wrote, "whilst scrubbing in the church [Clara] slipped and knocked her elbow on a bench and broke her arm." According to the diary, Clara didn't tell the sisters "until the arm pained her so much she could hardly dress herself." They sent her to a hospital in Omaha, where her arm was put in a cast. "After we removed it [the cast] things were not as they should be so we prevailed on her to return to hospital. She had several sores on her body, the doctor who examined her also found she had appendicitis. When they operated they found the [intestines] were decayed because she had tuberculosis of the stomach. There was nothing they could do, she died a few days later." The sister historian added, "A requiem was held. She was the first Sioux girl to make a vow of chastity. She is buried near the sisters in the cemetery."

Trachoma, often called "sore eyes," a bacterial infection that could lead to blindness if left untreated, was endemic in the schools. The nun's diary describes the excruciating treatment in which the children's inner eyelids are repeatedly scraped with a scalpel. During one round of treatment, a government doctor visited the school, treating more than ninety children for the disease. They lay in beds packed into the darkened school's parlor, where they remained for several days. The sister historian complained that nothing else could be accomplished at the mission due to the treatments. She expressed annoyance that the "government seems very much interested in the corporal benefit of the Indians." Notes of student deaths appear

mostly in passing: "seven students died during first year of school";
in 1913, the sister historian notes that an eight-year-old boy dies from
eating elm blossoms; an entry in 1918 reads, "the flu came . . . among
the Indians were many deaths . . . we had funerals every day."

Information on the number of Indian schools, students, and subsequent deaths is incomplete, but according to new accounts gathered by the National Native American Boarding School Healing
Coalition and the 2022 Department of the Interior's *Federal Indian
Boarding School Initiative Investigative Report,* more than five hundred federal or religious boarding schools operated in the United
States—such as Carlisle and Haskell—with capacities for up to one
thousand children each. It's estimated that nearly ten thousand children attended Carlisle over its thirty-nine-year history. The number
of Indian deaths either during or after attending Indian boarding
schools and rates of disease and death of family and community
members infected by students could be in the tens of thousands.

Preston McBride, an assistant professor at Pomona College in
California, who spent years researching boarding school deaths for
his doctoral dissertation, estimates that as many as forty thousand
Native children died while attending boarding school and thousands of others died after going home sick.

"Sending sick students back to their communities made them
deadly pathogen carriers," McBride wrote in his dissertation. "Indeed,
school superintendents routinely infected Indigenous communities
across the United States by sending ill children and young adults
home. When terminally or terribly ill students approached death,
superintendents sent them home to possibly infect others and
die." McBride, of Comanche descent, combed through school and
national archives as well as census data and news reports of four federal Indian boarding schools: the Carlisle school in Pennsylvania; the
U.S. Indian Industrial Training School in Haskell, Kansas; Chemawa
Indian School in Oregon; and the Sherman Institute in California.
He examined records from 1870 to 1934 and used the information
from the four schools to arrive at his estimate of deaths.

McBride's findings already far exceed the 973 boarding school deaths found by the Department of the Interior investigative reports, including volume two that was released in July 2024. His research found that official records list that 831 students died at just the four schools he examined, and that 3,947 students were sent home from the schools during this period, mostly because of illness. "I took all the archival material I could find and compared it to school superintendent reports sent to the commissioner of Indian Affairs," McBride told me in an interview. "Death rates were routinely underreported across all four schools." He was also able to determine that at least 1,000 died after being sent home sick, in addition to the number of students reported to have died while enrolled at the school. "Accurate numbers are hard to come by," he said. "I describe most of the deaths as 'administrative disappearance.'"

There is every indication through archival reports and communications that government leaders were well aware of the role schools played in spreading disease and death. In the early days of federal administration of boarding schools, the government required schools to submit periodic reports about student attendance. The reports took the shape of preprinted forms that included columns for student names, tribal affiliation, age, grade, date of graduation, runaway or withdrawal from school, and death. While researching boarding school records at the U.S. National Archives and some Christian missionary collections, I noticed that sometime around the late nineteenth century some of the forms no longer contained the column labeled "died." Did deaths decrease to a level deemed unworthy of reporting? Did someone in the Indian office experience a spasm of conscience over relegating the death of a child to a simple hash mark on a government form? Or was the practice an outright attempt to cover up the high rates of death and disease?

The complete story lies somewhere in the National Archives' Record Group 75, the vast collection of federal Indian records spread throughout the agency's more than forty locations throughout the country. In a telephone interview in July 2024, I asked assistant secretary for Indian Affairs Bryan Newland if he could account for the disparity in the number of children who died at boarding schools found by researchers in his office and the numbers found by McBride. "We did the best we could with the resources, time, and information we had, but we've been clear that there's a lot more information that can help fill in the details," said Newland, a citizen of the Bay Mills Indian Community. "There's a lot of work left to be done." In Newland's defense, his office was tasked with examining the entirety of federal boarding schools in a span of three years.

McBride said tuberculosis was "hands down" the number one killer at schools and on reservations during the period he studied. Tuberculosis developed through what he called a "disease synergy," in which waves of measles, pneumonia, and other diseases worked in concert to weaken the immune system, making people susceptible to more dangerous diseases. "Children don't just die," he said. "Once children get beyond age five, they are among the healthiest demographic of any population. Between the ages of eleven and thirteen children are the healthiest they will ever be. Yet this is squarely the age when Native children died at boarding schools." McBride noted a bitter irony in his research about the historical treatment for tuberculosis. Before the use of antibiotics in the 1940s, the gold standard treatment for patients sick with the disease was advising them to live in tents to afford maximum exposure to fresh air. "Basically, they were telling people to go live in tents, which the Lakota were already doing before government officials forced their children away to boarding schools," he said.

At a time when rates of tuberculosis among Indians began to rise rapidly, the federal government responded by doubling down on assimilation-style policies including mandating compulsory attendance. Indeed, the last forty years of the nineteenth century were devastating for Indians, wrought by federal assimilationist policies that brought Indian country to its knees. Although a number of treaties previously included compulsory education, in 1891 the federal government passed a compulsory education law that allowed authorities to withhold food and rations from families or arrest parents who refused to comply. The law also permitted government agents to kidnap children in order to send them to school. In 1894, a group of nineteen Hopi men from Oraibi, Arizona, were sent to prison for refusing to send their children to a government boarding school forty miles away from their village. Meeting organized resistance from parents, the local Indian agent called for support from the U.S. Army. Troops arrested the "hostiles" and, without benefit of trial or legal representation, sent them to Alcatraz Island, then a military jail. They were released about one year later and allowed to return to their village. Although the men claimed that government leaders promised their children wouldn't have to go to school, the promise was not kept.

In the post–Civil War era, tuberculosis was primarily a disease of the city, associated with crowded, filthy living conditions inhabited mostly by the poor and immigrants working for low wages in the country's growing industrial economy. A tuberculosis diagnosis in those days was essentially a death sentence; in the late nineteenth century, 450 Americans, mostly between the ages of fifteen and forty-four, died of the disease every day. Most scientists then believed that tuberculosis was hereditary, a reflection of poor constitution and biological inferiority rather than contagion. This belief was driven by the emerging pseudoscience of eugenics, a term coined in 1883 by Sir Francis Galton, an English explorer and anthropologist who was also a cousin of Charles Darwin, the naturalist who authored *On the Origin of Species.* Galton and other eugenicists misapplied Darwin's theory of natural selection or survival of the fittest to explain high rates of illness and social disparities among the poor and people of color as a matter of heredity of "bad genes." White leaders of the era enthusiastically embraced eugenics theory, citing it as proof of already existing societal beliefs in the superiority of the European population and culture and the physical, social, and mental inferiority of people of color. Within this narrative, white people represented the apex of human development and civilization, an especially reciprocal notion supporting already in-place policies forcing Indian assimilation. Whites were far more inclined to attribute health disparities to heredity rather than differences rooted in race and class. Eugenicists believed that elevated social positions and wealth of Nordic, Ger-

manic, and Anglo-Saxon peoples were attributed to their superior
genetic makeup rather than advantages bestowed by the coincidence
of being born wealthy and white. Although Robert Koch identified
the tuberculosis bacillus in 1882, proving the disease is transmitted
by contagion, the eugenics theory had grown legs and persisted well
into the twentieth century. Indeed, even after contagion was accepted
as the vector for tuberculosis, the theory of eugenics continued to
inform government policies surrounding social welfare and medical programming. Many prominent Progressives including scholars
and scientists supported eugenics and sterilization as a scientific way
to reduce suffering and improve the common good by improving
human heredity through the social control of human breeding. It's
difficult to imagine today, but eugenics ideals and theories influenced nearly every area of social reform, science, and medicine; this
was not a fringe movement. Hundreds of college courses at mainstream universities were dedicated to the subject. Theodore Roosevelt, W. E. B. Du Bois, and Margaret Sanger as well as organizations
like the General Federation of Women's Clubs and many religious
groups were also supporters.

Conditions at Indian residential schools in Canada, rates of
tuberculosis, and reliance on eugenics to guide policy were similar
to those in the United States. In 1879, Nicholas Flood Davin, a lawyer
who was elected as a member of the Canadian Parliament in 1887,
was charged with investigating U.S. boarding schools as an answer
to Canada's shared Indian problem. Favorably impressed with institutions like Carlisle, Davin recommended a similar system. Both
countries relied on research such as the joint report released by the
First International Eugenics Congress and the American eugenicist
Bleecker Van Wagenen in 1912, *Preliminary Report of the Committee
of the Eugenic Section of the American Breeders' Association to Study and
to Report on the Best Practical Means for Cutting Off of the Defective
Germ-Plasm in the Human Population,* to inform federal policies. Van
Wagenen's report included ten remedies for "cutting off the supply
of human defectives," including involuntary sterilization and euthanasia. In the 1927 case *Buck v. Bell,* the U.S. Supreme Court found in

favor of states' rights to compulsory sterilization of people with sup-
posedly "undesirable traits," such as epilepsy, feeblemindedness, and
criminality, which ultimately translated into use primarily against
women of color, including Indians. Thirty-two states passed such
laws. In 1974 a D.C. District Court ruled against use of federal funds
for sterilization.

Residential school researchers in Canada have identified far
more damning and widespread archival evidence of governmental
collusion with eugenics-driven responses to tuberculosis infection
among Indian people. It's likely that since Canada began addressing its residential school history in the early twenty-first century, the
research there is more advanced than in the United States. As in the
United States, Canadian authorities were well aware of the disparities in infection and death among the Indian population. Dr. Peter
Bryce, chief medical officer of the Canadian Departments of the Interior and Indian Affairs, sent several reports about high rates of illness
and death from tuberculosis among Indians in residential schools
and on reserves after conducting research on the population in
1905 and 1906. His 1907 *Report on the Indian Schools of Manitoba and
the Northwest Territories* was published without its recommendations,
which included access to physicians and improved sanitary living
conditions. According to Bryce's 1907 and 1909 reports, the mortality rate among residential school students, mostly from tuberculosis,
was nineteen times that of the general population. The government
failed to acknowledge Bryce's findings or act, but the doctor continued to submit his annual reports. Finally, disgusted by government
inaction, Bryce self-published his report in 1922 after his retirement,
The Story of a National Crime. Duncan Campbell Scott, deputy superintendent of Indian Affairs from 1913 to 1932, wrote in response to
Bryce's findings, "It is readily acknowledged that Indian children lose
their natural resistance to illness by habituating so closely in the residential schools, and that they die at a much higher rate than in their
villages. But this alone does not justify a change in the policy of this
Department, which is being geared towards 'a final solution of our
Indian Problem.'" Scott was an aggressive supporter of the residential

schools and was instrumental in expanding the system. Although Bryce's self-published report gained some traction in the press, the issue quickly fell from public attention. No official action was taken. Worse, in the 1930s and 1940s civil servants concocted a special category of tuberculosis that allegedly affected only the Native population. According to them, "Indian TB" was a unique, more virulent form of the disease to which Indians were more racially susceptible. Although the outright euthanasia of Native people, as recommended in Van Wagenen's report on eugenics, was ultimately rejected on moral grounds, the notion was clearly on the minds of many in leadership such as Scott. Adolf Hitler was greatly influenced by eugenics research and utilized methods suggested by Van Wagenen such as euthanasia in the form of genocide (the final solution) and sterilization among Jewish people and other so-called undesirables during the Nazi regime.

Even today, the vestiges of this pseudoscience continue to live on in American society, which penalizes the poor for the physical and economic outcomes of poverty as though they were fated by poor biology or personal choice. According to the tenets of American exceptionalism, all citizens are equally situated to gain wealth and status by simply pulling themselves up by their bootstraps, even if they lack boots. Or feet. By the beginning of the twentieth century, it seemed to the American public that Indians—like those in Zane Grey's 1925 novel *The Vanishing American*—were destined for extinction. Despite the rapid onslaught of assimilationist policies like boarding schools, however, Indians adapted as they have since time immemorial.

At boarding schools, they watched and listened and, as my mother would say, learned how to talk to white people. Paradoxically, white people managed to learn almost nothing about Indians. Instead, they clung to mythologies created by other white people in popular culture of Indians as destined for extinction or food for playacting an imagined past to enrich America's illusions of exceptionalism created out of a primitive wasteland.

Although unintended by Pratt and other white reformers, board-

ing schools offered students a new common racial, pan-Indian
identity, a source of pride, common experience, and purpose. Many
boarding school survivors returned to become leaders in their communities, uniquely situated to negotiate the seam between white and
Indian communities. The boarding school experience helped ignite
generations of Indian activists and advocates, Red Progressives such
as the writer Zitkala-Sa (Red Bird), whose English name was Ger-
trude Simmons Bonnin, of the Yankton Dakota Tribe, Marie Louise
Bottineau Baldwin of the Turtle Mountain and of Chippewa Indians, Dennison Wheelock of the Oneida Nation, and Luther Standing
Bear of the Lakota Nation. These leaders and many others sought
equal rights and treatment for themselves and their communities. In
1911 they formed the Society of the American Indians, a pan-Indian
group made up almost entirely of boarding school survivors. The
society went on to advocate for Indian citizenship and other reforms.
And George Little Wound, who was sent home sick from Carlisle,
survived. He carried on the efforts of his father, Chief Little Wound,
in tirelessly lobbying the government to build schools on or close
to reservations as a way of reducing illness and death. Chief Little
Wound died in 1899, but his son successfully helped in establishing
a day school in the mid-1930s in Kyle, South Dakota, on the Pine
Ridge Reservation. The Little Wound School, named after George
and his father, is a tribally run institution still in operation today.

As the Progressive Era took hold in America, Indians worked to
turn power, using their newly acquired knowledge of settler systems,
to their favor. But Indian advocates soon found that there were limits to ideals of racial equality even among white reformers in the
Progressive movement. Many embraced the deeply entrenched racist
beliefs based on eugenics. Reformers such as Estelle Reel, superintendent of Indian education from 1898 to 1910, blamed boarding
school graduates' failure to succeed in the white world on eugenics.

Despite all the boarding school teachings about the American
system of government, equality, and freedom, it became abundantly
clear that these tenets applied to Indians only insomuch as they
accepted their place in society as a marginal class, forever occupy-

ing the category of a conquered race. For Indians like my mother, being pulled away from their families, beaten, humiliated, isolated, told they were less-than, and then told that even the diseases that threatened them were somehow their fault became, over time and over generations, something *inside* them rather than a colonial process being *done* to them. No amount of my mother's hand-wringing could erase the stain, nor that of white reformers.

As assimilationist policies continued to diminish Indian wealth, the communities came to rely on boarding schools to care for the growing numbers of needy children. By the time my mother and her siblings came to St. Mary's in 1930, the sisters were well established in Odanah, offering the child-care choice of last resort. Bernice and her brothers and sisters lived at St. Mary's year-round; there was no other place for them to go. Order was the order of the day at the Sister School, where the nuns adhered strictly to their civilizing and proselytizing mission. The sister matron rang the morning bell promptly at 5:00, according to my mother. The girls' dorm was large and drafty, but it was so crowded with single beds one could scarcely walk between them. Curled up tight against the cold, sometimes two to three children to a bed, the girls knew better than to delay; the sister matron was quick to use a wooden switch on malingerers. The girls fairly jumped from the beds into their clothes, eager for the warmth. My mother described how they washed at a communal sink using shared towels; my mother learned to clean her teeth with the towel; there were no toothbrushes. After making their beds, they lined up in preparation to march to the little church, about one-quarter mile away, for morning Mass. Each motion—lining up, marching, sitting, eating, sleeping, washing, praying—was governed by the bell.

The nuns were at war against disorder, dirt, and laziness, traits they believed were endemic among Indians. The phrase "dirty and lazy" preceded directions and criticism. The schedule and curriculum at the Sister School were designed to root out these enemies of civilization and Christian decency. The nuns were impatient with the children, quick with a slap or a well-aimed pinch. Those who dis-

obeyed or were slow at their lessons or work were publicly shamed
in various ways: forced to kneel for hours, forced to wear a dunce
cap, denied food, publicly beaten, or locked in the cellar. The nuns
created a closed Catholic world where only English was spoken and
only complete obedience was tolerated.

After Mass, the children lined up once again and marched back
to the school for breakfast, usually oatmeal or corn mush and tea
or something they called blue milk, akin to skim milk. By 8:00 a.m.
the workday began. Girls worked in the laundry, mending, washing,
and ironing clothing and sheets, or in the kitchen, washing dishes,
hauling water, and cleaning, lots of cleaning. The nuns demanded
special attention to the floors, which the girls scrubbed daily always
on hands and knees in a kind of purifying supplication. Boys and
girls both worked in the garden, weeding and hoeing. Boys milked
the cows and maintained the school's farm, chopped wood, and
helped with repairs and construction. At noon, the children lined
up for dinner, typically bread and soup. Lining up again, they made
their way to classes in reading, religion, penmanship, math, and civics until 3:00 p.m., when they broke for recess for a blessed hour of
ball or reading, Bernice's favorite activity. Sometimes she snuck back
to her bed in the dorm, lounging and reading a novel, eating the
precious crackers Pa sometimes brought. Occasionally she missed
some of the crumbs after shaking out the sheet, but she didn't mind;
they reminded her of Pa. There was a miniature woodstove among
the school's toys, and when she was very young, she and the other
girls built fires in the little stove, baking potatoes stolen from the
garden or the cellar. After recess there was more work until supper,
bread, more soup, and sometimes a little meat. Then it was study and
prayers; kerosene lamps out at 9:00 p.m. It stayed light enough in
the warmer months to read her novels for a few minutes until it got
too dark or the sister matron surprised her with a whack on the bed
frame. There was little in the way of vocational training, although
Auntie Lucille grew adept at tatting lace for sale to white donors
and tourists. Bernice, with her small, quick hands, created beautiful
loomed beadwork, also for white people. The nuns praised her hard

work and attention to detail, but their words were tainted. Although she welcomed and sought their praise, she was secretly shamed by it. Mostly she found it best to keep her head down and avoid attention altogether.

The children relied on their big brother, Don, four years older than Bernice. The nuns were especially harsh with Rags, the youngest, who was about three years old when the children entered the school. Rags was small, wiry, dark, and scruffy. Always on the verge of losing his pants. He irritated the nuns with his ongoing cries for Ma. One evening he slapped at the sisters when they tried to make him eat a supper of stewed onions. Infuriated, several nuns took him in hand, holding him down while forcing the onions into his mouth as he choked and sputtered. Don rushed to help. Pushing them away, he began swinging his fists and landed a terrific blow to one of the nun's chests, knocking the wind out of her. The other nuns retreated as she gasped for breath. Falling to their knees, they began to pray loudly over Don, insisting he was possessed by the devil. *It didn't do any good, though,* Mom told me later, laughing. It didn't do Rags any good either; Don escaped and ran all the way back home. My aunt Pat, just a child, remembers that their dog started barking and there was Don, dressed in his pajamas. He'd run all three miles from the Sister School on that bitter cold winter night. He told their mother how the sisters had nailed Rags to the dining room table because he wouldn't eat stewed onions for dinner. The nuns left him there, nailed to the table, overnight. Later, hearing about Don's skills with his fists, one of the priests recruited him for the school boxing team. The priest also included Don in an Indian dance troupe he'd organized to tour the region raising money for the school. Scrappy and resourceful, Don was constantly on the lookout for food for his siblings. When he weeded the strawberry patch, he'd stuff his mouth and pockets with the sweet fruit, later sharing it with them. Sister would yell, *Donald, what are you doing?* Barely able to speak with a mouthful of berries, he'd answer, *Mmmm, mmm, nothin', Sister!* Being children—and maybe also because they were Ojibwe children—they were stubborn in their search for joy and mischief. The nuns strictly forbade speaking the Ojibwe language, but they said nothing about pig Latin. The children soon realized that the German and French nuns, for whom English was often a second language, couldn't understand their childish wordplay, especially if they spoke quickly. *Ooodgay orning-may, ister-sey hithead-say* (Good morning, Sister Shithead), they'd say sweetly to the sister matron. The sisters suspected there was something subversive about the word game but were unable to sort it out. The children also delighted in ringing the daily Angelus, fighting over the privilege. The bell signals the Catholic call to prayer that begins, "The angel of the Lord declared unto Mary," but the best part was riding the upward return of the bell rope, which lifted them off the ground. And there was the kindly priest who sometimes gave candy to the little kids. They would swarm around him, calling, *Father, Father,* as he reached into the large sleeves of his friar robes. *Well, let's see what I have,* bringing out handfuls of small sweets. And there was Sister Amanda, a young, lively nun who was a favorite among the big girls. They taught Sister how to do the jitterbug, but Mother Superior Sister Catherine barged into the room, slapping the young nun soundly across the face. *Oh, please don't cry, Sister,* the girls said, trying to soothe her. But Sister Amanda left the school soon afterward.

There were no more visits from Ma or other family members. Only Pa came to see them. He brought maple sugar candy from his sugar bush, crackers, and other small treats. *My father was named Joseph, and like Saint Joseph, he was a carpenter,* my mother told me. Cele, however, was loud, hateful, and mean, forever belittling and criticizing Joe for his drinking and failure to hold down a job.

Pa was a happy-go-lucky kind of drunk, she said during our nighttime visits. She often described the final awful fight between Joe and Cele that ended the marriage. My mother laid the blame for her abandonment squarely with Cele and her extended family. Perversely, according to my mother, Cele's family hated Joe because he was from Red Cliff, a neighboring Ojibwe reservation.

I remember once Pa came home drunk, happy, and singing. My mother got mad and hit him over the head with a beer bottle. He sank right down on the ground. I screamed and screamed and screamed. I thought she'd killed him. I could feel her fists clench tightly in the dark as she relived the moment. We waited together for it to pass. I held my breath. At last she continued. *After that they broke up and we went to live at the Sister School. My mother's relatives were just like her. All they did was criticize; they never helped him. If they helped us kids, they made us feel like dirt. Pa was the only one who ever cared about me.*

He was the one who visited us and wanted to get us away from those nuns, she continued. The nuns kept a strict eye on the children during Pa's visits. *They treated us like prisoners, sitting in on all our talks; they were scared we'd learn something Indian,* she later said. Perhaps it was the nuns' fearful measures to keep culture and language away that further sparked the children's interest in all things Ojibwe. For instance, she recalled that the nuns hired an Ojibwe man to create paintings to sell to tourists. *He painted scenes from Ojibwe life and would tell us all about the old ways and teachings,* she said. The nuns shooed them away, but they visited the artist as often as they could, eager for his stories.

When life at the Sister School grew unbearable, Don would organize an escape; he and his siblings would run away to find Joe. Joe was one of those old-time backwoods Ojibwe who preferred to rely on traditional hunting and gathering. He also kept a still back in the Bad River sloughs where he made homemade whiskey, selling it from his shack. Bernice loved her father above all others. *Pa had a little tavern where he sold his homemade brew; he'd stand me up on the bar, and I'd sing "All Around the Water Tank" for the people.* As a child, I imagined her as an Indian version of Shirley Temple in a white dress and black patent leather shoes. Like Little Miss Marker, she was the star of the show, saving the adults from their misguided lives. The tavern, I learned later, was a dirt-floor shack; the bar consisted of two barrels with raw boards laid between them. When he was sober, Joe would take the children berry picking in the woods, patiently explaining the Ojibwe words for plants and their uses. When Bernice cried from hunger, he would brew her tea from the leaves of a special tree until they sold enough berries to buy food. *He always called me my girl,* she said. Don helped Pa bring whiskey back from the still, but soon Pa would get too drunk to help, often falling down in the boat. The children were forced to look for food, and the reservation police would find them, alerted by the sisters, and they would be taken back to school. It was an ongoing pattern throughout her childhood.

At first Bernice welcomed the small treats or used toys and clothing brought by white donors to the school. They were usually white women, over whom the nuns fawned, lavishing them with praise for their Christian generosity. She recalled how a tall white lady visiting the school clucked her tongue, watching Bernice deftly looming beads. As the woman leaned down close to inspect the work, Bernice saw that her eyes were filled with pity. Unexpectedly, hatred washed over Bernice; she pulled away from the large pink face. And then there was the white family who spent their yearly Christmas Eves at the school, entertaining and feeding the students. *We were supposed to be so goddamned grateful for that crummy, secondhand stuff they gave us,* she said. *We were always writing thank-you notes and begging letters to the donors.* She wanted to spit in the faces of those sanctimonious white ladies. They and the nuns were so sure of her inferiority and of their supremacy. Those lessons in civics class about equality and rights, she realized with disgust, clearly weren't meant for Indians. But she made up her mind; one day she would be the one those nuns respected and to whom they ingratiated themselves. Like all Indians who went to boarding schools, she learned to analyze white people, their habits, their facial expressions and body language, their coded speech. She learned their predilections, dislikes, and fears. Bernice learned one of the most important Indian boarding school lessons: not necessarily how to be civilized and assimilated, but how to talk to white people. This is how she survived, and this was how she eventually triumphed.

FOUR

RAGE FOR SURVIVAL

There's an old joke about Ojibwe men's notoriously flat asses. It's said they made the mistake of getting into arguments with Ojibwe women who proceeded to chew those impudent asses right down to the nub. Joking aside, Ojibwe women are known for their fierceness. That's how we survived. It's little wonder, then, that women like my mother turned to what they knew best in order to survive the crushing experience of boarding school. Beginning in her early teens, Bernice grew more aware of the injustice and hypocrisy of the crushing charity of the Sister School. She claimed her power and dignity in the only way she knew: through defiance, anger, and resentment. Rage will, it seems, keep you alive. In so doing, she set a course for revenge. Her vengeance would be disproving all the prejudices the sisters held about Indians as lazy, dirty, and biologically inferior. She started work on the outsized chip she forever carried on her shoulder, sometimes nearly collapsing under its weight. *I made up my mind!* was her go-to phrase, which she repeated her entire life and—increasingly as she got older—to prompts only she could hear. Today, when all troubling behavior seems to be medicalized, psychologists have created a diagnosis, a label, for this behavior: oppositional defiant disorder. Traumatized children, they say, sometimes grow defiant as a means to control anxious or dangerous situations. In that context, defiance isn't abnormal; it's an understandable reaction to powerlessness, a means of protection. Broadening out that understanding further, oppositional defiant disorder is a natural response to conquest, especially when the oppressor makes an ongoing fetish of their domination.

The nuns always made us feel "less than"; Sister Catherine would tell us we should fall to our knees every day in gratitude for charity from the church, she told me during our nightly talks when I was young. The arrogance of the school's day scholars, who lived at home, was especially hard for her to bear. There was a girl whose mother carefully braided her hair every day before school. "Braids Girl" sashayed into class every day wearing a clean ironed dress; sometimes with a small, folded hankie pinned near the hem. Seeing my mother eye the hankie, Braids Girl said, *My ma puts this on for me.* Braids Girl fingered the piece of cloth and said, *Too bad your ma doesn't come around.* The girl took pleasure in reminding Bernice of her mother's absence. One afternoon, Bernice was sweeping out the cellar as punishment; Braids Girl hung on to the doorjamb, swinging her legs into the open space. *Bernice was bad; she has to sweep the dirty old cellar,* she teased in a singsong voice. Barely stopping, Bernice swung the broom hard at Braids Girl's face, knocking her to the ground. Startled, the girl sat silently for a few moments, her mouth opened wide until she jumped to her feet. Bawling loudly like a calf, she ran to the sisters' convent. Bernice watched her retreat and followed along slowly. Sister was holding a raw piece of meat to Braids Girl's eye as she sat in a kitchen chair. *Bernice, how could you do such an awful thing?!* the nun demanded. *Well, she shouldn't have teased me,* Bernice said. It was a long punishment: Bernice had extra cleaning duties for a week and got a thrashing with the belt besides. But Braids Girl had a big black shiner and stopped teasing my mother.

After finishing eighth grade at the Sister School, Bernice lived with her father, Joe, in his dirt-floor shack in Odanah. Even though they were among the poorest of the poor, she was careful about her appearance; she kept her meager wardrobe immaculate, homemade dirndl skirts and white blouses, forever pushing back against the "dirty Indian" trope. Her famous haughtiness was aimed not only at the nuns but also at the Ojibwe community that had grown too poor to provide traditional social supports for children and families. The betrayal cut her to the quick; if they truly loved her, she felt, they would have found a way. One day, she vowed, she would show them all. Aloof and pretty, she attracted male attention, especially from white men. She described how the boys from Odanah grew furious seeing her dance with a handsome Swede in Ashland. The men began to fight; the Swede had a knife and stabbed a boy from Odanah. She earned a reputation as a troublemaker.

Later, responding to a drunk white guy pawing at her as she sat in the train depot in Ashland, she brushed his touch from her arm. *Keep your goddamned dirty white man's hands offa me!* Auntie Lucille, fearing a confrontation, urged Bernice to be less combative. *I don't care. Who do they think they are anyway?* she said.

St. Mary's School didn't officially participate in the outing system like that at Carlisle and Haskell, but white people from the area frequently contacted the sisters when looking for laborers. Bernice graduated from eighth grade at St. Mary's around age thirteen; at that time, the sisters recommended her for a housekeeping job with a wealthy white lady in the nearby town of Ashland. She lived in a small room by the back door; after serving the woman, she took her own meals on a low table in the kitchen. She used a special silver device called a crumb sweeper to clear off the tablecloth between dinner courses. The lady was a lawyer, one of the first women to pass the bar in the state, and a "true lady." One day the lady came home unexpectedly, finding my mother and her friends in the house's fancy parlor. Laughing loudly, they failed to hear her enter. Mom's friend Beanie boldly smoked a cigarette with her big feet propped up on the carved coffee table. The lady lawyer let her go after that, but Bernice often recalled details of the woman's speech, mannerisms, and dress. According to my mother, she was *quality.* She became a model for Bernice's self-invention.

By the early twentieth century, after more than five decades of the great federal assimilation process at boarding schools, Indians grew inured to the experience. For better or worse, being exiled to boarding schools had become normalized in Indian country, almost a rite of passage. By the 1920s it's estimated that 76 percent of Native children had attended boarding school. Although many Indian people succumbed to the steamroller of assimilationist policies either through death or the loss of language and identity, many survived, learning to protect culture and traditions in ingenious ways.

Like my mother, they set about reinventing and making a way for themselves in this new reality. Indians' ability to discern the nuances and parameters of white society was remarkable. The rules of the game required not only knowledge and intelligence but also the ability to smooth over white fear and fragility while convincing white people of Indians' humanity. After decades of federal boarding schools and associated daily contact with white people, Indians used that experience and their famous adaptive skills to survive in this new society. In 1917, for the first time in more than a hundred years, the birthrate surpassed the death rate among Indians. Newly educated Indians and white Progressives began pushing for reforms in the military-style boarding school model that emphasized constant drilling and marching and mostly failed to adequately prepare Indians for participation in white America. Very slowly, the federal government's approach to Indian education began to change. In the early twentieth century, Progressives began describing the practice of forcibly separating children from their families for extended periods as "so monstrous and so un-Christian." Zitkala-Sa, who graduated from a boarding school in Indiana and later taught at Carlisle, wrote scathing essays for *The Atlantic*, including "The School Days of an Indian Girl," in which she described the emotional pain of separation from her family and succumbing to the "iron routine" of boarding school life. Educators were also promoting ideals of the Progressive child study movement, which celebrated primitive cultures' emphasis on family and natural growth. Considered out of step with new education theories, Lieutenant Pratt, the destroyer of all things Indian, was invited to resign by Commissioner of Indian Affairs William Jones in 1904. By 1909, after more than 4,000 students attended

Carlisle, only 532 received diplomas, then the equivalent of a grammar school education. In a stunning example of magical thinking, architects of the boarding school system made only the most meager, poorly thought-out plans for graduates to reap the rewards of the assimilation process. Students returned to communities where there was no use for the skills learned at school and little access to capital or loans with which to begin farming or other trades. White reformers had also failed to take into account the barrier that racism played in keeping Indians out of jobs. In the end, they blamed the failure on Indians themselves.

On the positive side, the strict military structure of boarding schools helped prepare students who either were drafted or enlisted in the military. A Cherokee man enrolled at Chilocco Indian boarding school in Oklahoma described the military atmosphere at the school: "We started drilling at five o'clock in the morning; I later joined the Marine Corps and did twenty-eight years with the Corps. You hear people talk about how tough boot camp was, that was a breeze after Chilocco!" In some cases, Indians trained at boarding schools fared better in the military than their poor white untrained contemporaries. They qualified for jobs as carpenters' mates, shipwrights, blacksmiths, and electricians. About 30 percent of the adult male Indian population, double that of all American men, served in the military during World War I. Most Indians, however, were assigned to the infantry, often in the most dangerous duties such as scouts and snipers nearest the front. Racism and pop-culture beliefs about Indians' warrior nature fueled these actions by white leadership. Their casualty rates were five times higher than the American Expeditionary Forces as a whole. Although they were not yet recognized as U.S. citizens, Indian men were required to register for the World War I draft. In 1919, Congress granted citizenship to those who served in the military, about five years before the federal government conferred the same for all adult Indians in 1924.

In the twentieth century, Indians grew emboldened by tenets of the Progressive movement. Two hundred seventy-six students signed a petition requesting an official government investigation of Carlisle school, complaining about brutal corporal punishment, too great an emphasis on sports, and woefully outdated vocational training that failed to prepare students for jobs and life after graduation. The superintendent of Carlisle and several administrators were dismissed after the investigation; many other employees received stiff reprimands. Once considered the best model of assimilation and salvation for the American Indian, Carlisle Indian school closed in 1918. After decades of navigating the boarding school experience, Indians began slowly making the schools their own while simultaneously turning the power to claim their new roles as American citizens.

In 1926, "all Indian trails led to Lawrence, Kansas," when students and faculty dedicated Haskell's now-iconic arch and a new football stadium, the first lit arena in the region. Athletics, especially football, were popular at Indian boarding schools in the 1920s. Now Haskell had its own stadium where the team could host home games. White fans flocked to boarding school games, part of the new nostalgia for Indians of the past; here at Haskell they could safely imagine the game as a pseudo battle, a reenactment of the Indian wars. Media of the day declared the weekend celebration the largest gathering of Indians in peacetime, predicting more than eight thousand people from various tribes would travel there to camp on the forty-acre plot of campus land set aside for that purpose. The headlines contained the typical corny racist memes of the day: "Primitive Tribe Coming"; "More Than 8,000 Redskins from All Over U.S. Will Be Present at Dedication of New Haskell Institute Stadium." Officials at the Indian Bureau were eager to showcase the school's "successful" assimilation and civilization programming in which students were transformed from primitive Indians into productive participants in the democratic process. The celebration included a parade through the city of Lawrence with floats titled "Indians of the Past," with Indians dressed in traditional regalia, contrasted with "Indians of the Present," which carried Indians dressed in office and work attire holding signs reading "blacksmith," "electrician," and "steamfitter," indicating "progress of the race." Students put on a huge buffalo feed for their visiting relatives camped near the stadium and hosted a giant powwow that managed to scare the white visitors.

"Knees bend grotesquely; moccasined feet descend toe downward; arms rise and fall. Beribboned weapons are twirled and swung menacingly. But the dance is stopped before the ecstasy comes. Enough is enough," wrote a journalist with *The Kansas City Times*. After Indians were safely conquered and no longer posed threats to white property and enterprise, white people grew nostalgic for an Indian who never was. They were eager to be thrilled by the threat we once represented. Boarding schools, keen to profit from the emerging white imperialist nostalgia market, often staged orations of *The Song of Hiawatha* by Henry Wadsworth Longfellow and pageants with "real" Indian dancing and reenactments of primitive life. I like to think, however, that Indians at the Haskell celebration largely ignored the white tourists. Under the cover of providing entertainment, Indians camped, visited, ate, and danced, embracing the opportunity to spend time with friends and relatives.

The Haskell Fighting Indians beat the Bucknell College Bisons 36–0 that weekend in the first football game played in the new stadium. The celebration was a triumph. The triumph was a triumph: Haskell students proved that they could at once be both American and Indian. The arch, described by officials as one of the first memorials for World War I veterans, and stadium were paid for entirely by Indian donors including two former students, Agnes Quapaw Hoffman and Alice Beaver Hallam, both of the Quapaw Nation, now wealthy from profits from their mineral rights. The arch, officials claimed, was a declaration of patriotism, an embrace of civilization, and a rejection of all things Indian. They were only partly right. The Indian students and visitors were indeed Americans expressing their patriotism. But, overlooked by the white people there, the Indians were also celebrating their heritage through a newfound sense of common purpose and pan-Indian identity. In their own way, Indians were actively repudiating the eugenics-driven belief that they were biologically and intellectually inferior to white people. In the process, they made Haskell their own. The name still runs deep in Indian country; scarcely an Indian family in America lacks a tie to the school somewhere in its family tree. In 2009, I visited the school as part of a writing project for Haskell's 125th-year commemoration publication. To walk on the athletic fields of Haskell Indian Nations University is to walk in the footsteps of some of the greatest American Indian athletes of all time. Billy Mills, who won an Olympic gold medal for the ten-thousand-meter run; Jim Thorpe, football star and Olympian who was the first president of the American Professional Football Association (later the National Football League); John Levi, football and baseball player; and others are all part of the Haskell athletic legacy. Congresswoman Sharice Davids and the National Indian Gaming Association chairman, Ernest Stevens Jr., are among notable former students as well. This is Haskell Indian Nations University, part of the U.S. tribal colleges and universities system, where Indians can pursue four-year degrees in Indigenous and American Indian studies, elementary education, business administration, and environmental science. The old arch still stands, occupying a central spot on the campus. Sitting near the edifice where tall pines cast shadows against its concrete face, I watched the flow of campus life. College students, as they do everywhere, hurried by distractedly, absorbed in the demands of classes, life, and, increasingly, the future. The arch's original symbolism as a metaphoric passageway to assimilation has passed into obscurity, but it's a potent reminder of how hard Indians have fought to stake their claim in America while still maintaining their identity.

Indian boarding schools, especially before 1940, could undeniably be violent and dangerous with a primary focus on eradicating Indian identity. Discipline was brutal. The most draconian punishment was whipping, universally feared by students, especially boys. Annie Bigman described seeing the adult teachers at Oklahoma's Rainy Mountain Boarding School whip the boys: "When they whip 'em, some would half kill them." Her fellow student Bert Geikoumah agreed: "Well, they whip you hard. Boy they don't monkey with you. They whip you." Despite the hardships, however, some former students spoke fondly of their days at the institutions where they forged lifelong friendships and even met future spouses. Heading to far-away boarding schools also offered escape from desperate economic conditions and limited opportunities on reservations. Moreover, they offered travel and adventure for some eager young folks, especially teenagers. Thomas Wildcat Alford, Shawnee from Oklahoma, recalled his train ride to the Hampton Institute in Virginia in the late nineteenth century: "I recollect the impression made on my mind as we traveled over the beautiful country, and through well cultivated fields, past beautiful homes and through busy bustling cities and small towns. All was strange to our eyes, accustomed only to the western prairies and lowlands or rolling timber hills. A wonderland indeed!"

Although quality training and education were often lacking, some students went on to work in government Indian Service jobs. By 1899, 45 percent of these approximately twenty-five hundred jobs in the Indian school service were occupied by returned boarding school students. And for many, the mission to eradicate Indian language and culture failed. At Chilocco school, for instance, students organized clandestine peyote meetings and all-night stomp dances. A student at Riverside Indian School in Oklahoma recalled, "I didn't learn my Indian ways at home; I learned them right here" at Riverside. Parker McKenzie, who attended Rainy Mountain in Oklahoma, described the institution's unsuccessful war against Native languages. One student caught speaking her Indigenous language was forced to hold quinine tablets in her mouth as punishment. "Kiowa remained the dominant language when away from campus," McKenzie said. When he wooed his future wife, also a student at Rainy Mountain, he would send her messages written in a phonetic version of the language he created himself. This, he said, kept teachers from confiscating the notes and reading them aloud to the class. McKenzie's syllabary later led to the first written form of the language. Students bonded with members of other tribes, using traditional skills such as storytelling and dark humor to transcend the daily attacks on culture, language, and family. In typical Native fashion, they tagged the most hated teachers with descriptive nicknames. Frank Mitchell, who attended the boarding school at Fort Defiance, Arizona, recalled calling an especially mean and unattractive woman teacher "The Woman Who Makes You Scream" in the Navajo language. Francis La Flesche of the Omaha Tribe of Nebraska described how he and other boys concocted a scheme to gain a half holiday at the Presbyterian Indian mission school in Nebraska. La Flesche, part of a self-described gang of Omaha boys, "the Big Seven," scattered corn outside a flimsy section of the school farm's pigpen. Later, during geography class, the superintendent burst in shouting the pigs had broken loose and needed to be rounded up. "We did not wait to be ordered a second time; all afternoon we chased pigs and had a glorious time," he said. La Flesche went on to become one of the first professional Native American ethnologists. He is best known for a voluminous dictionary of the Omaha language. Julia of the Turtle Mountain Band of Chippewa described how she ingeniously survived brutal punishments at St. Joseph's Indian School. She accidently broke an egg while helping the nuns cook breakfast. Enraged, one of the nuns threw Julia in the cellar, locking her away for three days. "I was so weak, I had to go to the infirmary," she recalled during a discussion with Lajimodiere, author of *Stringing Rosaries,* a collection of interviews with boarding school survivors. It became a painful pattern between Julia and the nun. After a while, however, she hid a can opener in the cellar so she could open cans of food when she was sent there. "I thought, boy, this girl isn't going to starve anymore!" Seeing a window high up in the cellar, she noticed legs walking past. So she created steps to the window using stacked cans. "I hollered out and there was [some] boys," she said. Knowing they were hungry, Julia opened up cans of fruit and other food, passing them to the kids outside. Shared adversity helped create a social glue among Indians that in turn emboldened them to stake their own claims to the rights and promises guaranteed in the U.S. Constitution to all Americans. Equality was a concept Indians could get behind.

And so they did, in ways that continue to surprise and inspire even today. Although Indians were forced to make accommodations to an oppressive system, they survived and even prevailed in many ways.

I was surprised to learn that my grandma Cele was among the many unrecognized early champions of Indian rights. I stumbled across her name completely by accident as I pored over 1920s-era records of congressional hearings dealing with misuse of Indian trust and treaty funds and corruption within the Bureau of Indian Affairs. It was late at night and my eyes were burning from hours of staring at the tiny print when the name "Cecelia Rabideaux" grabbed my attention. Initially, I thought my tired eyes were deceiving me. Here was the name of the woman my mother hated, the bad mother who abandoned her children. With little in the way of legal, economic, or social protection for Indian women in those days, Cele was placed at an untenable moral impasse: physical survival or motherhood. She chose survival; my mother never forgave her and seldom spoke her name. Cele married a white man named Herschel and started a new family; she died in 1956, a year before I was born.

I knew little about Grandma Cele except that she was loud and profane and baked excellent pies. Uncle Russell, my mother's half brother, confirmed this. He recalled sitting at the table with Cele and the family when their father, Herschel, began choking on one of her pies. Still angry at Herschel's previous night's drunkenness, Cele shrieked at him, *Choke then, you sonovabitch!*

I was surprised to see Cecelia Rabideaux described as a "responsible woman" and chair of the local League of Women Voters during a 1926 floor debate in the House of Representatives regarding the corrupt judicial practices of Bureau of Indian Affairs reservation superintendents. Cele had written to James Frear, representative for Wisconsin's tenth district, for help, describing how her brother Paul was arrested without warrant or due process and jailed seventy miles away from the Bad River reservation, on the Lac du Flambeau reservation. Like many Indian people during that era, Paul was arrested and incarcerated at the whim of a reservation superintendent. As part of the Code of Indian Offenses, enacted in 1883, government reservation agents appointed Indian judges to enforce their judgments against Indian citizens. Typically, judges were paid $10 per month and almost always supported the agents' agendas. Agents in need of workers for reservation projects, for instance, often simply arrested people and forced them to work as part of their sentence. According to the record, Uncle Paul and some friends were partying with some women on the Lac du Flambeau reservation. One of the women was later found to be in a "delicate condition"; she named Paul as the culprit. As a result, the judge issued an order for Indian police on the Bad River reservation to arrest and transport Paul to Lac du Flambeau. Grandma Cele took the train to Lac du Flambeau and confronted the superintendent, insisting she be allowed to see her brother. She found him languishing along with several other Indian men and women in a tiny, filthy jail cell with a ball and chain fastened to his ankle. Eventually, Wisconsin's governor, John Blaine, carried Cele's protest all the way to President Calvin Coolidge. Afterward Uncle Paul was "permitted to escape." As a result of Cele's intervention Uncle Paul walked free.

In her sworn, notarized testimony, Cele reported she'd asked the police in Bad River to produce a warrant for Paul's arrest. When the white government farmer who occasionally acted as community police officer told her one wasn't needed, she asked, "How is that?" How did Cele, a twenty-four-year-old Ojibwe woman with less than a ninth-grade education, know about due process? In civics class at the Sister School, Cele learned about this most fundamental guarantee of the U.S. Constitution, the due process clause, which provides that no state shall "deprive any person of life, liberty, or property, without due process of law." America in the 1920s was a turbulent age for Indians and women, a time in which long-accepted social and economic norms were undergoing marked transformations. Women and newly educated Indians, keen to reap the rewards of the American promise of equality, boldly challenged long-standing traditions surrounding race and gender. Cele was in the middle of it all. She was an eighteen-year-old single mother in 1920 when women gained suffrage. Not long afterward, in 1924, Native Americans were declared citizens of the United States.

Greater surprises about Cele came later. According to the archives of the Wisconsin League of Women Voters, the village of Odanah on the Bad River Ojibwe Reservation is the birthplace of the first Indian League of Women Voters, established in October 1924. Ellen Penwell, membership and events manager of the League of Women Voters, sent me links to the organization's original newsletter, *Forward*. "Most stirring to the imagination is the recent report of the formation of the first Indian League of Women Voters composed of 86 women of the Odanah tribe of Wisconsin." "In Odanah, there is a band of serious thoughtful women who are just as interested in having everything right for their children as we are for ours. They want the right to be heard in court on the same terms as the white race. They want a doctor, a home for the old people. They want a voice in the village government that they might improve the condition under which they have to live."

Although Cele isn't named in the 1929 *Forward* article and the tribal affiliation of those founders of the first Indian League of Women Voters is incorrectly listed as the "Odanah tribe," she was almost certainly one of the "band of serious thoughtful women" described there, as evidenced by the statement to Congress. It was the work of Indian women such as Cele and members of the Indian League of Women Voters who aided in forwarding the Wheeler-Howard Act of 1934, which ended federal allotment of Indian lands and stressed self-governance.

John Collier, a white sociologist and social worker, drove many of the changes. Earlier he had become the face of Indian reform as the leader of the American Indian Defense Association founded in 1923. Collier opposed assimilationist policies such as the Dawes Act and criminalizing Indian culture and spirituality. He was an idealist with a deep belief in the power of human community to work toward utopia. He was a fan of William Wordsworth and shared the poet's love of nature and the human relationship to it. A trip to the Taos

Pueblo in the early 1920s convinced him that Indians had a great deal to teach modern man about the importance of creating and maintaining community. It was at Taos that Collier witnessed the tribe's Red Deer Dance; he later wrote of the experience in his memoirs: "The discovery that came to me there, in that tiny group of a few hundred Indians, was of personality-forming institutions, even now unweakened, which had survived repeated and immense historical shocks, and which were going right on in the production of states of mind, attitudes of mind, earth-loyalties and human loyalties, amid a context of beauty which suffused all the life of the group. What I observed and experienced was a power of art—of the life-making art—greater in kind than anything I had known in my own world before." Taos, he wrote, "led me to say within myself, with absolute finality about the Indians: *This* effort toward community must not fail; there can be no excuse or pardon if it fails." Collier threw himself into fighting for reform of federal Indian policy. He and other advocates lobbied government leaders to reform policies that reduced Indian landholdings and undermined culture. Yielding to pressure from reformers and the public, the Department of the Interior secretary, Hubert Work, commissioned a comprehensive study of federal Indian policy, published later as *The Problem of Indian Administration,* commonly called the Meriam Report.

The report was named after the study's director, Lewis Meriam, educated at Harvard and George Washington Universities with a PhD from the Institute for Government Research. Meriam was a brilliant statistician who had previously worked at the Census Bureau. He assembled a team of researchers including Henry Roe Cloud of the Ho-Chunk Nation, the first Indian to graduate from Yale. Cloud, a former boarding school student at Genoa Indian school, lectured extensively about the inadequacies of boarding schools, opposing the notion that Indians were suited only for vocational training. He was later appointed head of Haskell Institute, then the largest off-reservation high school, and finally supervisor of Indian education for the Bureau of Indian Affairs in Washington, D.C. Cloud was one of the driving forces behind the Wheeler-Howard Act or Indian

Reorganization Act (IRA) of 1934, granting home rule to tribes and replacing the Dawes Act. Meriam and his team, which included an economist, medical doctor, and experts in family life, agriculture, land tenure, law, and education, traveled to nearly one hundred reservations, schools, hospitals, and agencies in several states over a period of seven months as they gathered data for the 847-page report. The results, published in 1928, were described as a "stinging reproach to a niggardly and exploiting government." The first sentence of chapter 1 begins with a damning description of the failures of federal Indian policy: "An overwhelming majority of the Indians are poor, even extremely poor, and they are not adjusted to the economic and social system of the dominant white civilization."

The sections examining Indian education were especially critical. It read in part, "On the whole government practices may be said to have operated against the development of wholesome [Indian] family life. . . . [T]his worst of its features still persists, and many children today have not seen their parents or brothers and sisters in years. . . . The government has in effect destroyed Indian tribal and community life without substituting anything valuable for it." Researchers found that much of the hard physical labor at the schools was being performed by children eleven years old and younger, many of whom were malnourished. "The labor of [Indian] children as carried on in Indian boarding schools would, it is believed, constitute a violation of child labor laws in most states." The Meriam Report affirmed the complaints Indian families and students had been making for years, among them that the federal government neglected to provide Indian children with even the most basic necessities in schools where they resided. Researchers found deplorable health conditions including overcrowded dorms, unsafe buildings, poor and inadequate food, and unnecessary corporal punishment. Strict rules, they noted, were often enforced through "solitary confinement and corporal punishment, such as flogging, withholding of food, whipping and slapping, or cuffing." Schools were overcrowded by 40 percent or more, with two to three children sharing beds in some cases. Further, the overcrowding coupled with unsanitary conditions like filthy latrines and the practice of sharing towels and other personal items allowed contagious disease to sweep through the populations. Basic classroom instruction was limited to half the school day with the remainder given over to work. Researchers also took issue with the grinding regimentation and military-style drilling in the schools, which they said effectively dampened the children's spirits and negatively affected health. Missionaries, they found, often employed people as teachers who had only the most elementary education themselves. "It is quite possible for missionaries without the personal qualifications necessary for work with the Indians to maintain themselves indefinitely in isolated locations," researchers wrote. They also found the mission schools had no supervisory mechanisms and failed to maintain any minimum educational standards for students. "From the point of view of education the Indian Service is almost literally a 'starved' service," the researchers concluded. They didn't, however, recommend that boarding schools be discontinued. Rather, they advised the government to increase funding, eliminate routinization, limit attendance to children in sixth grade and above, reduce labor, add more relevant vocational training, increase recreational activities, create community day schools, and introduce courses relevant to Indian culture. The Meriam Report drew great media attention and public outrage; President Herbert Hoover's administration was shamed into almost doubling spending at Indian schools between 1928 and 1933.

In the same period, the government closed twelve boarding schools, leaving sixty-five. Over the next eight years, those institutions were replaced by nearly a hundred community day schools. Change, however, in terms of the culture of the schools, was slow to come. Throughout the 1930s schools were still supported by student labor; many of the old-guard teachers and administrators failed to embrace the Meriam Report recommendations and continued on as usual. Schools gradually shifted away from the strict military model, however, and began incorporating recreational and athletic activities such as showing movies and holding socials that included both genders but without dancing. Most of the recommended changes in the Meriam Report related to increasing efficiency rather than calling for an end to assimilationist education policies. Indian education continued to primarily focus on preparing students to enter mainstream society.

In 1933, President Franklin Delano Roosevelt appointed John Collier commissioner of Indian Affairs, where he served until 1945. Many conservative political leaders considered Collier a firebrand, a fanatical Indian reformer blinded by his own bias. Collier brought great change to federal Indian policy, championing Indian New Deal programs including passage of the Indian Reorganization Act in 1934. Under the IRA, Indian land allotment was abolished and a process for restoring tribal land was created. The act also recognized tribal governments, offering incentives for adopting U.S.-government-style constitutions and governing councils. Many tribal leaders complained, however, that the IRA forced tribes to accept westernized versions of governance while ignoring traditional forms already informally in place. Although the IRA was transformative, it retained the traditional paternalistic relationship between Indians and the federal government. The constitutions were boilerplate documents and in many ways were and continue to be wholly inadequate.

Collier also pushed for tolerance of Indian religion in schools as well as inclusion of a curriculum teaching traditional Indian arts and crafts. Some schools in the Southwest employed local artisans to teach rug making, silversmithing, and pottery, helping to elevate the growing Indian art movement in the United States; Collier also helped create the Indian Arts and Crafts Board, an entity charged with improving the quality of Indian art and setting standards for authenticity. His recommendations surrounding religion, however, mostly went unheeded.

Collier advocated for better training for teachers, a more natural setting for students in which they were raised at home with family while attending school, appropriation of funds to encourage traditional arts and crafts, and more acceptance of Native language and culture. Ultimately, however, the schools mostly failed to reinforce traditional culture but changed their curriculum to focus on Progressive education ideals such as citizenship. Collier's policies did not include abolishing boarding schools, but the heyday of off-reservation boarding schools came to an end at the close of the 1930s. The Johnson-O'Malley Act, or JOM, was part of the Indian New Deal and reflected a growing trend of Indian enrollment in public schools. By 1938, 51 percent of Indian children were enrolled in public schools. The JOM, which Collier helped steer through Congress, offered federal funding to public schools to support Indian education and health care. Indian lands are exempt from property taxes, so the intent of the JOM was to compensate school districts with large Indian populations for funding normally gained from property tax revenues. Under the rules of the act, school districts were to use the funding to pay for lunches, transportation, social welfare, health care, and other needs for Indian students.

Problems began almost immediately. There was little oversight of the unnecessarily complex program, and schools already strapped for dollars during the Depression often simply used the money to offset budgets; Indian parents had no say in choice of programming or how the money was allocated. Mismanagement of policy and funding under the JOM went on unexamined for decades. It wasn't until 1969 that the government evaluated and investigated the outcomes of the legislation. The congressional report *Indian Education: A National Tragedy, a National Challenge,* also called the Kennedy Report after Senator Edward M. Kennedy, chairman of the Senate Subcommittee on Indian Education, would find that "it is doubtful if the needs of these Indian children are being met any more than they were thirty-five years ago when the Johnson O'Malley Act was passed."

During the Great Depression, boarding schools provided an unexpected lifeboat for Indians, a means to house and feed their children. My mother used to joke that Indians had already been experiencing an economic depression for decades by the time it hit white people. Because on the margins, the fallout from the crash hit Indians especially hard. The possibility of starvation was real. Many people had no choice but to place their children in the schools in order to ensure they were fed and clothed. By 1933, the number of children in boarding schools was greater than in 1928. According to Collier's 1936 end-of-year report, the total student enrollment of American Indians was about twenty-six thousand in the 249 government schools then operating.

As in most Indian communities, times were tough in Odanah during the Depression. No longer earning as much selling his bootleg whiskey and now drinking more, Grandpa Joe had little to offer Bernice after she graduated from the Sister School. She nearly died from an overdose of ether given to her at the Hayward Indian hospital during an emergency appendectomy. *I was out for three days. Both Pa and Ma were there when I woke up; they thought I was dead,* she told me. Reluctantly, she went to live with Cele and her new husband, Herschel, in their boardinghouse in the timber boomtown of Winegar, which the timber baron W. S. Winegar named after himself. The town changed its name back to Presque Isle in 1955. Although Cele might have been trying to make up for those lost years when her children languished in the Sister School, Bernice would have none of it; it was simply too late. After graduating from eighth grade at St. Mary's in the late 1930s, Bernice worked as a maid until she was fired. Then she lived with Cele and Herschel for a few months. *All she wanted me for was as a babysitter,* she told me. Herschel and Cele worked hard, and the boardinghouse was popular among the town's lumberjacks. Herschel bought Cele her own car, an unheard-of luxury for an Indian woman in those days. Shamelessly, Cele shouted obscene greetings to friends as she drove her car through town.

Hey, you old sonovabitch! How the Christ are you, anyway? she'd yell.

Bernice sank down as low as possible in the passenger seat, mortified by Cele's behavior. Cele had successfully negotiated a good life in the white man's world, but she remained unapologetically true to herself. Rejecting the stifling norms of white ladylike behavior, she was independent, loud, and vulgar. She answered to no man, not even Herschel. But Bernice had bigger plans, plans that included more than simple survival: she was aiming to conquer the white world on its own terms. She was shamed by Cele's Indianness. Still angry and wounded over Cele's abandonment, Bernice rebelled when Cele tried to parent her. Bernice was still a young teenager, and Cele intervened when older male boarders grew too familiar with her daughter. *She was always jealous of me, trying to boss me around.* In the end, Cele packed her off to Flandreau Indian School in South Dakota. Flandreau, which still functions as a federal Indian boarding school today, opened in 1893. By 1931, however, it had transitioned to an accredited four-year high school, no longer serving elementary students. Bernice often spoke fondly of her years at Flandreau, where she met Indians from all over the United States. It was her first time away from Odanah, where everyone intimately knew everyone's family and circumstances. Bernice was amazed by the wide expanse of the prairies so different from her home in Wisconsin; she told me of the brutal blizzards there when cattle froze standing in the fields. She described making friends with girls from other tribes and how they'd laugh and teach each other the latest dance steps. She was a young woman now and an old hand at navigating boarding school life. Bernice enjoyed the school's weekend social dances for students and trips into town. She flourished academically and socially at Flandreau, where she was on equal terms with the other students. At Flandreau she got a taste of life without the constant brand and shame of being unwanted, a charity case, an orphan, or, as my cousin Marylu would later describe her, a "throwaway kid," after a 1980 TV investigative report about foster kids destined to languish in the system. Bernice was not eager to be cast into that role again where everyone seemed to look at her with pity or, worse, the certainty that all her grand plans would fail and she'd end up poor, with a pack of kids to raise. Joe sent her a pair of real silk stockings for Christmas during her last year at Flandreau; they were among her prized possessions and signaled her entry into womanhood. *I babied those stockings for such a long time, stitching every tiny run or tear,* she told me. After graduation, she returned to Odanah confident in her future. That future quickly came to include Joe.

Bernice moved in with Joe, intending to stay for only a few weeks until she could move to southern Wisconsin, where her siblings Don, Lucille, and Rags lived. They had good factory jobs down there. There was nothing happening in Odanah. Folks got by hunting, fishing, and harvesting wild rice, and fewer than one thousand people lived there then. I found an old University of Wisconsin Extension office handbook on Indians from that era. "The Bad River reservation of Chippewas is undoubtedly one of the most economically depressed Indian communities in Wisconsin.... Odanah offers virtually no steady jobs." Her sights were set on making a life for herself away from the reservation. But until then she casually accepted a date with George C. Bernice wore her famous silk stockings on that first date, giving George a hint of her style and sophistication. All the Odanah girls were after George, called Cycie, pronounced "psyche," short for "Cyclone." He was, in her words, *very flamboyant,* a charismatic figure given to grand gestures, always surrounded by admirers. On that first date he screeched to a halt in front of Joe's shack in a borrowed Model T, loaded with friends. She smoothed her dress over the precious stockings as she squeezed into the front seat, barely settled before George raced the car out of the yard. Soon they arrived at the dump, where a few boys grabbed shotguns as they spilled out of the backseat. They hollered loudly, shooting the rats that nosed through the piles of burning trash. With a start, she realized this was the date destination. *I was overdressed,* she later told me dryly. But there was something irresistible about George. Her eyes went a little blind as she described him to me many years later. She gazed into the distance, vulnerable and unguarded. George was *a big, tall man,* a very important point for her. So big that he blotted out all her uncertainty, shame, and fear. Being with George was like being part of something grand, something bigger than herself. Everyone was drawn to him. He is remembered among elders who knew him as being *very jolly with kids.* But George was also cruel and violent, especially when he drank, which was often. Her description of George was remarkably like that of her father, although, as my cousin Delphine recalls, Grandpa Joe was "a short little shit."

Enduring his drinking and violence was the prerequisite, the price of his love and attention. It was a familiar price, the only emotional transaction she knew, and one she would pay over and over again as an adult for George's affection. Some people said George witched her. His family was known for their proximity to fireballs, potent messengers that worried the people. Bernice seemed to disappear from family and friends overnight; she gave birth to a baby boy, my brother Larry, and went to live with George's people, old-time backwoods Ojibwe who dwelled apart from the community. Failing to hear from her for months, her siblings Don and Lucille traveled to Odanah; they found her with George's family, her face covered in bruises as she nursed her child. George had recently been arrested and wasn't home at the time, so Don and Lucille bundled her and Larry into a car and took them to southern Wisconsin. It was here she met and married my father, Gordon. She was eighteen; Gordon was thirteen years her senior.

Charles Gordon Pember, known as Gordon to friends and family, was born in 1916 near the corner of Truth and Charity Streets in Shullsburg, in the "Driftless Area" of southwestern Wisconsin. During the ice age, glaciers failed to cover the area, leaving hills and forested ridges intact and creating an undulating sea of alternating mounds and rises. Immigrants from Wales and Norway were drawn there in the nineteenth century to farm and labor in the lead mines that dotted the landscape. The lyrical names of his childhood homes in Browntown, Gratiot, New Diggings, Lead, and the long-ago forgotten hamlet of Dill belie the pain of his birth. He was born with a clubfoot, which frightened his young parents, first-generation Norwegian and Welsh immigrants. When he contracted polio at age two, they were torn apart. My paternal grandfather, George Pember ("Pa," to us), was a gambling addict and fled the family home. Ma took her only child to Shriners Hospital in Minneapolis and found jobs nearby cleaning houses. My dad recovered after a couple of years in the hospital but developed kyphosis, severe curvature of the spine. He was a hunchback, a cripple. This was an era long before basic civil rights were even considered for the disabled. At best, they were pitied; at worst, disparaged, objects of ridicule.

Despite early suggestions that he might be better off in an institution, Ma (Cora) refused. Her education was limited, and English was her second language, yet she knew her son deserved the same opportunities as his peers. Relatives said that when neighbors would complain, saying she should help her child as he struggled to perform tasks, she would state firmly, *He's got to learn to do things for himself, or he'll never get along in the world.* Pa eventually returned, and he and Ma worked various farms "on the halves" (sharecropping) near the Pecatonica River to ensure my dad could attend school. Ma had a saddlemaker fashion a leather brace for her son so that he could stand up independently. Cora and George's families were poor, but they stood by Gordon. Despite his physical challenges, Gordon was smart and impish, with a thick shock of red hair. Like the red-haired boy protagonist in O. Henry's famous short story "The Ransom of Red Chief," he was mischievous. An Anglo trickster.

According to family legend, he nearly choked his grandfather by dropping a handful of popcorn into the man's gaping, sleeping mouth. *Get this young 'un away from me, Cora, he's tryin' to kill me!* the old man sputtered. People often assumed that his physical deformity was mirrored in his mind somehow: that he was mentally deficient just as he was physically handicapped. Not true. He fought back by working harder than most of his peers, graduating from high school, and securing a job as apprentice to a dental technician. Creating dentures then, without the benefit of modern technology, was a demanding craft requiring great skill and an eye for perfection.

He excelled at the work but yearned for acceptance as a man in the able-bodied world. To that end, sometimes he behaved a little wildly, drinking in roadhouses and hanging out with Indians. While drinking at Slick's tavern, located in a battered log cabin in Janesville, he tripped and fell down on his way to the men's room. The stiff leather brace he wore for his back kept him from getting to his feet. Like an abandoned turtle on its back struggling to right itself, he lay there for quite some time. Tipsy bar patrons laughed and waved off his calls for help. He was a drunken cripple, probably crazy too, so they simply stepped over him.

Fortunately, my uncle Don was also on his way to the men's room. Although drunk himself, he saw that all my dad needed was a little help and offered him his hand. After getting to his feet, Gordon said, *A hundred men stepped over me before you came along. By God, I'm gonna buy you a drink!* And so, according to my mom, *they were off to the races.* Dad started hanging out with Ojibwe folks, who have firsthand experience in struggling to get to and stay on their feet. They are a little less eager to judge another man's limits. Uncle Don introduced Gordon to my mom, Bernice, a nineteen-year-old beauty, alone in the world and fresh off the rez. Gordon fell for her, hard. He was moved to protect the petite, emotionally fragile girl. When he proposed to her, Bernice said, *What do you want with me? I got this kid.* Gordon pointed at Larry, whom she held in her arms. *That's my kid,* he responded simply. Gratefully, she accepted his promise of shelter and safety. They married after a beery celebration weekend in the wild town of Dubuque.

Dad worked hard, always trying to keep the nagging suggestion at bay that he wasn't fit, physically or as a man or both. He was quick-tempered and eager to take offense at a world that frequently scorned him. Armed with their insecurities, Gordon and Bernice set out to make a life for themselves.

Ma and Pa, my father's parents, loved and accepted my mother, proud of the couple's determination and success at creating a family. Ma's large extended family, however, which included five sisters, was a bit skeptical of the unlikely match. Small and dark, my mother stood out among the large-boned, ruddy Norwegians at family gatherings. *My, ain't it hot, though,* they'd fret as they sweated and pulled at their girdles. My mother remained cool, aloof as she helped carry heavy platters of food to the tables.

I remember my aunt Calma shaking her head disapprovingly as she watched me play. *She's awful dark,* she fretted. The adults scrutinized me during these visits as I sat on the floor, stupidly happy to be the center of attention, any attention. My mother smiled tightly, saying little. But she neither defended nor retreated; she stood her ground, our ground. Later, as I listened to her comments and tone of voice during the ride home, it was clear she secretly disdained them as ill-bred and narrow-minded. *I guess Calma doesn't think too much of us,* she huffed. *Well, at least I know how to dress.* I was too young to understand the dissonance, but I sensed their disapproval of our family; to them, everything about us was wrong in a very fundamental, inescapable way. I found our white relatives' gazes uncomfortable, but I enjoyed their rambling farmer lives where I could tumble with cousins in the hay mows and run freely.

My parents' relationship was more partnership than marriage, at least for my mother. Although she respected my father and was grateful for his kind, steady nature and unflagging support, I never saw them share physical affection. But they seemed to genuinely enjoy each other's company; I often found them seated at the kitchen table late in the evenings chatting over coffee or beer. My mother was young and attractive; she frequently attracted attention from men, a big point of pride for her. She often described to me how men would hit on her when she and Dad were out together. They'd ask, *What are you doing with HIM, anyway? I tell them, Hey, he treats me good; that's why I'm with him!*

They bought a small one-bedroom house, a shack really, and set up housekeeping in Janesville. Located close to a railroad yard and roundhouse, with a section of track less than twenty feet from the front door, the little house seemed in danger of shaking apart as trains lumbered past day and night. There was no indoor plumbing; baths were taken in a tub set up in the kitchen on Saturday nights. The little tan house was located on Pearl Street in a neighborhood of Sicilian immigrants. Our mixed-race family fit in easily among the small, dark Sicilians and their large broods of children. The Castagnas, Tortorices, Buscemis, and Angelillos loved my hardworking parents, who gardened and scratched out a living alongside them. Old man Castagna made potent homemade red wine that he shared freely with his neighbors. Although they spoke little English and my parents spoke no Italian, my mother and the Sicilian families seemed to share understandings. My father, however, was often perplexed by their words. Mr. Castagna kept chickens and asked my father one day, *Hey, Gord, you wanna the ax (eggs)?* My dad answered, *No, I got an ax.*

No, no, the ax, what the chicka lay! Mr. Castagna replied impatiently.

Dad worked long hours at the dental laboratory, and Mom cleaned offices and worked at a factory canning vegetables. Sometimes Dad hunted deer and pheasant. Their enormous garden thrived; my mother, with help from Ma, canned and preserved the bounty. In this way, they fed our family.

Occasionally, Grandpa Joe would show up unexpectedly. Sometimes he would stay for weeks, helping my parents fix up their home, building cabinets and making repairs. I met Joe only briefly when I was about three years old; it must have been 1960, sometime in the late summer. We traveled to Odanah with the express purpose of presenting me to Grandpa Joe for the first time. The trip in my parents' Ford was a long drive in those days on two-lane highways that wound through the little towns and villages of northern Wisconsin. We drove the entire day. Toward evening, the forest began to thicken and dwarf the road. We were leaving the familiar behind; it gave me a thrilling yet ominous feeling. We finally stopped at a tourist hotel for the night a few hours south of Odanah. The room was shabby and smelled of its many former guests. We couldn't afford to eat at restaurants, so Dad cooked our meals at roadsides with supplies he kept in the trunk of his car. He was proud of his little Sterno-powered stove, mismatched plates and silverware, tins of Vienna sausages and pork and beans all stored in a black battered suitcase.

In preparation for meeting Grandpa Joe, my mother bought me a little robin's-egg-blue woolen suit from the St. Vincent de Paul thrift store. It hung on a nail on the back of the bedroom door, ensconced in a dry-cleaning bag for weeks before the trip. On the morning of our visit to Grandpa Joe's house, she dressed me carefully in the little vest with a bird embroidered over one breast and the matching pleated skirt, completing the ensemble with a white Peter Pan–collared blouse, white ankle socks, and black patent leather shoes. She pinned a little white hankie near the skirt's hemline. *Now, don't monkey with that,* she instructed. I loved her excitement and attention but grew shy and tongue-tied when she proudly placed me before Grandpa Joe. He seemed ancient to me with his sparse, grizzled gray beard and white hair. Seated in an old armchair, he laughed delightedly as he spread his arms wide, welcoming me in Ojibwe. I didn't understand the words and was terrified by his toothless smile. I remained frozen, bewildered, and unsure of what to do. My mother nudged me angrily toward him. *Give Grandpa a hug, now,* she instructed me pettishly. I don't recall if I hugged him or not. His house, however, was a wonder to me in which a rooster strutted boldly across the kitchen table and a whole pack of dogs crowded around the back door. My mother expertly cleared a path for us through the sea of wagging dog tails. *Heyah, heyah,* she called to them sternly.

My brother Bill has more memories of Grandpa Joe. He recalls him as quiet, gentle, and patient, always taking time to listen to his grandson. One day, however, Grandpa Joe would be gone, a pattern repeated over and over with my mother's relatives. Sometimes cousins would stay for a year or more, even attending school along with my brothers. Visits from our Indian relatives were thrilling, unpredictable, tinged with danger, a counterpoint to the ordered new world my mother had created for our family. Indian relatives didn't announce their visits in advance. They simply showed up. Sometimes our mother was reluctant in welcoming them at first, but then they would all start laughing, and magically we were all Indian again. On random mornings, aunts or uncles would appear on our couch. Their eyes closed, they slept like the dead, the smell of stale beer and whiskey emanating from their gray-tinged skin. These relatives would leave abruptly; no explanations were given.

But my parents were busy pursuing the post–World War II American dream in which everything suddenly seemed possible. It was a time of endless possibility, of personal reinvention, when Americans were encouraged to forget the painful past of the war and march forward, to grab the good life with both hands. But the promise of equal opportunity, self-determination if one worked hard enough, was at best overstated for Indians. At worst—inconsequential. Most

Americans believe we live in a meritocracy, but for Native folks it was more like a demeritocracy: everything was a strike against you. Our mother, like other boarding school survivors, became a shape-shifter, transforming herself according to her surroundings. Even as our family ascended the ladder of social and economic success, our mother's mind was engaged in a kind of ongoing intrapsychic conflict. On the one hand she encouraged us to conform to the white world, but at the same time she not so secretly despised us for trying. As a child, I found it a tempting, perilous cipher, one I was constantly trying to unravel.

In one of my earliest memories, I am seated on the floor, tightly wedged into a kitchen corner next to a cabinet, as far away from adults as possible. From this vantage point I can safely observe them and their drama as I try to make sense of their world. In this memory, I am crying my eyes out over a terrible injustice. A woman squats down to my eye level and takes my photo. The woman with the camera was my beloved aunt Betty, Uncle Rags's wife, who was babysitting the extended family's children. Rather than scold me, she playfully documented my overblown childish dramatics. Looking back as an adult, I'm certain the injustice was a trivial event; I was unhurt. But the memory is still vivid for me today. Filled with a crushing belittlement and dismissal, I felt utterly powerless, crammed in my corner seated on the brown linoleum floor. I still have the photo she took that day; my fingers are in my mouth as I try to stem the flow of snot and tears.

ASSIMILATION
REVISITED

uring World War II and into the 1950s, federal Indian policy took some giant steps backward. "'De-Indianizing the Indian' was back in fashion." Although it had never truly fallen out of fashion, assimilation once again became the stated mission of the federal government. A House Select Committee on Indian Affairs in 1944 offered recommendations on "the final solution of the Indian problem," which was essentially assimilation in a new package; its name was termination. By 1948, Congress directed the commissioner of Indian Affairs to develop criteria for withdrawing federal recognition and services from tribes. Under termination policies, Indians, trust land, and reservations would cease to exist; Indians and their children would be absorbed and, under the policy of relocation, relocated to cities. Once again, the goal of the federal government was to assimilate Indians into the dominant society through semi-forceful removal, enticements to move to cities, and education policies. Several community day schools as well as boarding schools were closed with the intention of encouraging Indians to attend public schools. However, enrollment in boarding schools increased in the late 1940s and early 1950s. The postwar economic bang experienced in the rest of the country was barely a whimper heard in Indian country, much of which still struggled along without basic necessities like running water, reliable heat, and electricity. During this era with its emphasis on social conformity and growth of the white middle class, challenges to the status quo were discouraged. Of an Indian population of approximately 400,000, 44,000 saw active duty during World War II, but Indian veterans found themselves mostly excluded from education and mortgage benefits guaranteed by the GI Bill. Between 1953 and 1968 more than one hundred tribes were terminated from federal assistance, their governments dissolved, and land and properties ordered to be distributed to their citizens. Several tribes, such as the Menominee Indian Tribe of Wisconsin, regained federal recognition after the policy was abandoned in the 1970s, but many continue to work toward restoration today. In conjunction with termination, the government enacted the Urban Indian Relocation Program in 1952. Under the voluntary program, Indians received financial assistance to move to metropolitan areas such as Denver, Los Angeles, Cleveland, and Seattle. The Bureau of Indian Affairs helped with finding jobs and housing in the new locations. The plan was for Indians to disappear into the great American urban diaspora of people of color. Many of our relatives took advantage of the relocation program, usually moving to Chicago; "going down Chicago," they called it. Most participants found that they simply exchanged rural poverty for urban poverty; many returned to their home communities. Marilyn Miller, Lac du Flambeau Ojibwe, recalled her first night in Chicago after relocating from the reservation in northern Wisconsin in 1967. She and her family—two parents and ten children—took the long train ride into the city.

"Our apartment was not in the shining skyscraper I had in mind when we moved to the city," Miller says. "We didn't have a doorman like Buffy and Jody in the TV show *Family Affair*. Everything was dirty, so dirty that on that first night my mother covered everything with sheets before she even let us lie on the floor. Our first apartment was a third-floor walk-up. Everything was noisy and dirty. What a disappointment!" The BIA sent agents to reservations to recruit participants for the program. The agents carried recruiting materials showing chamber-of-commerce-style photographs of parks, schools, and affordable homes. The pamphlets also showed pictures of successful relocatees in their new city homes seated in living rooms with television sets, their children wearing clean clothes and new shoes. It's estimated that around sixty thousand Indians moved to cities between 1950 and 1980, many as part of the relocation program. Although 35,000 children in the 1960s still attended boarding schools, by 1969 about two-thirds of Indian students in the United States attended public schools. Overwhelmingly, people viewed relocation as a chance for "better." In those days on the reservation, "better" translated to what would be defined today as "decent."

The realities of city life for Indians fell far short of the glossy BIA pamphlets. Many became victims of crime or succumbed to alcoholism and other misfortunes, falling through the cracks. In the end, they simply joined the sea of other low-income brown folks struggling to survive in an unfamiliar big city. Marilyn Big Bear (Odawa) remembers the old days when the Uptown Chicago "Indian bars" served as the unofficial community centers. "Let's see, there was Dago Mary's, the B-29, Club Erin, Dead Man's Bar, the Wooden Nickel, My Place and others. They were all on Clark St. (in Uptown)," Big Bear recalled. "You could cash your checks there. Of course, a lot of people ended up spending a lot of money in the bars. Those bars owed a lot to Indians." I recall hours drinking grape pop in those bars when we visited relatives down Chicago. People lived on the North Side in those days in nearly identical shotgun-style apartments with rotted, splintery wooden fire escapes. It was impossibly glamorous to me as a child, but my mother disliked the grim, gritty surroundings that offered little upward mobility or even comfort. After losing the often-seasonal jobs secured by the BIA, many relocatees sought work at daily pay services. After cashing their checks at Indian bars each day, some fell prey to an awful cycle and never clawed much more than a bare subsistence life out of the urban soil. Many people returned to their reservations, overwhelmed and demoralized by the city's challenges. Some tried the adventure of relocation several times, often choosing different cities. Miller was living with her two daughters when I interviewed her in Chicago. They described their current life as often being caught between two worlds. Miller's family moved back to the reservation for a time in the 1970s, and she recalled missing the freedom of the city. She also found herself impatient with the racial intolerance of rural whites and increasingly aware of a "glass ceiling" on the reservation for Indians. As an adult, she moved back to Chicago, where she raised her two daughters and earned her BA and master's degrees. Ultimately, for her, the relocation program was a failure. The stats back it up. The gentrification of the Uptown neighborhood has pushed most Indians to cheaper, less safe areas of the city. Miller lives with her two daughters and granddaughter in a three-bedroom apartment outside Uptown. Her daughter Alicia, who has a BA, was downsized from her teaching job with Chicago Public Schools and was looking for work. "Like many Native Americans in the city, we are just a smidge above poverty line. Despite all our efforts, our children are only a tiny bit better off than we were," Miller says.

The desire for community and culture, however, so tied to place in Indian tradition, kept Indians forever connected to their home reservations. But relocation, like boarding schools, also later served to politicize Indians. They grew more educated and began connecting the dots of oppression shared by other communities of color, thus giving birth to another generation of activists who later joined the civil rights movement's quest for racial equality. Several of the founders of the American Indian Movement, including Russell Means, Oglala Lakota, who helped found the Cleveland American Indian Center, were products of the relocation program. Others include Karen Diver of the Fond du Lac Band of Lake Superior Chippewa, raised in Cleveland when her family relocated there. She went on to serve as chairwoman of her tribe. Wilma Mankiller of the Cherokee Nation grew up in San Francisco and went on to become principal chief of the Cherokee Nation.

Shortly after I was born in 1957, Dad went into the dental technician business for himself. He did well. The family moved to a two-story house on the east side of Janesville, where many of his dentist clients and other professionals lived. Covered in artificial brown brick siding, our house on Oakland Avenue clung to the very fringes of a nice neighborhood where the homes were large with splendid wraparound porches. Our house was nestled among properties that were carved up into rental units and sat at the bottom of a ravine as if it had somehow rolled to a stop there. There was no backyard, only a pad of blacktop. The roof of the garage nearly touched the ground in the back. One could climb up and slide down the peaked roof where the gravelly shingles would tear out the seats of our pants.

There was no formal announcement of the move to Oakland Avenue. One day, Bill found himself next to our dad as he worked on plumbing in the basement of an empty house. Soon afterward, the family simply moved there, our new home.

If leaving his beloved vegetable and flower gardens and lovingly tended fruit trees heavy with apples and peaches on Pearl Street bothered my father, he never let on. Instead, he bravely tackled the steep, inhospitable earth surrounding the new place. The land was far too limited and precipitous for vegetables or fruit trees, so he planted flowers in small beds. He even tried terracing the sheer cliff behind the garage with lumber and garden soil. He tried to enlist Bill's help, but my brother viewed it as a fool's errand and refused. Nothing grew there.

Our father was happiest in a garden and loved all that grew from the earth.

I saw him at his angriest when I damaged the large maple tree in our front yard by repeatedly running my metal wagon into its trunk. It was a brilliant crisp Saturday morning in the fall when I jumped from our back door outside to claim my holiday. Wearing my favorite shirt decorated with a sailor motif and my ragged cutoff shorts, I was shocked as he grabbed me by the scruff of my neck, lifting up my entire body. He paddled me so soundly and fiercely that I forgot to cry. Dad made me help care for the tree's damaged bark as he tenderly wrapped it in brown butcher's paper, as though he were bandaging the limb of a loved one. It must have been a difficult move for my mother as well; she was no longer surrounded by friends and neighbors. No one here shouted over a back fence offering wine or eggs. We stood apart at the new house, where all the neighbors were white, mostly European and Nordic descendants of ancestors who'd immigrated to America generations ago. People stared at our family.

I roamed the neighborhood, one day joining kids at one of the grander homes. Mary T. said to me, *My mom says you can't play here because your mom's a nigger.*

What's a nigger? I later asked my mother.

Where did you hear that word? It's a bad word; don't say it.

I explained. She flew into a rage.

That goddamned prejudiced white bitch! I should slap the shit right outta her!

Nothing more was said, but I got the message. Something was wrong with us, and it had something to do with how we looked. And of course there was something wrong with my father's body. *Hey, what's wrong with your dad's back? He looks like the hunchback of Notre Dame!*

It was safer to stay close to home, playing with kids living in the nearby rental properties, kids of single divorced mothers like Eunice "Eunie" S. Eunie and her three daughters lived in a cramped second-floor apartment carved out from a single-family home. She teased and sprayed her auburn hair into a sturdy beehive style before heading to her job waitressing at the Town and Country restaurant downtown. Sometimes Eunie would step outside onto the landing of the rickety wooden steps leading to the apartment brazenly clad in a black bra and half-slip. Determined to get in the last verbal shot at her retreating ex-husband after his visits with the girls, she'd shriek, *Shitass! Shitass!* as he raced to his car, his shoulders hunched protectively. I had great regard for Eunie, who reminded me of my aunties; she took no shit, and she always welcomed me into her home.

My mother grew determined to claim her place in the American dream, and one year she decided we were rich. She arranged a trip on a jet for me, my dad, and herself to California to visit her old friend Muriel from Odanah, who also boarded at the Sister School. Muriel lived in Glendale. I was ten years old. My mother often spoke of outrageously ambitious plans that never materialized, so I didn't take her seriously. One could fantasize forever about such a thing without any hope of it happening, but to my shock and delight this dream actually came true. We stayed with Muriel, who now called herself Misty, which we were harshly instructed to call her at all times. Misty was a real taste of the rez, loud and vulgar. Unlike my aunties who had the gift to jolt me to attention, Misty seemed genuinely dangerous. She was married to a white man called Big John with whom she had a son, Johnny, then about three years old. Big John owned a bar, a modest beer and shot joint on Central Avenue north of Compton. Misty worked as a nurse's assistant. It was rumored she had deserted at least two other families with children back in Odanah. A handsome young single Indian man whose identity and role in the household was tantalizingly unclear also lived with Big John and Misty.

Johnny, like his dad, was huge, far outpacing most three-year-olds in height and weight. He was also the naughtiest kid I'd ever met. Johnny raced through the giant (to me) California supermarkets popping the pop tops from cans of soda and beer. Woe to any adult who dared to comment to Misty about Johnny's behavior! She chewed people's asses completely off. But Misty was excitingly worldly; I soaked up every nuance of our time together. Once I accompanied her and my mother to visit an Indian man who was a hairdresser; he was called Geoducks, a fussy gay man who kept an immaculate apartment in Hollywood. I strained to hear Misty and my mother's whispered conversation; it was something about Geoducks's fellowship in a sort of secret thrilling society, but I couldn't make out what it was. He didn't appear very glamorous to me and was crabby when I touched one of the ornaments in his apartment. But my mother spoke highly of Geoducks. The haircut he gave her, she said, was the best she'd ever had.

Later, Misty and Big John took us all to Disneyland. Another impossible dream suddenly made possible. But the dream soon devolved into a long, hot day of standing in massive lines for the rides and attractions. Misty, however, had a work-around; she'd simply barge into a place near the front of the line. I was deeply uncomfortable with this practice. One of the first lessons I learned in

Catholic school was how to queue up for everything from lunch to using the bathroom. Rushing a line is tantamount to a mortal sin, a serious violation of social and spiritual order. After pushing us into a lineup for a now-forgotten attraction, she left Johnny and me to weather the comments and glares from put-upon parents. I still recall the flinty power of a white lady's voice, polite but withering, as she told us it *wasn't very nice* to push into line and instructed us to go to the end. I led Johnny back to our parents. By now I was crying. My mother slapped me across the face, hard. Misty, however, didn't miss a beat. She grabbed us both by the hands and led us back to the line, demanding to know who told us to leave; although I was now dazed into silence, I managed to point out the unfortunate woman. Misty proceeded to push us in front of the same white lady and her family. *If any goddamned white bitch tries to run you off again, I'll slap the shit out of her!* Nothing in that middle-class white woman's life could have prepared her for Misty's racial pushback and the direct threat of physical violence. Suddenly Disneyland was no longer a safe, protected world dominated and defined by white society. Clearly shaken to the core, the woman and her family were speechless. The wait seemed to go on forever. I still don't recall the name of the ride or attraction. Back at Misty's house, she and my mother roared with indecent laughter over beers at the kitchen table at the memory of the white lady's face.

At home in Wisconsin, my father's day began before I rose in the morning; he seldom returned before I went to sleep. On weekends, he tried to repair all the things that didn't work in our house. His repair jobs were notoriously bad; refusing to buy anything new, he was as frustrated with his patch jobs as the rest of us. His cussing took on a familiar singsong quality as he hammered away: *Goddamned, no-good, dirty, rotten son of a bitch!*

The song ended with a terrific final blow that often destroyed his work. We would shake with stifled laughter until red in the face. Dad had a temper, but he was also a magnanimous sort of man. On Sundays he would sometimes let me join him after Mass when he stopped off at the Eagles Club for a shot and a beer. His sport coat, vest, and tie were subdued in color and of good quality. Leaning against his side as he sat at the bar, I breathed in his smell of soap, Camel straight cigarettes, and Old Spice. Even as a child I was impressed and proud of his courtly manner, which even extended to the lady barflies who hustled drinks from him. I didn't see him during the week, since he worked long hours. Although I didn't understand it until much later, I was angry with him about that for a long time.

My father mostly left the child rearing and household to my mother, who created an impenetrable, shadowy world ruled by herself and my eldest brother, Larry. Larry was a secret kind of special in our house, one we were forbidden to question or discuss. He stood apart from Bill and me. While we both struggled with our weight, Larry was tall and trim. His movements and walk had a liquid kind of grace, his feet seldom stepping wrong. He reminded us of a movie star or fashion model, so effortlessly handsome standing in our kitchen. Our mother would jump to her feet when Larry entered the room, shooting dagger eyes at us if we interrupted their conversations. As adults my brother Bill and I joked that Larry was like a visiting dignitary in our home. One Saturday, the family returned after a short trip together without Larry; he'd stayed home to mow the lawn. I was very young, around four years old, and rushed to the bathroom after the long drive. Larry's mangled sneaker lay on the bathroom rug, covered in blood. Bringing it into the kitchen, I said, *Larry made a big mess in the bathroom.* Our mother shrieked and slapped me full across the face, shouting, *What the hell's the matter with you?!* We learned later he'd gotten his foot caught in the lawn mower and a neighbor took him to the hospital. It was a bad cut, but he recovered fully. Being a child, I assumed the accident was my fault and spent many hours afterward trying to figure out my role in hurting the person she loved above all else. I idealized him! Just walking with him was a treat as I absorbed the stray crumbs of approval given to him by the world. I even pretended not to mind the cruel nickname, Slim, he gave me. He was an engaging talker, and people were drawn to him. But he was also cruel, a bully who belittled and hurt us. Playfully throwing me in the air as a baby, he cracked my head on the ceiling. He and my mother laughed at my cries. I craved his attention as I craved hers and was grateful even when he was mean to me. Secretly, however, I was suspicious of her blind love for him; he was her crucible into which she poured herself.

The rest of the family were perpetual outsiders, sometimes regarded as threats to their carefully guarded, ill-defined world. As for him and our father: they maintained an uneasy détente. Bill and I were part of her new life, her creation proving she was equal to the white lady donors at the Sister School, but Larry was her defiant Ojibwe pride, symbolizing her visceral love of George, her father, and her race. Her relationship with Larry was pathological; it was as though, in raising him, she were trying at once to re-create her father, Joe, and her lover George. Although we didn't know Larry was adopted until after my father died, I learned Larry was the spitting image of George. As an adult, I saw George once at a powwow from a distance. He was tall and despite his years still possessed a charisma and danger I could sense even yards away. Fiercely protective of her eldest son, my mother allowed her world to revolve around him, often to the exclusion of my brother Bill, who was two years younger than Larry. Bill was a sensitive, intelligent boy. He was terribly wounded by her incomprehensible, casual cruelty, withholding of affection, and constant criticism.

Men were the heroes in her world. Women were treacherous, deceitful, and cruel. She rationalized men's violence toward women as guileless, forgivable, misguided gestures of love.

My father, however, refused to hit her. During drunken arguments she repeatedly dared him to strike her. *Just go ahead and hit me, then!* she would scream.

Looking down at his hands, Dad simply shook his head. Larry, however, had no problem hitting people, including me, his wives, his girlfriends, and even our mother. She accepted and almost welcomed his hostility. Although I admired Larry and longed for his attention, he frightened me. I didn't share my mother's cognitive confusion of love and violence. I learned to read his mercurial moods and degrees of drunkenness so I could stay out of his reach. Mine was an unsafe world, all the more dangerous because even the act of recognizing the threat was a sort of blasphemy.

By the time I was around ten years old, Dad's business was doing well, so well that my parents could relax a bit. On weekends, they began to spend time at taverns with friends. Deemed mature enough to care for myself, I was permitted to stay home.

It was a wintry Saturday afternoon; I was home alone sitting on the couch with my dog, watching TV. There was a terrific stomping outside the front door. Although the door was heavy and had many layers of thick black enamel paint, its lock gave way and Larry and a friend stumbled inside. Larry was in his late teens, recently divorced from his high school sweetheart and mother of his son; the marriage had lasted only a few months. In its aftermath, he was trying to work and live on his own, but he frequently turned up unexpectedly at our house. He began serving various bids in prison at this time. Sometimes he stayed at our house only long enough to do a load of laundry or eat a meal, but sometimes he remained with us for weeks at a time. On this particular day, Larry or his friend violently kicked my dog in the mouth with a snow-covered shoe as he barked at them. Yipping painfully, he spat out a mixture of snow and blood. Both men smiled at me, but their eyes were bleary, unfocused, volatile. *Where's Mom and Dad?* Larry asked. *Out,* I said.

He laughed, a little menacingly. I paid close attention to the tenor of his laughter; his humor usually involved pain for others. I needed to leave. Putting on my winter coat and boots, I leashed the dog and began to walk to a friend's house. Walking for hours, I couldn't find any neighbors at home; ice began to form between the dog's foot pads, so I carried him. It grew dark and colder, but finally I saw that my parents' car was in the driveway and I returned home. *Where were you!* my mother demanded. I could see she was a little drunk, so I said calmly, *Oh, just out for a walk.* Sensing my unease, however, my dad asked if something was wrong. *Did Larry do something?* he asked. At this my mother flew into a rage. She spat at him, *You filthy-minded, dirty* ... Words eluded her. Sputtering, she retreated to the bedroom, slamming the door.

My father said nothing. His loyalty to her was unshakable, rooted in something unspeakable from which he protected her. I honestly don't recall if anything really happened, but around this time I begin having a nightmare that occasionally occurs even now. The thick door to our house, with those familiar layers of black enamel paint, figures largely in the dream. The door's big locks look sturdy, but they are worn. I slam the door hard, checking and rechecking the lock, but somehow it always pops open; there is no protection from the indistinct threat that is never identified. In real life at that time, however, my parents no longer left me alone. I traveled with them to the taverns, where I drank orange pop, ate Slim Jims, and watched the Hamm's beer sign twirl behind the bar. There was a singing bear on the sign; the lyrics to his song were printed there, emerging from his lips: "From the land of sky-blue waters / From the land of pines, lofty balsams / Comes the beer refreshing / Hamm's, the beer refreshing." On TV, the jingle included a background of campy, Indian tom-tom music.

I took books along on these trips. If it was warm, I sat in front of the tavern, reading late into the night under a streetlight.

At home I sharpened a lead pencil into a daggerlike point and wrote microscopic messages and insults to my family on the wall next to the stairs leading to the second floor of our house. *Shit! I hate you! You're assholes!*

Painfully ascending the stairs for his Saturday night bath, my father failed to find my graffiti messages. Nor did my mother. No one saw them, but I knew they were there. My tiny insurrection in that heedless world.

Larry and my mother were united in an ill-defined, unspoken rebellion. Accordingly, he acted out. In drunken blackouts, he attacked people. As a teenager he was arrested repeatedly for kiting checks, robbing a liquor store, and other poorly planned crimes. Our mother maintained his innocence in the face of overwhelming evidence to the contrary. *Oh, if only they'd leave him alone,* she cried, when police came looking for him.

His cocky self-assurance didn't help him with the authorities, and although he was still only a teenager, no more than seventeen, the court sentenced him to a prison bid in Green Bay. I was about four years old when we began visiting Larry in various prisons that my mother described as "colleges." The prison at Green Bay occupied an entire city block. It stood like a gray cement cube of despair, surrounded by turrets and guards with automatic weapons. It was an institution designed to hold older criminals, guilty of violent, physical crimes. The things he saw and the things they did to him there were beyond his experience or imagination. He fell to his knees in the dark green prison uniform, burying his face in our mother's lap during that first visit.

She tried to get him transferred. Leon Feingold, an attorney whose office she cleaned, suggested she appeal to her state representative. The Feingolds, parents of the former Wisconsin senator Russ Feingold, would be lifelong friends to my mother and offer her advice and support. Good liberal Jews that they were, they also urged her to get involved in civil and social justice issues. She eventually joined an organization of Democratic women, campaigning for Lyndon Johnson.

Now she had a tangible cause, defending Larry from a racist justice system. After months of worrying, frantic phone calls, and letter writing, she successfully had him transferred to a minimum-security facility that served younger men. How I loved the trips to the prisons! There were endless lines of vending machines and big mounds of change to keep me occupied.

Larry cultivated an image as a rebel, a dangerous man. Homemade prison tattoos decorated his arms and hands, "hate" and "love" spelled out on the fingers of each hand. Like my mother's other relatives, he would appear unexpectedly after long absences, blown up against our door like a dead leaf. Seeing him approach, I would run out to meet him on the sidewalk, throwing my little-sister arms around him. I worshipped him. I feared him. And I never saw how utterly lost he was.

Our mother set about reinventing herself after our move to Oakland Avenue; she was determined to gain acceptance and respect in the white world. She emulated the white wives of the professional class, dressing stylishly in classic, conservative, muted tones, which flattered her petite figure. She tried to make me a part of the transformation, but my size, stubbornly straight hair, and ethnic features were barriers. The selection of dresses in the "husky" department at Sears was limited. My hair refused to hold a curl even after repeated Toni home permanents. The curls began to droop even before the stink of the treatment's chemicals dissipated from the kitchen.

Undaunted, she joined a working-class Catholic parish, St. Patrick's, near our old neighborhood, where she enrolled me in school. We went to Mass every morning at 6:00. I was the only child she enrolled in Catholic school; conversely, she tolerated my brothers' infrequent attendance at Mass. I was the one immersed in all things Catholic. I see now that she was, in her way, providing me with the best possible tools for an Indian woman's success in a white world.

Life for me at St. Patrick's was not a happy time; the nuns created a joyless, disapproving atmosphere where students were encouraged to tattle on one another. Discipline was harsh and sometimes included corporal punishment. My mother was frequently at odds with the nuns, muttering about their hypocrisy, racism, and sanctimony. She not so secretly disdained the other families at the school, mostly workers at the local Chevrolet plant, and their small-minded, provincial hopes and dreams for their children. I, however, would be different. She encouraged my love of books, writing, and music. Together we watched Leonard Bernstein's Young People's Concerts on television. Inspired, she rented a piano and paid for my weekly lessons. She described me to others as an "inner-lectual."

During one of my classes at St. Patrick's, the nun asked everyone to stand and declare their heritage. Everyone said "Irish," "Polish," or "Norwegian." When my turn came, I said "French" as my mother had instructed. French was foreign, exotic, a bit swarthy perhaps, but acceptable. My classmates, however, were skeptical.

At recess, kids said, *French, huh!? Well, you got nigger lips, Pember!*

I covered my mouth with my hand during the entire seven years spent at the school. But my mother threw herself into her new plan, frantically volunteering at charities for children and campaigning for Lyndon Johnson's presidential election. She was constantly in motion, unavailable.

She also took in various homeless people, mostly single mothers with young children. Some of her charges were shady characters; our family secretly wondered about her motives. She seemed to be atoning for an unnamed crime, but she found no salvation, only frustration and disappointment. A pattern soon emerged. She focused on fixing their lives, constantly on guard against any of our comments that might suggest criticism. She would often chide me, seemingly unprovoked, *You have no idea how it is for them. You've never had to live like that; you've always had everything!*

Soon, however, the families would disagree with her in some way or fail to show sufficient appreciation, and they would be gone. In the meantime, I searched our house for her love. Sometimes I rummaged through her dresser drawers, savoring her little jewelry box with its dainty lock and a tiny bottle of real French perfume; its scent mysteriously stirred the blood. In the bottommost drawer I found several feet of beaded loom work coiled together like beautiful snakes. Intricate yet strong, the lengths were a tactile joy. I wanted to make my own creations. There were only a few remaining loose beads, so, incredibly, she let me cut apart her loom work. It was slow going using my little scissors, but I managed to extract most of the beads, enough to fill a half-gallon-sized Tupperware container. Typically, my ambitions overshot the reality of hard work. The holes in the tiny beads required using wire-thin needles, and I soon tired of the tedious work. She had intended to make the beadwork into belts for all the men in our family. In the end, the shame of being Indian overshadowed her pride in her handiwork, and she allowed me to destroy it. But all that denial stuck in her craw. Her secret pride in all things Ojibwe somehow leaked out; she taught me our ways in stories and lessons carefully embedded in the ordinary course of our lives. At night, strings of lights, rather like phosphorescent snakes, would enter my room. Coiling and uncoiling, they made their way across the ceiling. Haltingly, I described the visions to her. After some thought she said, *They want to protect you; they won't hurt you, but don't ever tell anyone else you see them.*

Although she made no conscious choice of doing so, she shared that knowledge with me in the only way she knew, through story. Her knowing was also not conscious; it was embedded in her Ojibwe worldview, a view unshakable and immune even to years at the Sister School and other assimilationist institutions. To me, she imparted a transcendent, undeniable, stubborn belief in our ways. I began to see this was our power. Long ago, our ancestors understood that the brain is driven to tell stories and passed along our culture and traditions in that way. For instance, older people like to tell stories over and over again, and young children like to hear stories repeated often. There is a lock-and-key mechanism for transmission of oral culture across generations. My mother's gift of storytelling activated a latent Ojibwe worldview for me, that we are a part of, rather than apart from, the earth and creation. It was her ability to empower through story that guided me. Unfortunately, she didn't share these gifts with my brothers. Perhaps she chose me because I was the daughter, the only girl, and she knew as an Indian woman I'd need all the strength I could get in order to survive in the white man's world.

She told me stories about the spirits and gave me "old teachings" about how Indians loved the land and the animals. Never wasteful, they used all parts of animals that were killed. She taught me that refusing a gift from an Indian was a terrible insult, like a slap in the face. Every morning we discussed our dreams, the symbols we'd seen and what they might mean. Cavalier assimilationists were so blinded by their racist assumptions about Indians that they assumed we could be made to forget our families and heritage by a few years of separation. Remarkably, even though my mother was raised in the Sister School, where Ojibwe language and practice of culture were forbidden, she absorbed the power of our ways and passed them on to me. She did so through the inventive, unheralded ways our people resisted.

I later found an example of that resistance in an unlikely place, the motherhouse of the Franciscan Sisters of Perpetual Adoration in La Crosse, Wisconsin. There it was: hidden in an old report in the archives. The sisters allowed me access to their rather thin holdings, consisting mostly of a few scrapbooks and quarterly rosters of students who attended the school. Details about individual pupils were scant. I was tickled, however, to find my grandmother's name, Cecelia Moore, listed on a roster. She attended the school's day program from 1911 until February 1916, when she abruptly left at age thirteen. In the roster's preprinted column regarding her reason for leaving, St. Mary's secretary wrote tersely, "no good reason." How could it be otherwise?

The resistance or what my mother would have described as Indian bullheadedness emerged in a remarkable collection of documents and reports created from 1936 to 1940 as part of a federal Works Progress Administration (WPA) project coordinated by Sister Mary Macaria Murphy, principal of St. Mary's School. Titled simply "WPA Indian Research Project: Bad River reservation, Odanah, Wisconsin," the multivolume report documents vast aspects of Ojibwe life in the region, the industrial year, health data, history of the tribe's political structure, military records of local men, and traditional Ojibwe cultural and spiritual ways.

President Franklin Delano Roosevelt created the WPA during the toughest years of the Great Depression as a means to gainfully employ citizens and build public infrastructure such as school buildings, hospitals, bridges, airfields, roads, and sanitary lines. The WPA also sponsored projects in the arts, employing tens of thousands of actors, musicians, writers, and artists. Several Bad River citizens were employed to research and write reports on Ojibwe culture and spirituality; the tenor of the work, however, was clearly influenced by Sister Murphy's point of view as a white Catholic nun. Most of the essays on culture are shaped by reductionist ethnological studies of the day, emphasizing the view that Ojibwe traditions are part of a rapidly dying primitive past that was giving way to the modern assimilated Native American. But the text provides invaluable information about Ojibwe ways and teachings with titles like "Dreams— Their Significance," "Indian Prophecies," and "The Indian Doctor."

Some of the best examples are the interviews of tribal elders. W. P. Bigboy interviewed Mrs. Newago, an elder and longtime member of the traditional Ojibwe Midewiwin, or Great Medicine Society. Mrs. Newago laments the changes in the clan structure since the coming of so many Europeans. "In the early days," she said, "not many birds were claimed as 'doodems' or totems for clans." It was her opinion, however, that as people intermarried with whites, especially the French, they were considered to belong to the chicken clan. Bigboy wrote, "Whether in ridicule or otherwise, the fish and reptile clans began to appear among the chickens when Indians from other sections or tribes started to mingle and marry among the Chippewa." Mrs. Newago said, "A lot of these inductions in new clans or doodems were through the efforts of some dissatisfied or disgruntled persons who believed they could further their interests through the induction of new clans." Bob Wilson, one of the Project's authors, wrote about dreams and their significance. He wrote, "Dreaming was the Indian method of securing preternatural powers which are not transferred directly to the dreamer but are contained in a vision telling him how to secure the power. An old woman would get a dish of food ready with a piece of charcoal on one side and give them to youths in her wigwam, giving them choice of food or charcoal. Those who fasted too long grew unbalanced thus food given every fifth day and the face was blackened." Blackening the face offered spiritual protection, according to Wilson. Florina Denomie wrote about Indian doctors and medicine men: "By means of a shake lodge, the medicine man determines the illness or affliction. But the Indian doctor, after determining the pains that afflict you, endeavors to cure you by using various herbs, roots, and barks. For centuries, the Native Indian has depended upon the ability of the Indian doctor for welfare of himself and family. There is no person with an MD affixed to his name to whom he could turn." Angeline Cedaroot described Indian prophecies in her interview: "The Indian knew about all modern inventions that you see today. When I was a little girl I saw pictures of airships and that was long before they were ever heard of. It was the custom of Indians to preserve the memory of their dreams by picture writing. The Indians on Bad River preserved their dreams by writing them on a large flat rock. The dream was written on this rock to give the dreamer greater powers." The WPA project also included notes from "Missionary Labors of Fathers Marquette, Menard and Allouez in the Lake Superior Region," written by Chrysostom Adrian Verwyst, who served as parish priest in the Bayfield and Ashland areas from 1882 to 1912. Verwyst wrote about the Ojibwe habit of seeking guidance through dreams: "They shrink not from suffering much on account of those foolish divinities for they fast in their honor to ascertain the issue of their affairs. . . . This is not very hard work for a poor fellow with empty brains, wholly exhausted by fasting and who thinks of nothing else all day long but what he may dream about. . . . Their knowledge of medical science consists in ascertaining the cause of sickness and applying the remedy. . . . All this shows how far these poor people are from the kingdom of God." In addition to graphically depicting historically conflicting worldviews between white Europeans and Indians, the WPA project reflects the stubborn superiority of settler-held beliefs even among those professing missions to help us.

I was disheartened by one of the listings in the project's index, "Why does paganism still exist among the Chippewa?" (The term "Chippewa" is an Anglicized version of the word "Ojibwe.") Dan Morrison, a Bad River Ojibwe man, answered the question in a short essay that is included in the report. "There are still a few pagans on the Bad River reservation," he wrote. "We find that a large percentage of Indians, irrespective of the development of their minds, who do not have enough ambition to think for themselves; it is only natural that this class should follow along the lines of least resistance and while the principles of Christianity have been expounded in their presence they still continue in their belief in paganism and tradition as the latter is easier to follow."

Later, I shared my archive findings with my cousin Delphine. As a young mother, Delphine lost her leg after a car accident with a drunk driver. Recently she lost her other leg to diabetes. She is gently bickering with her partner, Albert, when I arrive. *Here, hand me my pros-*

thetic; I need to kick your ass! she threatens. Seated around her kitchen table, I read Morrison's words aloud to her and our friend Jan Smart, also from Bad River. After a few moments of silence, Smart said, "Oh, he was probably Mide." At this we all burst out laughing. She was referring to the Great Medicine Society, an Ojibwe spiritual fellowship that predates European contact by hundreds of years. Despite the efforts of Christian missionaries, the society continues today in many Ojibwe communities. Suddenly Morrison's dismissive essay emerged to us as an act of resistance. The WPA project was created in a time when it was a federal offense to be caught engaging in traditional Indian spiritual practices. A bit of additional research corroborates our suspicion that Morrison was conducting a form of covert rebellion. In 2013, Chantal Norrgard described the WPA project in the chapter she wrote for a collection called "Beyond Folklore: Historical Writing and Treaty Rights Activism in the Bad River WPA." She wrote, "In contrast to the project's official purpose, the writers saw it as a means to look back on the persistence and integrity of their community and to address political and economic issues they faced at the time."

According to Norrgard, Morrison's father, John, attempted to get aid from the federal government when the J. S. Stearns Lumber Company "swindled timber money from Ojibwe and sold commodities at inflated prices." John, and likely his son Daniel, were ordered off the reservation at gunpoint by lumber company men because of their efforts to assist tribal members and address treaty rights violations through their writings.

I visited Bad River's tribal historic preservation officer, Edith Leoso, who confirmed our theory. She received me in her pleasantly cluttered home, where we chatted over coffee. "Many not-so-devout Christians were still doing Ojibwe ceremony, but they did so secretly," Leoso said. But surely, I asked her, in a small, tightly knit community like Bad River everyone must have known about the activities of their neighbors. Leoso believes that it was an open secret that people, especially elders, were keeping the Great Medicine Society alive. "To tell on someone at that time was to risk their lives," she said. "Our people just don't do that." Leoso also clarified that "elders were respected, plus people really didn't want that worldview to be completely annihilated."

The federal Code of Indian Offenses enacted in 1883, which created the Courts of Indian Offenses, outlawed Native cultural practices such as dances and ceremonies and other activities celebrating Native spirituality. Two of the nine rules included in the original code state:

> "The sun-dance," the "scalp-dance," the "war-dance," and all other so-called feasts assimilating thereto, shall be considered "Indian offenses," and any Indian found guilty of being a participant in any one or more of these "offenses" shall ... be punished by withholding from the person or persons so found guilty by the court his or their rations for a period not exceeding ten days; and if found guilty of any subsequent offense under this rule, shall by [sic] punished by withholding his or their rations for a period not less than fifteen days, nor more than thirty days, or by incarceration in the agency prison for a period not exceeding thirty days. . . .
>
> [W]henever it shall be proven to the satisfaction of the court that the influence or practice of a so-called "medicine-man" operates as a hinderance to the civilization of a tribe, or that said "medicine-man" resorts to any artifice or device to keep the Indians under his influence, or shall adopt any means to prevent the attendance of children at the agency schools, or shall use any of the arts of a conjurer to prevent the Indians from abandoning their heathenish rites and customs, he shall be adjudged guilty of an Indian offense, and ... shall be confined in the agency prison."

Although the code was amended in 1933, eliminating references to customary Indian practices, it was not until 1978, with the passage of the American Indian Religious Freedom Act, that Native peoples could freely and legally practice their own religions.

Leoso also explained that the "Indian pageants" performed at St.

Mary's for the entertainment of donors and tourists were actually an opportunity for elders to pass on songs and teachings from the society. During the late nineteenth and early twentieth centuries, the white public developed a taste for Indian pageants as entertainment such as *The Song of Hiawatha,* published in 1855. According to Leoso, her grandmother told her of how the sisters and white audiences at St. Mary's Indian pageants had no idea that the Ojibwe elders were in fact conducting ceremony right under their unsuspecting noses. "Our ancestors risked their lives and freedom to pass along the songs and protocols of ceremony," she said. The elaborate rights of the Great Medicine Society, for instance, are conducted solely in the oral tradition in the Ojibwe language; it can take days or even weeks to complete them. Preservation of such traditions involved a concerted, coordinated community effort that remarkably went virtually undetected by government officials and missionaries.

Dora Mosay Ammann of the St. Croix Chippewa Indians of Wisconsin remembers well the great lengths to which her parents resorted in order to preserve their spirituality. Ammann's father was Archie Mosay, Nibaa-giizhig, Evening Sky. Mosay was born in a wigwam in 1901 near Balsam Lake, Wisconsin, speaking only the Ojibwe language until age ten. The St. Croix Ojibwe are descended from those who refused to leave their ancestral homes for settlement on reservations in the nineteenth century; they remained and tenaciously kept to their traditional ways. Ojibwe traveled from throughout the region to seek Mosay's help and advice in spiritual matters until he died in 1996 at age ninety-four. But in the 1950s, even one as revered as Mosay had to contend with the white man's rules and regulations. Refusing to send one's children to school and church could attract attention from child welfare authorities who could easily claim parents were neglectful. "We lived with that constant threat of being taken away from our family and sent away to foster care or the Hayward Indian School," Dora said. "It's hard to believe sitting here now, but this happened not so very long ago, during my own lifetime." Dora shakes her head, looking off into the distance as we sit in our camp chairs. It's hot and muggy, but here in the shade, surrounded by friends and relatives, we're safe and protected. I've known Dora for some time now. She is over eighty but remains remarkably unchanged with each passing year, as though immune from time. Dora is a humble, reassuring presence, a *mindimooyenh*, an elder woman, "one who holds things together." She is a boss lady, a leader in the Great Medicine Society.

"We were put here to keep our ceremonies alive," she said. Dora's Ojibwe name is Ashazhawaagiizhig, Crossing Sky Woman; she has been part of traditional spirituality her entire life. When she was a child, however, the people conducted ceremonies way back in the woods, far away from roads, in order to remain undetected. "Mom and Dad dressed us up every Sunday and took us to church even though we weren't Catholic." The act was an important protective measure; she recalled witnessing the removal of children from a community family.

According to Dora, the mother grew ill from tuberculosis and was sent away to a sanitorium by Middle River, Minnesota; in her absence the father, Benny, struggled to care for their children, feeding them, sending them to school, and keeping them clean. "There were no washing machines then; all the neighbors tried to help, but it was a lot of work." Dora speculated that someone at the school must have reported the family to county social workers because one day sheriff deputies came to take away the children. "Benny was so angry people had to hold him down to keep him from attacking the police," Dora said. "I'll never forget the sounds of his hollering and the women wailing and crying; it was just awful." People went to find Benny after he'd disappeared into the woods for several days. "They were afraid he might have committed suicide." Although he tried repeatedly, Benny was never able to get his children back; they were sent to white foster homes. His wife died in the sanitorium, and he was never allowed to see the children again. "He hitchhiked to Minneapolis and stayed drunk until he died," Dora said. "Benny used to come back here sometimes; my parents were always sympathetic to him and tried to encourage him to stop drinking." Dora paused, the pain of the memory still palpable. But soon, she was distracted from her musing; someone gestured to her. Nimbly, she rose to her feet; her expertise was needed. As she left she said, "Without our spirituality we have nothing; this is what I try to teach the young people."

Like most Ojibwe women, my mother had a marvelous sense of the absurd, and we often laughed until we were breathless over images and events, like the story of Dad, who in frustration flattened a brand-new stovepipe replacement by jumping up and down on it. Afterward, red-faced and exhausted, he realized he'd have to buy another pipe. He said, *Well, I feel better anyway.* Housework was also one of her medicines; she taught me to scrub the floor, iron clothing into perfect creases, and sew. We fell into a rhythm then with the sun casting long shadows on the linoleum floor of our kitchen. Labor was her love language; we laughed together easily.

She described the old-time Indian nicknames from her youth, Pinochle Gus, Tudda-bean, Tootsie Porkchop, and the improbably named Shit Reilly. Seeing him as an adult in Chicago, Uncle Don loudly called out, *Hey, Shit!* Shit, whose real name was Sheldon, quickly silenced Don. *Shhh, be quiet, they don't call me that here!* Don replied, *Sorry, but I never knew you as anything other than Shit.*

We made occasional trips to Bad River when I was a child, but the visits seldom ended well. My mother always arrived in high spirits, happy to be home. Here she and her relatives laughed raucously with an abandon we seldom heard in Janesville. For a delirious instant, her laughter in Odanah made anything seem possible. She secretly hated our white man's house and its carefully delineated yard. For a moment, back in Ojibwe country, her cheeks would flush and she would toss her hair. First, we would stop and "greet the lake," Gitchee Gumee, the great sea that welcomed us with its deep glug-glug voice and gentle hiss when its waves retreated from the sandy beach. She would gaze out toward that perfect line between water and sky, her thin arms wrapped around herself; we could see she was home. I loved the freedom of the reservation, where everyone seemed to be a relative. I ran with my cousins through the untended fields. Two dogs, one white, one black, the Love Dogs, joined our adventures. They ran as one, in constant physical contact with each other. We explored abandoned houses with nails dangerously sticking up from their floorboards. We climbed on old army trucks parked and forgotten there by the U.S. government. No adults shouted warnings. Sometimes, however, I felt oddly off kilter as though everyone knew something that I didn't. Exhausted, we would fall asleep in a pile on a living room floor as the adults played cards. I loved hearing the rhythm of their play, a soothing, reassuring pattern that lulled us to sleep. *Aye!* followed by a hand slap and then the waves of laughter, *haw, haw, haw!* By the early morning hours, the laughter took on a bittersweet quality, a soft *heh, heh, heh* tinged with regret. As the night wore on, the crowd of shorty Pabst beer bottles on the kitchen table grew.

But suddenly the rhythm would change.

They would accuse her of trying to act white by marrying my father, and they would talk loudly about subjects that were clearly off limits to us, her children. *You think you're too goddamned good, huh? You forget we know all your shit, Bernice!* She would rage at them, shooting dagger eyes, and drag us all off in a huff. Those long drives home were silent.

At home, I lingered in our town's little Carnegie library. There was a large red leather wingback chair that I loved in the corner of the children's library. Its walls were covered in murals of characters and scenes from fairy tales. The book-lined library was a safe place; I explored the world from the red chair.

Ours was a house of readers, filled with books and newspapers. My parents and brothers, especially my mother and brother Bill, were always reading, books, newspapers, magazines. They would discuss events of the day, principally issues surrounding civil rights and social justice. I loved the righteous tone of those discussions about racial and economic equality; my family's opinions frequently put them at odds with our white neighbors, placing our racial differences front and center. I listened to their loud, passionate talk from my place under the table. A fire began to build in my child's belly, a fire that would purify our family and shine a light on all the wrongs and injustices that the world ignored. Writing would be the fire.

Before I learned to read, I knew the power of the written word. I knew it even in those long hours under the table, making symbols of my own design with my black crayon.

I hated St. Patrick's with its cloying, circumscribed instruction, so I eventually persuaded my mother to send me to public school for eighth grade. I was unprepared, however, for the racism there: no longer coded or quiet as it had been at St. Patrick's but in-your-face, go-fuck-yourself racism. School administrators assumed I was academically challenged because I wasn't white and placed me in classrooms for "slow" students. Later, however, after they saw my scores on a general IQ test, I was placed with the college-bound students whose classism made it nearly intolerable. When the mean girls ganged up on me, I waited for their leader after school and kicked her ass, warning there was more to come if she didn't back off. I earned a reputation. I was becoming like my brother Larry. I drank and experimented with drugs. I hated the dull, uninspiring coursework and would simply walk out of class and spend the afternoon reading in the library. I stopped caring about attendance or graduation or any of the white world's expectations. Frequently, police would have me removed from class for questioning about crimes I didn't commit and about which I had no knowledge. School administrators assumed I was guilty and facilitated the police.

I savored my notoriety and created my own version of the chips Larry and my mother carried on their shoulders, and we bonded over our ill-defined insurgency. My mother recognized my rebelliousness and youthful independence. But she lacked the parental ability to create boundaries and let me drink with her. Alcohol and excessive drinking were at once tools for survival and the means to protest a racist world. To the horror of relatives, I got so drunk at a family wedding that I spent much of the evening vomiting out of the open car window as my mother drove. She belittled me the next morning in front of our family: *You gotta learn how to hold your liquor!* Eventually, I ran away at age thirteen.

I found my way to Milwaukee, where I was arrested and placed in a juvenile detention center for several weeks. It was there I had my first pelvic exam. The elderly white doctor openly expressed disgust at my body, considered too mature for my age, to the guards in the room. He seemed well past retirement age; he was very careful not to touch me or the other girl prisoners, using a pencil to lift up our hair; I remember wondering what state one had to be in to fail his exam. *The doctor was very disgusted with you,* the nurse hissed into my ear. *Maybe he needs to find a different job,* I retorted. I was later transferred to county jail and sentenced to probation for being "incorrigible."

Although I bragged at school about the adventures, I found the whole experience less thrilling than I'd anticipated. Jail was miserable and boring. Education there consisted of reading aloud from poorly written 1950s romance novels, watching TV, and doing embroidery. Girls used the large needles to scratch deep cuts into the hidden folds of their arms and backs of their necks, a form of self-mutilation that far predated white girls' highly publicized cutting habits in the 1990s. The girls at the detention center showed me how to tattoo using the needles, thread, and ink from broken disposable pens. I spent my days gouging the word "squaw" into my forearm, an attempt to make that derogatory term so often used against me my own. But the letters of my mark were uncertain and scraggly, nothing like the bold blue lines of Larry's prison tattoos. In addition to the words "love" and "hate" on the fingers of each hand, he wore a girl's name, Marylu, and a large four-leaf clover with the letter *F* in each corner on his arms. The latter, he said, stood for *find 'em, feel 'em, fuck 'em, forget 'em.* Back home, I hid my tattoo from Larry. But seeing it later, he snorted in derision.

The population at the girls' detention center was overwhelmingly Black; in our boredom, the girls taught me to help with their hair. We applied so much pomade to a white girl's head that her hair looked as though it were made of molded plastic. It was here I met fifteen-year-old Cassandra; she was married to her adult male guardian, who had her arrested for running away. Cassandra threw herself to the floor as she acted out her story for us, how she kicked her husband/guardian and the police as they wrestled her into a police car and her response to the nurse's pelvic exam. *I'm gonna piss in*

Author crying in the corner. Age 4.
(*Courtesy of author's personal collection*)

Sister Mary Catherine Buckley, Mother Superior at St. Mary's Catholic Indian Mission School in Odanah, Wisconsin, on the Bad River reservation. Photo by Father William Hughes, 1931.
(*Courtesy of Bureau of Catholic Indian Missions, Marquette University, Raynor Collection*)

Nuns and Ojibwe children in front of St. Mary's, Odanah, Wisconsin, date unknown. (*Courtesy of Bureau of Catholic Indian Missions, Marquette University, Raynor Collection*)

Left to right: Sister Mary Chrysostom, Sister Mary Catherine Buckley, and Father Emeran Fox (far right), other nuns unnamed, at St. Mary's Catholic Indian Mission School in Odanah, Wisconsin, on the Bad River reservation. Photo by Father William Hughes, 1931. (*Courtesy of Bureau of Catholic Indian Missions, Marquette University, Raynor Collection*)

Exterior of St. Mary's Catholic Indian Mission School, Odanah, Wisconsin, 1930. (*Courtesy of Bureau of Catholic Indian Missions, Marquette University, Raynor Collection*)

Girls' dorm, St. Mary's Catholic Indian Mission School, Odanah, Wisconsin, circa 1930. (*Courtesy of Bureau of Catholic Indian Missions, Marquette University, Raynor Collection*)

"This is the way some of our boys look on a summer's day." St. Mary's Catholic Indian Mission School, Odanah, Wisconsin, Bad River reservation, 1930. (*Courtesy of Bureau of Catholic Indian Missions, Marquette University, Raynor Collection*)

Children at St. Mary's Catholic Indian Mission School, Odanah, Wisconsin, Bad River reservation. Photo by Father William Hughes, 1932. (*Courtesy of Bureau of Catholic Indian Missions, Marquette University, Raynor Collection*)

Sonny Smart and Joe Rabideaux in Chicago, date unknown. (*Courtesy of author's personal collection*)

Cele and Herschel Spencer with sons James and Russell near Lapwai, Idaho, date unknown. (*Courtesy of author's personal collection*)

Mary Pember and dog Hansy,
Janesville, Wisconsin, circa 1961.
(*Courtesy of author's personal collection*)

Bernice and Gordon Pember, early years of relationship, circa 1946.
(*Courtesy of author's personal collection*)

Larry Pember, Janesville,
Wisconsin, circa 1963. (*Courtesy of
author's personal collection*)

Bill Pember, Janesville, Wisconsin,
circa 1965. (*Courtesy of author's
personal collection*)

Bernice Pember and Donald Rabideaux, brother and sister,
shores of Lake Superior, Bad River reservation, circa 1983.
(*Photo by Mary Annette Pember*)

Mary Pember's brother, Bobby C. (right), with unknown friend, Chicago, date unknown. (*Courtesy of author's personal collection*)

St. Mary's Catholic Church on the Bad River
reservation in Wisconsin, 2020.
(*Photo by Mary Annette Pember*)

Shrine in front of St. Mary's Catholic Church
on the Bad River reservation in Wisconsin. Artist unknown, 2020.
(*Photo by Mary Annette Pember*)

Aunt Pat (Moore) and Bernice Pember, Bad River reservation, circa 1987.
(*Photo by Mary Annette Pember*)

your face if you don't let me alone, she said. We attended "school" for about an hour and a half each day with the appropriately named Miss Lamb. She was the very picture of a kindly old Quaker lady in her high-necked blouses, cameo, and tartan wool skirt. When Cassandra read aloud from our assigned book, "Bob was so romantic he swept my feet off!" I stifled a chuckle. I couldn't believe no one else laughed. Catching Miss Lamb's eye, however, I noticed her smile. I was a little shocked to learn several girls had hatched a plan to jump Miss Lamb and escape when we were alone with her. One day I sat down at the old tinny upright piano outside the classroom, playing Beethoven's "Für Elise." Cassandra was amazed. *Damn, you're some kinda Indian girl!* she said.

Back home, I read a great deal, Hemingway, Gardner, Kerouac, Wolfe, Ellison, Bradbury, Jackson, Capote, Steinbeck, Kesey, and others. I longed to leave Janesville for a place where I could be a part of something grander, no longer singled out as "exotic" or "other." In the whiteness of Janesville, I could never be fully human. I was an Indian, inferior and broken. Determined to thrive, I planned my escape.

In the spring of ninth grade, I left home for nearly a year, hitchhiking west to Omaha, Denver, Salt Lake City, Los Angeles, Berkeley, and Seattle. The early 1970s were the days of crash pads, communes, grassroots organizations, free clinics, and food pantries catering to disenfranchised and drifting youth. In Janesville, I was a pariah, but as an Indian on the street I found recognition, even cachet. These were the days of the occupation of Wounded Knee; people were interested in me, my knowledge, and my opinions. I began calling myself Mary White Feather and wore an old, tattered serape and a badly made leather headband. I made my way across the country along with groups of other young people who, like me, were on the run. In Denver, I joined a sort of loosely formed mobile commune led by an older man and his gay lover. Unlike us, in our ragged patched jeans, the lover traveled with a garment bag. He would magically emerge from gas station bathrooms impeccably dressed as though on a European holiday. He was Indian and we bonded immediately, laughing like girlfriends. We watched the hills, covered in velvety grass, undulate past the car windows. When the cops stopped us, I pretended the lover's bag filled with cosmetics belonged to me. Taking one look at my makeup-free face, the cop threw the bag back into the car. *Here, take it, faggot.* I parted with them in Salt Lake City, eventually making my way to Berkeley, where I met Arnie B. while smoking cigarettes on the steps of the student union at UC Berkeley.

Arnie grew up in Queens. He'd fled his life as a young Jewish professional with a wife and young son. An insurance salesman, he was arrested and convicted of embezzling money from the company, gambling it away at the track. His father was a sports bookie who, despite numerous arrests, somehow maintained a respectable family facade. The family had moved often during Arnie's childhood, from fancy apartments to cheap flats, depending on his father's prospects. After great expense to Arnie's family for attorneys and putting up their home for bail, he got away with a few months of probation and a promise to pay the company back. He got a job driving a cab, smoked a great deal of weed, and dropped acid. One day, however, he simply decided to step off and began hitchhiking west. He was twenty-eight years old, a big man with thick bushy hair. Arnie was funny and New York loud with an opinion on everything. We panhandled and sold hash, mixing with the street people on Telegraph Avenue. Initially I told him I was seventeen, later sixteen, until I finally confessed that I was fifteen. *Just stop, I don't want to know,* he said. I talked Arnie into signing on to my mad plan to hitchhike to Alaska. Many of the people who gave us rides laughed out loud when hearing about my plan. I reminded them of a character from the then-popular film *Five Easy Pieces.* In one scene, the actors Jack Nicholson and Karen Black pick up a pair of stranded young women, one of whom has long dark hair and olive skin. Tough and irritable, she goes on and on about the modern world and its "filth" and repeatedly declares she's headed to Alaska because it's cleaner. "I saw pictures; it's very white there," she said. "Yeah," Nicholson responded. "That was before the big thaw." But it wasn't Alaska's cleanliness that attracted me. I just wanted to keep going. When the land ran into the Pacific Ocean, I turned right toward the north to get as far away from Janesville as I could.

We reached Seattle, where Arnie caught hepatitis, so we hitch-hiked south to Hollywood to seek help from his brother Spence, who worked at a music industry magazine. We showed up unexpectedly at Spence's office in a sleek high-rise, where Arnie introduced me. Taking in my serape and headband, Spence said, *Oh, nice Jewish girl, huh?* Spence took Arnie aside, gave him a $20 bill, and dismissed him. We were living in the car of our new friend, Thaddeus, who'd just arrived in Hollywood from his hometown of Akron, Ohio. Arnie was very ill now and stayed curled up asleep in the tiny backseat of the old VW Karmann Ghia as Thaddeus and I explored the city. We loved the Hollywood Walk of Fame, plopping ourselves down on the sidewalk squares of stars we recognized and admired. We both loved music and sang along loudly to the car's radio until Arnie shouted for us to shut up. Thaddeus taught me how to keep time silently to the music by flaring my nostrils. Thaddeus was fun and extravagantly gay; soon we grew very attached. He drove us back to the Bay Area, where he took a room in Oakland. One glorious day, Thaddeus and I hitched to San Francisco so he could see the city. I took him to Golden Gate Park near the seawall, showing him the man-made mountains, created from rebar and cement like giant papier-mâché sculptures along the hillside. We climbed down to the ruins of the old Sutro Baths, built into the rocks where the sea waves crash up through hidden passages. Jumping on a rock, Thaddeus stood on its flat top, extending his arms, shouting *yes!* just in time to be drenched by a wave. We wandered to Geary Street and its shopwindows filled with beautiful, layered cakes. We shared a slice of cake at one of the cafés, bolting out the door after leaving all our change on the counter. Near dusk, we hitched back to Oakland. An old battered white pickup truck gave us a ride, slowing down just long enough for us to jump in. We laughed as we tumbled together onto the bed of the truck. I wrapped my serape around us as we sped across the Bay Bridge, the neon ablaze along the city skyline. Back at his crib, he tried to make love to me. Thinking he was joking, I laughed out loud mid-kiss, which pissed him off and hurt his feelings. He threw me out into the Oakland night, where I walked the evening away past the hookers' stroll on San Pablo and the titty bars, their doors held open by bar stools to let out the smoke.

Street life was dangerous, the risk of rape or attack constant, especially for an unattached woman or girl. Social services finally found a hospital to take Arnie as he recovered from hepatitis, and I found myself without male protection; occasionally I would hitchhike to the hospital, about twenty miles south of Oakland, to visit him. A lone man picked me up near Merritt College as I returned home one night; as soon as I got in the car, I knew I'd made a mistake. *Do you go to that school up on the hill?* he asked ominously. Rather than heading north, he abruptly turned in to the southbound freeway entrance toward Hayward. Silently, I waited until he exited the freeway and came to a stop sign where I jumped out; he caught me around the neck, his long fingernails digging into my skin, and I seemed to dangle precipitously between the car's interior and the road for what seemed like forever. A car approached the four-way stop from another direction and I began to scream; the man let me fall to the ground, where I continued to scream hysterically. He drove away. I ran to the approaching car, which was filled with local teenage boys high on LSD. They gazed at me for some time, their mouths open in wonder. *Wow,* one of them finally said. They ended up driving me all the way home to Oakland, where we'd rented a closet with a loft bed from Arnie's friend Bobby for $30 a month. Bobby was a former junkie who somehow managed to secure monthly Social Security disability payments. Mostly he stayed clean in a now-quiet life in his squalid apartment. But sometimes he chipped when addicts came around asking him to help score. I liked living at Bobby's with its bed safely hidden high up in a narrow closet. Life developed a rhythm. I sold hash and LSD on Telegraph Avenue. I used some identification found in one of our former squats to enroll at the local community college. I enrolled in a music class, jamming on piano with other students. I moved easily through the world; authorities took no interest in an Indian child roaming the streets. Adult, mostly white men, however, were keenly interested. I often wondered why they didn't pursue relationships with women their own age. Sometimes the men wanted to marry me, which made me laugh. And sometimes I had to accept their advances as a necessity to that life. Overall, I met very few adults during that time who behaved like adults. An older girl, however, hearing my story, insisted I call my parents and let them know I was alive. I recall the rush of relief my mother breathed over the phone that day and remain ashamed about my behavior even years after apologizing.

After his recovery, Arnie began dropping a lot of acid, seeking some sort of transcendence from his old life in Queens. He sat in a seated yoga pose, suddenly inhaling and widening his eyes in response to some vague internal revelation for which he had no words. He grew violent and erratic. Frightened, I spent more time away from him. One day while partying with his friend Charlie, he poured a can of gasoline over his head and self-immolated. He died later at the hospital. I heard later that Charlie sustained extensive third-degree burns while trying to help Arnie. I didn't see it happen.

I'd had enough; I called my parents and begged them to buy me a plane ticket home. I later earned a high school equivalency diploma, enrolled in the two-year University of Wisconsin Rock County extension school (U-Rock) in town, and began to write about my life and experiences out west. I failed the first introductory grammar test miserably. I was crestfallen and ashamed, dissolving into tears as I begged the school counselor to let me withdraw from the class. Instead, she arranged a meeting with the teacher Dick Strack, who waved away my concerns. *Don't worry, you can learn grammar, I'll teach you,* he said. *You already know how to write.* I was elated. Professor Strack praised my writing, comparing some of my sentences to Hemingway, one of my great idols. Shyly, I shared the news with my mother. *Self-praise stinks!* she almost shouted, holding her nose. I dreamed of earning a four-year degree at the main campus in Madison but lacked high school algebra and geometry credits. I needed tuition for one more semester, but she refused to help me pay for it, considering so much schooling a waste of time. Why didn't I pursue vocational school, she wanted to know. If I got training in interior decorating, I could help out in her used-furniture business, a recent

scheme. *You could earn money and have nice things,* she said persua-
sively. But I was awakening to something more. I followed threads
in the random books I read at the library; allusions led me to other,
more complex subjects in philosophy, sociology, and literature. I
stumbled upon the poetry of Dante, Baudelaire, Rimbaud, Emily
Dickinson, T. S. Eliot, discovering them on my own like an explorer.
I was unsure where it would all lead, but I found the path irresistible,
a precursor to what she called my incessant poking and prodding.
Interior decorating versus higher education—it became a huge point
of contention between us. She forbade Dad to help me; although I
could see it pained him, he went along with her. My only posses-
sion of any real value was the used piano Dad bought for me a few
years earlier, so I sold it to pay the $300 tuition. She reproached me.
You know, Dad is really hurt that you're selling your piano. In the end,
administrators at U-Rock added two courses just for me, Algebra 091
and Geometry 099. For that semester, I was the only student of the
mathematics professor Rajindar Luther, a kind, patient soul. I did
not score well but managed to pass both courses and enrolled at the
University of Wisconsin–Madison. My now-husband, John, helped
me move from Janesville to Madison. I met John at U-Rock while he
taught a geography class for a professor who was on sabbatical. John
was a graduate student, working on his PhD in geography at the
main campus in Madison. It was 1981. The first time I saw him, John
was leaning against the blackboard at the front of my introductory
geography class. His ankles were crossed in a way that emphasized
his thigh muscles, thick from years of bike riding. He stood there as
only a white man can, effortlessly sure and at ease in his body and
the world. I hung around his classroom and flirted with him until
he asked me out. John was the first white man who didn't treat me
like a foreigner, an exotic piece of ass to be conquered. Prior to graduate school, he'd spent four years in an isolated village in Iran working as a Peace Corps volunteer. As the only foreigner in the village,
he quickly learned what it was to be other, exotic, and maybe not
entirely human to the locals. John understood racism in ways most
white men don't. Plus he was educated, smart, and worldly; I found

him impossibly sexy. He shared my passion for social and racial justice and commitment to challenging institutions that supported and benefited from that inequitable status quo.

Cerebral yet affectionate and caring, John offered me the emotional safety and support I needed to navigate college and break away from my beginnings. I learned later that he earned his undergraduate degree at the Maryknoll Catholic seminary, a society of priests dedicated to serving as missionaries to the poor especially among Indigenous peoples. Although he decided against taking the vows of priesthood and turned away from Catholicism, he remained tied to the tenets of Maryknoll's liberation theology, which emphasizes the liberation of the oppressed. It was a relationship ripe for dysfunction, but that came later. And so I moved to Madison and grew into the "inner-lectual" my mother had imagined I was. I gained skill in language; now I could challenge the racist systems under which she suffered. Secretly she was proud of me, but she never said so. She grew defensive and angry when I used words and terms she didn't understand. *Don't think you're better than me,* she'd huff. Her inexplicable attacks wounded me. Our relationship was always uneasy; it was a long time before I learned how and why she was a prisoner of her illogical, cruel ways.

SIX

INNER-LECTUAL

The University of Wisconsin in Madison is not far from Janesville, only about forty miles. But for me it was a million miles different from Janesville, where most people dreamed of working at the Chevy plant. Madison represented abstract thought and concepts that could take me beyond my immediate experience, birth, and race. My years there during the 1980s were transformative. This was an era ignited by the civil rights movement of the 1960s, which gave birth to the 1975 Indian Self-Determination and Education Assistance Act, which allowed tribes greater autonomy in directing federal programs, services, and funding and opened up more educational opportunities for people like me in the form of funding and support. It was a heady time to be an Indian college student. Our demands for self-determination were beginning to be heard. We emphasized tribal sovereignty, railing against decades of disempowerment, disenfranchisement, invisibility, and injustice in relation to American culture and government. The influence of the Red Power movement, when Indian activists seized the abandoned federal prison Alcatraz on an island in San Francisco Bay for use as a school, cultural center, and museum in 1969, was still palpable. Activists claimed the site by "right of discovery," offering to buy it from the government for $24 in glass beads and red cloth—the price settlers allegedly paid tribes for the island of Manhattan. Although the effort ultimately failed, the occupation of Alcatraz became a rallying cry regarding government disinterest in Indian affairs and people.

In 1972, Indian activists from the Trail of Broken Treaties, a caravan organized to protest government inaction toward Indians, took over the Bureau of Indian Affairs building in Washington, D.C., occupying the office for more than a week. Organizers demanded redress for the government's failure to uphold treaty promises and presented a document to the federal government known as the "Twenty Points Position Paper," in which they demanded repeal of the termination policies, restoration of the treaty-making process, recognition of existing treaties, protection of religious freedom, and funding for health care, housing, and education in rural and urban Indian communities. At the time, the press focused on damages done to the office, obscuring the activists' demands. The government declined to prosecute the protesters, who were allowed to return home. But many of the demands from the "Twenty Points" paper were eventually addressed in government policies.

In 1973, Indian activists led by members of the American Indian Movement occupied Wounded Knee, the site of an infamous massacre of as many as three hundred Lakota in 1890 by the U.S. Army on the Pine Ridge reservation in South Dakota. The occupation, which lasted seventy-one days, focused the world's attention on American Indians and the failure of the U.S. government to honor treaties and other policies. Two Indian men, Frank Clearwater (Cherokee and Apache) and Lawrence "Buddy" Lamont (Oglala), were killed and many others were wounded by law enforcement during the occupation. Two years later two FBI agents were killed at a ranch—Ronald Williams and Jack Coler—on the Pine Ridge reservation. Leonard Peltier, Turtle Mountain Chippewa, Lakota, and Dakota, a member of AIM, was tried and convicted for the murders. He remains incarcerated fifty-one years later and has lost repeated requests for clemency despite support by the United Nations and many prominent social and racial justice leaders.

My professors at the University of Wisconsin were the warriors who helped set that transformative change for Indians into motion, including Ada Deer of the Menominee Indian Tribe of Wisconsin, the first woman to chair her tribe and first Native woman to head the Bureau of Indian Affairs. Ada took the lead in reversing termination and regaining federal recognition for the Menominee. There was also Truman Lowe of the Ho-Chunk Nation, sculptor and curator of contemporary art at the National Museum of the American Indian. And there was Dorothy Davids of the Stockbridge-Munsee Band of Mohican Indians, professor of education and community development, who (among others) took me under her wing, lifted me up, and helped me find my way. I met Indian students from all over the United States who, like extended family, gave me love and support. The women's rights movement was also gaining momentum; in 1981 the Supreme Court overturned laws giving husbands' unilateral control over property jointly owned with their wives.

My classes with Gerda Lerner, a founder of the academic field of woman's history, were thrilling. Lerner was a taskmaster, a stickler for detail who constantly reminded us that those who challenge the status quo of institutions must be thorough in their scholarship. In her books and lectures, Lerner possessed what her colleague Linda Gordon called "a relentless focus on power and a grasp of the interrelatedness of its various forms—class, race, and sex." She urged us onward when we complained about the many barriers women faced in education, describing how as an undergraduate she pasted class notes around her house so she could study while cleaning and caring for her children. How I longed to be among the group of young women who trailed after her, brilliantly discussing our class readings. Shyly, I hovered around the edges, but Lerner recognized my hunger, encouraging my participation and valuing my insights. Teachers like Lerner and Deer gave me the language and confidence to intelligently challenge racial and gender inequities.

Campus was a sanctuary for me, but initially I felt intimidated by the huge freshman lecture halls filled mostly with white upper-middle-class students. They seemed so at home there.

I lived in fear of being found out, of being asked to leave because of my background and lack of high school experience. I sat on the edge of my seat in Betsy Draine's literature classes, captivated by her analysis of prose, poetry, and plays. Slowly, writing became more than an impracticable dream; it was possible. Although it was years before the popular use of the term "intersectionality," I made personal intellectual connections between the roles of history, politics, and power in relation to social and racial inequities. I joined Wunk Sheek ("human being" in the Ho-Chunk language), the Indian student organization, and was active in racial and social justice issues. College was tough going financially, but with the help of state and federal grants as well as a series of jobs including waiting tables and working for the telephone company and the state bureau of prisons, I graduated in 1985 with a BA in editorial journalism. I was the first college graduate in my family, an outcome of all the hard work of my mother and advocates before me.

The era of change that affected my life also featured passage of several landmark Indian policies, many of which were driven by an unlikely supporter, President Richard Nixon. Nixon credited his support for Indians to his relationship with Wallace Newman, his football coach at Whittier College. Newman was a citizen of the La Jolla Band of Luiseño Indians and frequently made personal appearances with Nixon during his campaigns for congressman, senator, and, later, president. Nixon was a third-stringer on the Whittier team and saw little playing time but adored Coach Newman, whom he likened to a father figure. "I think I admired him more and learned more from him than any other man aside from my father. He drilled into me a competitive spirit and the determination to come back after you have been knocked down or after you lose. He also gave me an acute understanding that what really matters is not a man's background, his color, his race, or his religion, but only his character."

Although primarily remembered for his involvement in the Watergate scandal and his subsequent resignation, Nixon was instrumental in reversing the policy of termination, enacting the Menominee Restoration Act, restoring the tribe's recognition that had been terminated, and the Indian Education Act of 1972, which authorized

a higher level of funding for Indian education and created a forum
for tribes and Indian communities to provide input on education
priorities. In a 1970 address to Congress, Nixon described his vision
for self-determination: "The time has come to break decisively with
the past and to create the conditions for a new era in which the
Indian future is determined by Indian acts and Indian decisions."

Nixon appointed Louis Bruce of the Mohawk Nation as commissioner of the Bureau of Indian Affairs, the third Indian to lead
the BIA since the agency was created. In 1970, Nixon signed a bill
returning the sacred Blue Lake to the people of Taos Pueblo. He also
signed the Alaska Native Claims Settlement Act of 1971, intended to
correct unequal state land claims and transfer land titles to Alaska
Native corporations and villages. Although he resigned from the
presidency before its passage, Nixon laid the groundwork for the
Indian Self-Determination and Education Assistance Act, passed during his former vice president Gerald Ford's presidency in 1975. Peter
MacDonald, former chairman of the Navajo Nation, is credited with
referring to Nixon as "the Abraham Lincoln of the Indian people."
Certainly an overstatement by most people's reckoning, but there
is no denying the pivotal role Nixon played in furthering tribal sovereignty and self-determination. Conversely, Nixon is also remembered for his role in overseeing the forced sterilization of more than
three thousand Indian women during and after his administration.
Although determined to defund the War on Poverty programs created by his predecessor, Lyndon Johnson, Nixon eagerly supported
family planning with an emphasis on sterilization, increasing funding through passage of the Family Planning Services and Population
Research Act of 1970. Soon a pattern of sterilization abuse at federal
clinics emerged in which women of color were targeted and denied
informed consent for the procedure. Many were threatened with ces-
sation of public assistance if they failed to comply. Several thousand
Native American women were sterilized, often without informed
consent, by the Indian Health Service during this period.

Other life-changing policy and legislation during the 1970s
included the American Indian Religious Freedom Act of 1978,

which returned basic civil rights, eliminated government's ability to interfere with exercise of traditional religions and spirituality, and ensured access to sacred sites. The awkwardly named but profoundly important Tribally Controlled Community College Assistance Act was passed in 1978. Usually referred to as the Tribal College Act, it helps fund tribally controlled colleges, providing access to postsecondary education and vocational training to Indian and non-Indian students in mostly rural areas. There are currently thirty-seven tribal colleges in the United States, including Haskell Indian Nations University, first founded as a boarding school in 1884. The Indian Child Welfare Act (ICWA) was passed in 1978 in response to inequitable removals of Indian children from their families. ICWA set standards for removal and placement of Indian children, emphasizing keeping them connected to families, communities, and cultures. In 2023 the U.S. Supreme Court upheld the constitutionality of the act after repeated attempts to overturn it.

I recall my mother's visits during my student days in Madison. She would arrive briskly at my door, always impeccably dressed, and she would sweep me and my hungry roommates out to dinner. Sometimes she grew tipsy drinking with us. She wanted to join our discussions about race, politics, and social inequities but had trouble grasping the concepts. She would grow angry and resentful, accusing me of thinking I was better than her. She twisted herself into that familiar "I made up my mind" posture, flipping her hair defiantly and rooting her butt down into a chair. My roommates and I discussed the historical roots of institutional racism, its impact on our current lives and American society, and the disconnect between Indigenous and white European cosmologies and worldviews. Determined to save face and prove she understood our conversation, she took on a knowing expression. She cocked her head, smiled wisely, and peppered the conversation with her verbal props "to a certain extent" and "ironic." I was embarrassed for her. But after she died, I found a yellowed, undated newspaper clipping among her belongings. In an effort to describe the barriers Native people experience in navigating white society, the columnist quoted Chief Dan George.

"I was born in an age that loved the things of nature and gave them beautiful names. I was born when people loved nature and spoke to it as though it has a soul," George wrote. "And the new people came like a crushing wave hurling the years aside and suddenly I found myself a young man in the midst of the 20th century. On our little reserves and plots of land we floated in a kind of grey reality, ashamed of our culture which you ridiculed. Do you know what it is like to be without moorings, to feel you are of no value to society? We were shrugged aside because we were dumb and could never learn." I was too arrogant in my youth to see she understood—far better than my roommates and I—the racism and inequities entrenched in U.S. institutions and society. She had lived through the moment of their creation. She simply lacked the words to discuss her experiences. Plus, she was far too busy trying to survive in that world to idly dissect the forces that created it.

My mother was always in a hurry in those days, her high heels clicking sharply as she walked ahead of Dad when he joined her during her visits or anytime our family ventured out together. *He doesn't like it when we wait for him,* she reassured us. But the expression of pain, pride, and resentment that swept over Dad's face said otherwise. We were forbidden to notice his labored breathing brought on by his disability. Discussing it would make it real; better to plow ahead, willing away anything that drew attention to deficiencies that might set our family apart. She had no patience for extended study or examination. Fearful she might glimpse the horror and embarrassment of her past, she chose rather to rush ahead, using her appearance and income to elevate herself. Dad helped her in her used-furniture business; haughtily, she began telling people she was a businesswoman. Later she decided to get a realtor's license, but the textbooks sat unopened on the dining room table for months and disappeared within a year. *You have to step fast when walking in a city,* she instructed me during our visits to Chicago. *And always look like you know where you're going.*

Conversely, she supported my growing interest in our Ojibwe heritage, something she secretly longed for her entire life. It was then

I began my interrogation, what my mother described as my incessant poking, into her life, her past, and our family in Bad River. We made frequent trips to the reservation to visit Uncle Don, Aunt Gertie, and other family. I played chauffeur, driving elders to bingo and other doings, slowly soaking up the past, the present, and the unspoken nuance of Ojibwe history and life. Sometimes we stayed with Auntie Pat in her little house set back from the highway. She told us stories about Aunt Lucille's ricing adventures. Lucille was mom's older sister. Lucille always came up to rice. *One time she wore these heavy wool men's pants that slid down to her ankles when the canoe got swamped. A man was trying to help her out of the water, but she was laughing just hard,* Pat told us. *Quit laughing, the man said, I'm trying to help you here. Lucille said, I'm afraid to get out of the water, I'm bare-assed.* We sat at the kitchen table just as the adults had when I was a girl and laughed at all the old stories. Auntie fed us wild rice and fried walleye, which we devoured wordlessly, lost in our Ojibwe feasting.

During my college years, I made several handmade books, including one in a typography class illustrating some of my mother's and Uncle Don's memories of their childhood. We revisited the sites where they hid away from the nuns when running away and the remains of Grandpa Joe's shack. I photographed them walking barefoot along the shore of Lake Superior, where they searched for eagle feathers as they had as kids. Uncle Don threw his head back as he laughed his famous laugh when we piled into his little motorboat. He steered us to Baby's Beach along the Bad River and finally out to its mouth where it meets the lake. We took languid drives with my cousin Annie and her little daughter, Brooke, who stood on the car seat next to her, holding on to Annie's earlobe for balance. Mom and Auntie Pat sat in the backseat enjoying the warm breeze through the open windows. *Say, Bernice, do you remember ole Tootsie Porkchop?* she asked my mom. Annie and I burst out laughing. *Tootsie Porkchop?!* we exclaimed simultaneously. These were the only times my mother didn't grow impatient with my camera and questions. But there was an unbodied, ambiguous quality to the reservation for me. So much was just out of reach, beyond understanding. One summer afternoon the air turned suddenly torpid and still, the sky taking on the green-ish glow preceding a tornado. But the rain that followed was unlike anything I'd seen before. It behaved like an angry being on a mission.

A wall of water shot up diagonally, as though pressurized, through the small gap at the bottom of a barely open window. The rain seemed desperate to enter the house.

Among my relatives, the unsaid seemed to hang forever in the air. Their quick side glances suggested that there was something more, on a deeper register, happening around me. And thus, my mother's past remained elusive, beyond reach, like a fish darting away through the muck.

Thankfully, my father was a silent, abiding foundation for the family. For me. Although unexpressed or rarely expressed openly, his love was incontrovertible, without condition of any kind. It wasn't until he died during my junior year in college that I realized the singular, priceless nature of that love. The knowledge that such a thing exists, that I am worthy of and entitled to it, has sustained me my entire life. I made it to Dad's bedside before he died. Although he didn't regain consciousness, I remained with him until his spirit left with a final gasp. My mother and Larry, however, fled. *Oooooooooo,* she murmured, shaking her head and flapping her hands as they ran down the hallway.

My father's death set off a revelatory chain reaction in our fam-ily. In reading his will, we learned that our mother brought Larry, another man's son, to the marriage. Our father had adopted him.

Her wall of secrets very slowly began to give way, but there was more to come, far more.

SEVEN

DRINKING TO LIVE

found my niche at journalism school, where I discovered the power and influence of newswriting and photography. I began my newspaper career immediately after graduation. Faculty and staff at the School of Journalism helped me secure a yearlong paid internship with a large media company with newspapers located around the country. But I needed a car. My fellow waitress Dee at Cleveland's Lunch, an aluminum-clad diner near campus, signed a note for a car loan at the university credit union. I bought an old Buick Skylark. Its frame was sprung from a rear-end collision and its suspension shot, it floated freely over the road. The trunk lid didn't entirely close and had to be tied down with rope. The trunk compartment filled with water when it rained, but it carried me to newspapers in Michigan, Pennsylvania, and finally Kansas City and *The Kansas City Times.* I still recall the wide, sweeping brass stair rails and grand entrance of the building, which housed both the *Times* and *The Kansas City Star.* I was thrilled to learn that Hemingway worked there as a reporter when he was starting out. In my mind, I had arrived. I fell in love with the adrenaline rush of chasing news and the freedom of venturing out into the world to gather stories, especially those centering on people. For some, newspapering included hard drinking, part of the decompression process after long hours covering a difficult story. In those days, there were usually bars located near newspaper buildings with names like the City Desk and the News Room where journalists gathered. I fell in with that crowd.

After my internship I joined John for several months in Nepal, where he was doing research in the high-elevation jungle surrounding the Dhaulagiri range in the Himalayas. His research focused on tree species there; citizens of the local Pun Magar tribe helped him. The Magars reminded me of my Ojibwe relatives; we shared the same silly, earthy sense of humor and appreciation for the absurd. It was fun to sit with our brother Bo Bahadur's two wives (everyone is a relative in the Nepali language) in their kitchen shucking corn and visiting. John hired Bo as his research assistant. Not many Magar folks take multiple spouses, but when Bo's elder wife, Tilu, found she couldn't have children, she suggested he marry her younger sister Sandevi. It seemed to work well for the family, although Bo said, *Whenever there's a vote, I always lose.* One evening I squatted on the earthen floor with the wives as they worked preparing dinner. Sandevi passed an especially loud and musical fart. Before we could react, Bo, who was standing outside the window, said, *Hajur? or what?* as though asking us to repeat a word. We laughed long and hard, repeating the story several times to appreciative visitors. Like Ojibwe, the Magars could be hard drinkers; I developed a taste for their homemade liquor, *raksi,* distilled from millet. I became a frequent guest at their house parties, where we made merry late into the night. In those days, I couldn't imagine life without alcohol and overlooked the risk of drinking raw liquor that the people stored in empty kerosene cans. Later, John and I decided to marry in Kathmandu, the country's capital. My friends and I devised an outlandish ceremony in which bride and groom rode an elephant from the wedding venue to the reception. I wore a red sari from Karnataka state bought during our travels in India. In Hindu culture, red is the color of marriage, symbolizing new beginnings, passion, and prosperity. It was an epic celebration; Bo and his wives joined us. The party went into the early morning hours.

Disgusted with my drinking, John went to bed. I stayed up, get-

ting blackout drunk on *raksi*. Staggering out into the street, I fell
down, unrolling my beautiful sari, six meters of silk, in the dirt. Seeing his face the next day gave me a glimpse of many mornings to
come. His expression of disapproval and apprehension tinged with
disgust grew familiar. But he said little. Thus began nearly fourteen
years of our alcoholic and enabler relationship, a long slow train
wreck that I was powerless to stop.

The drinking life takes a lot of skill and effort, especially if you
want to keep a day job and co-pretend, successfully, that you're a
functional adult. For instance, I changed my name in order to drink.
My byline was Mary Annette Pember when I worked as a staff newspaper photographer in the 1980s and 1990s. Until that time, I was
known to the world as simply Mary. But in order to keep drinking
and avoid getting fired, I landed on the idea of reinventing myself
as Mary Annette or M.A. to my newspaper colleagues. If callers to
my home phone asked for M.A. or Mary Annette, I knew the call
was work related, likely an order to cover a breaking news event. If it
was during my time off, I was very likely drunk and couldn't safely
drive, so I didn't take the call. John answered the phone when he was
home; when he wasn't, I let all my calls go to the answering machine.

In my defense, photojournalism in those days was nearly entirely
dominated by white men; newspaper darkrooms had a distinctive
locker-room ambience that wasn't welcoming to women. In many
ways I was supremely lucky to work at newspapers while they still
constituted an essential part of American life; the work really was
"the life of kings" and allowed entry into people's lives and environments that would otherwise have been inaccessible. As a young
woman, I was drawn to journalism as a means to shine a true light on
Indian lives, a light that would illuminate our diversity and humanity beyond the settler-driven stereotypes that often defined coverage
of our communities. I soon found, however, that success for a woman
of color often amounted to one's ability to function well within the
confines and parameters of mainstream journalism. I walked and
talked white; editors commented on my articulate speech. Most
important, I learned to shield their racial insecurity, to put them at

ease. Although they appreciated my work ethic, it grew clear that I would never gain access to their inner circle of confidence and trust where the great assignments were delegated. One day, late in my daily newspaper career, I pitched an Indian-focused story to my editor. He expressed concern that since I'm Ojibwe, I wouldn't possess the necessary objectivity to cover the story fairly. *What about the white male reporters who cover city hall, where employees and politicians are almost entirely white men?* I asked. *How is it you don't have similar concerns about their journalistic objectivity?*

Pember, he asked, *why do you always have to be such a smart-ass?*

Not long after that, I quit and began covering Indian people and issues for the ethnic press and other publications that would hire me. I never looked back.

Leading up to that moment, however, I had grown disenchanted and ground down by the entrenched sexism and racism. So, my drinking got worse. Drinking in my family was our only coping mechanism and I embraced it enthusiastically. And it worked. Until it didn't. Honestly, if it had worked, I'd still be drinking today. Alcohol was the answer to everything. I drank to relax, to celebrate, to socialize. I drank to ease the rage and anger over a racist, unfair world, my discomfort with myself, my family, and my mother, most of all. As a fellow recovering alcoholic described his end-stage drinking, *I drank because it was Tuesday.* The last days of my drinking before the millennium were joyless, empty times. When I opened my eyes in the morning, my brain would slowly reorder itself. Was I animal, vegetable, or mineral? I had hit bottom and reached out to Alcoholics Anonymous (AA). Alcoholics in AA frequently talk about hitting bottom, the thing or event that made them see they had to either quit drinking or die. For me, it was seeing myself in my daughter Rosa's eyes. I'd gotten blackout drunk during a family vacation when she was nearly two years old. I woke up with my face against the cool tile of the hotel's bathroom floor, where I'd passed out after vomiting. Looking in her eyes that morning reminded me of my little-girl self, the helplessness, the fear, and the smell, that awful smell, associated with my relatives. I didn't want her to have to live with those memories and trauma. So I called AA and went to a meeting. The people in AA weren't shocked or surprised by my story. If anything, they appeared underwhelmed; I was just another drunk. I heard far worse stories than mine in the rooms and came to see how incredibly lucky I was to have found what they call "the gift of desperation" before I'd killed myself or someone else. In the rooms of AA I found the help and support I needed to build a new way to live life without alcohol. Fortunately, I also had a safe home environment with a loving spouse and reliable access to food and housing, which helped make recovery possible. Recovery meant acknowledging my addiction as a part of me, a part that would always be there. I envision it as a windigo spirit, not unlike the one I imagined that tried to devour my grandparents. In Ojibwe cosmology, the windigo is a cannibal spirit, sometimes manifested as a monster that can also possess human beings, infecting them with an insatiable hunger that only grows even as it's fed. Those enslaved by the windigo begin to devour loved ones and eventually in desperation begin to devour themselves. My windigo resembles Warner Bros. Cartoons' Tasmanian Devil character. A tiny creature residing in the deepest part of my gut, it slavers and rants for more. It wants more alcohol, food, fancy shoes, and accessories or anything else that makes me feel good in the short term. Like every windigo, it's immune to rational thought or willpower; it's never satisfied. One must accept it. Failing to acknowledge and care for it only makes it more powerful. For me, the best defense is prayer, offering myself up to the great mystery, and willingness to be of service to my fellow humans.

John and I faced up to the disease that haunted our relationship, seeing that in many ways it was alcoholism and its roles of alcoholic and enabler, Indian and missionary, that first drew us together. We recognized that denial is part of the disease and we are still married today, nearly forty years later.

A major part of my recovery also involved creating a healthy relationship with my birth family, especially my mother. It was tough going at first; I was angry and filled with resentment and hurt over her harsh and baffling ways. My AA sponsor instructed me to pray for my mother every day. The prayers were to have no specific request for outcome. I was told to pray only that she would find peace. And so I prayed when she would suddenly decide to stop speaking to me over an unknown offense and when I grew exhausted by her defensiveness and paranoia. After my father died, she grew increasingly defensive and secretive, convinced Bill and I were after the modest inheritance my father had left. Fortunately, we'd learned and practiced to rely on our own resources long ago so it really wasn't an issue for us. Money, buying and selling, was her new obsession. She used it to lure Larry into accompanying her on trips to the reservation, where she resold piles of cheap goods purchased at closeout sales and garage sales. They set up shop in the old bingo hall on weekends. Larry got to know our relatives, and soon they invited him to ceremonies. But it was all lost on him. *All those Indians do up there is sit around in the woods and beat on drums,* he told me later. *What the hell good is that; there's no money in it.* As the years passed, she frittered all her money away in an ongoing series of ill-advised schemes and investments in decrepit rental properties, the goal mostly being to create a living for Larry.

All that remained by the year 2000 was her house, her car, and a few possessions. I was shocked to learn that when Uncle Don died, rather than distribute his belongings to the community (a traditional Ojibwe practice), she sold them, including his aluminum walker, at a garage sale in the front yard of the tribal elder's home. By then, her mental decline was undeniable: she'd begun showing signs of dementia; she was more erratic.

My brother Larry's death in 2004 hit her hard; she could no longer rely on the dependency and neediness that bound them together. Unexpectedly, she was left with me and Bill. She wasn't really prepared to love us in a healthy, reciprocal way, because it meant lowering her guard. Something for which she was radically unprepared. During family gatherings she would often grow angry at us for reasons we didn't understand. She would purse her lips and stiffen her spine in that particular way she had while rooting herself into the furniture. Raising her hands silently, gesturing as though in an internal argument, she let them fall abruptly. Her thin wrists landed sharply against her wristwatch with a distressing metal-on-bone crunch. Over and over again. Her rage and dis-ease, seldom articulated, seemed to emanate from her like a presence that seeped into every corner of the house. She clearly wanted to make us aware of her displeasure, but her silence told us that if we really cared about and loved her, we would already know what was troubling her.

Through all of this, I continued to pray for her and began to connect more seriously with Ojibwe culture and spirituality.

Sobriety is a prerequisite for participation in ceremony, so for years it held little interest for me; I'd politely decline the occasional invitations extended by friends and relatives. Fortunately, however, in my first weeks of sobriety, I scored a monthlong gig covering Ojibwe communities in the Great Lakes region. My first assignment was photographing Jim Simon Mishibinijima (Birch-bark Silver Shield Man) on Ojibwe Wiikwemikong Unceded Territory on Manitoulin Island in Ontario, Canada. Jim is a painter in the Indigenous Woodland or legend artists style, which is influenced by spirit writing. Before contact, Ojibwe used mnemonic symbols or spirit writing to record visions and teachings on birch-bark scrolls and rock faces throughout the Great Lakes region. My hands were still shaking from alcohol withdrawal and my legs were wobbly as I walked up to Jim's tiny studio far out in the bush. A big man, he stood in the doorway silently watching me approach. Holding up his hand, he said, *Wait right here. I have something for you.* He returned with some dried plant medicines and said, *I can see you're struggling.* After giving me instructions on what to do and how to use the medicines, he showed me his paintings and posed for photographs. I left Jim's studio in a daze. These medicines and teachings had been here waiting for me all along. I remember thinking, *If the Creator is going to this much trouble for me, maybe I better pay attention.* That was the summer of 2000; I've been sober ever since.

EIGHT

POKING TRAUMA

As part of the Rosalynn Carter Fellowship for Mental Health Journalism and other journalism awards, I spent a year taking a deep dive into trauma's effects on our minds and bodies and its ability to traverse generations. More specifically, I wanted to understand my mother and the effect of trauma on our family. I learned about historical trauma, the neuroscience of trauma and its physiological effects on our brains, and the science of epigenetics, literally above the gene. Epigenetics posits that we pass along more than DNA in our genes; it suggests that our genes can carry memories of trauma experienced by our ancestors and thus influence how we react to trauma and stress.

I spoke with mainstream mental health professionals and traditional Indian medicine people throughout Indian country. I also met with Mary Vicario, a licensed professional clinical counselor and certified trauma specialist who often consults with tribal mental health organizations. Vicario and other trauma experts helped me better understand the neuroscience behind my mother's behavior. I learned that children tend to blame themselves for abuse and neglect. Developmentally, young children think they control their world and are responsible for events, both good and bad. Fresh from the trauma of witnessing Joe and Cele's fight and her family's destruction, my

mother was abandoned by her extended family and placed in the
Sister School. Together, the events created a perfect storm of lifelong,
intractable trauma and shame. Witnessing Joe and Cele's last horrific
fight likely set off a whole cascade of neurological responses that forever altered her physiology, affecting her nervous system and mental
health for the rest of her life. In the moments of the fight, my mother's awareness descended into the most primitive part of her nervous
system, the cranial vagus nerve, a long nerve beginning in the brain
stem and extending all the way down into the large intestine. There
are two parts to the vagus nerve, the dorsal vagus and the ventral,
each with different functions. The dorsal vagus governs our freeze
response to danger. This response emerges after our limbic system's
messages of flight or fight have failed. The limbic system is a set of
structures on both sides of our brain supporting emotion, behavior,
motivation, long-term memory, and smell. They drive our behaviors
associated with survival.

Together, according to Vicario, the limbic system and the dorsal
vagus nerve constitute our brain's fear center. "Our limbic system
wants certain things to happen in a particular order when faced with
danger; first it directs us to flock towards safe people," she explained.
When safe people are not available, the limbic system directs us to
fight or flee. If these responses don't work, our vagus nerve takes
over, preparing us to die. The dorsal vagus nerve places us in a freeze
response, numbing our senses, essentially making us more comfort-
able as we die. When the dorsal vagus nerve takes over, the part of
the brain that records memory is often off-line, which explains why
my mother retained so few memories of her parents' violence. This
response is an example of trauma-related disassociation, a mental
escape when physical escape is impossible. When deep in the dorsal
vagal response, abused children are drawn to the most powerful person in the room as a means to protect themselves and ensure the least
amount of pain. Although that person, frequently the abuser, is the
most aggressive and powerful, they are seldom the safest.

Thus my mother created an adaptive strategy in which the most
aggressive, unsafe person in her life, her father, was her savior while

her mother, the victim, became the villain, responsible for not protecting her. We glorify the unsafe perpetrator because it's also a way
to stay safe. What a powerful message for a four-year-old to learn that
in order to be safe she has to align with the most violent person!
"Experiencing physical or emotional trauma early in life may disrupt
one's sense of consciousness and cohesive sense of identity," Vicario
said. Survival in my mother's childhood household depended upon
her inability to recognize the danger of her parents' violent relationship and the very real threat Joe's alcoholism presented to the family's survival. The full details of the drunken brawls between her
parents were never recorded in her biographical memory. "As a child,
she feared for her life and without thought went into a brain-stem
response; there was only overwhelming visceral input," said Vicario.
Her empathy for, and glorification and protection of, violent perpetrators would have dire implications for both her own and our family's lives for years to come. Whenever similar danger emerged again,
she would descend into a freeze response, rendering her incapable of
protecting others, even her own children, from violent perpetrators.
Larry symbolized unconditional love but a love forever tainted by
shame and secrecy. And in some twisted attempt to ensure safety for
our family, I think she helped re-create another violent perpetrator
in parenting Larry. Like George and Joe, he would grow to become
the strongest person in the room. And like his father and grandfather
before him, Larry was an unsafe savior.

Although we often suffer in obscurity, we seldom suffer uniquely.
It turns out, my family's experience is shared by many in Indian
country. In the late twentieth century Indian health-care professionals began applying the emerging theory of historical trauma to
describe high rates of shared physical and mental health disparities
among Native peoples. An early proponent of this theory, Maria Yellow Horse Brave Heart describes historical trauma as the "cumulative
emotional and psychological wounding across generations, including the lifespan, which emanates from massive group trauma." Brave
Heart, Hunkpapa/Oglala Lakota, is professor in the Department of
Psychiatry and director of Native American and Disparities Research

at the University of New Mexico. She and Lemyra DeBruyn, a medical anthropologist with the Indian Health Service, applied literature regarding Jewish Holocaust survivors and their descendants in describing the effects of historical trauma on subsequent generations.

In the initial phase, the dominant culture perpetrates mass trauma on a population in the form of colonialism, slavery, war, or genocide. In the second phase the affected population shows physical and psychological symptoms in response to the trauma. In the final phase, the initial population passes these trauma responses to subsequent generations, who in turn display similar symptoms. According to researchers, high rates of addiction, suicide, mental illness, sexual violence, and other ills among Indian peoples might be, at least in part, influenced by historical trauma. Supporters of this theory claim that many present-day health disparities can be traced back through epigenetics to a colonial health deficit, the result of colonization and its aftermath.

The American Academy of Pediatrics reports that the way genes work in our bodies "determines neuroendocrine structure and is strongly influenced by experience." Neuroendocrine cells help the nervous and endocrine (hormonal) system work together to produce substances such as adrenaline (the hormone associated with the fight-or-flight response). Trauma experienced by earlier generations can influence the structure of our genes, making them more likely to "switch on" negative responses to stress and trauma.

The now-famous 1998 Adverse Childhood Experiences (ACE) study conducted by the Centers for Disease Control (CDC) and Kaiser Permanente showed that adverse experiences could contribute to mental and physical illness. ACE assesses associations between childhood maltreatment and health and well-being later in life.

Indian people have known about the deadly fallout from trauma for a long time. Our health-care professionals and community leaders have been championing the importance of considering the deadly role historic and ongoing trauma and violence play in making us the gold standard for disease in this country.

With our high rates of addiction, suicide, diabetes, violence against women, and other ills, Indian people occupy ground zero for adverse childhood experiences. According to recent data from the U.S. Department of Health and Human Services and other federal health agencies, the rate of type 2 diabetes is nearly three times greater among Native people than nonnatives. Deaths from alcoholism are more than three times greater, fatal accidents one and a half times greater, and suicide four times greater.

Dr. Don Warne, Oglala Lakota, is among the Indian health-care professionals leading the charge in research on the effects of historical trauma. Warne is co-director of the Johns Hopkins University Center for Indigenous Health. Previously, Warne served as director of the University of North Dakota Indians into Medicine Program. During his tenure in 2021, UND's medical school received a multi-year $10 million grant from the National Institutes of Health (NIH) toward creating an Indigenous Trauma and Resilience Research Center. The UND professor of public health Ursula Running Bear's research, which connects boarding school attendance with chronic physical health outcomes, is included in the NIH grant. Running Bear is a citizen of the Sicangu Lakota or Rosebud Sioux Tribe. Her work is included in the Department of the Interior's *Federal Indian Boarding School Initiative Investigative Report.*

Learning about the neurological effects of historical trauma, epigenetics, and ACE helped me gain insight into my mother's behavior. Without the emotional or mental tools to process trauma, her shame shaped her entire life. And her physical reactions to intrusive memories, the wringing of hands, violently shaking her head, her constant flitting from one activity to another, were somatic attempts to process and eliminate the pain of past trauma. According to Bessel van der Kolk, author of *The Body Keeps the Score,* sensory information is blocked and frozen by trauma:

Traumatized people chronically feel unsafe inside their bodies: The past is alive in the form of gnawing interior discomfort. Their bodies are constantly bombarded by visceral warning signs, and in an attempt to control these processes, they often become expert at ignoring their gut feelings and in numbing awareness of what is played out inside. . . . The more people try to push away and ignore internal (physical) warning signs, the more likely they are to take over and leave them bewildered, confused, and ashamed. Victims of trauma may respond to contemporary stimuli as a return of the trauma, without conscious awareness that past injury rather than current stress is the basis of their physiologic emergency responses. Hyperarousal interferes with the ability to make rational assessments and prevents resolution and integration of the trauma. People's lives will be held hostage to fear until that visceral experience changes.

For my mother, the triad of bitterness, fear, and shame was a physical presence like thorns forever embedded in the soft tissue of her body. Repeated trauma and the lack of parental affection, essential to our physical development, blunted her ability to show affection and express empathy for her own children. Many survivors and their descendants have shared similar stories with me about the lack of affection and the harshness in their families. "We lost the bond and knowledge of family at boarding school. I see now that the behaviors such as the inability to show affection and the excessive cleaning were learned," Nitausha Williams told me in a telephone interview as I worked on an article about healing from boarding school trauma. Williams of the Dakota Yankton Sioux Nation has worked as a social worker in Sioux City, Iowa. Williams, her mother, and grandmother all attended Indian boarding schools. "I was raised with shame, anger, fear, and isolation," she said. But understanding the generational nature of trauma is helping her start her family's healing process. "At first my mother got angry with me when I asked her why she never hugged us or told us she loved us, but after a while she apologized and now we hug. It's uncomfortable for us, but we're getting better at it."

Denise Lajimodiere's parents both attended boarding school. Her father, she recalled, was an emotionally distant alcoholic and was often violent. During research for her book about boarding school survivors, *Stringing Rosaries: The History, the Unforgivable, and the Healing of Northern Plains American Indian Boarding School Survivors,* she learned that he nearly died from a beating during his years at Chemawa Indian School and her mother was routinely locked in a closet at her boarding school in South Dakota. While he was intoxicated he often told her, "I just want to be a man, not a fucking Indian!"

"I had to forgive my parents after I understood what happened to them," Lajimodiere said. "In many ways there has been a resounding silence across Indian country regarding boarding schools." She believes many survivors are stuck in secondary trauma and are unable to discuss what happened to them at the schools. "Before reconciling with the U.S. government we need to reconcile among ourselves first," she said, adding that Indians need to create our own means to address internalized trauma. "No one can do it for us: we need to do it for ourselves."

Chief Wilton Littlechild, former commissioner of Canada's Truth and Reconciliation Commission and residential school survivor, agreed. I first met Littlechild at the TRC's closing events in Ottawa in 2015. It was a busy time for the commissioners, but Littlechild made time for an interview with me. He was seventy then, but his stride was lithe and athletic as he led me to a quiet corner for our talk. A former hockey player at the University of Alberta, Littlechild described how sports helped him survive the trauma from abuse he experienced at residential schools he attended for fourteen years from age six through high school graduation. But he held none of the survivor fantasies depicted in Hollywood-style films about triumphing over adversity through inner strength and resolve alone. "Healing is an ongoing process," he said. "The pain doesn't magically disappear once you face past trauma." Littlechild has been working for more than forty years, both personally and professionally, on this issue. I interviewed him again in 2023 about his life and work. Although he was seventy-eight years old, he found that he's still working through the impact of his residential school trauma. After listening to the many stories of abuse during the TRC hearings, he found himself reliving the abuse he suffered even though he has had a lot of counseling. "It hit me pretty hard; it stays with you unless you find a way to unload the stress and pain," he said. For instance, hearing about children's graves found at the site of the Albuquerque Indian boarding school in 2021 reactivated painful memories of his residential school days. Littlechild earned his law degree at the University of New Mexico in Albuquerque. He decided to help in the search for children's graves in his own community in Maskwacis, Alberta, at the site of the Ermineskin residential school, one of the largest schools in Canada and the one he attended. "Just being able to push that machine [ground-penetrating radar] along the ground and praying really helped me," he said. But even today after so many years, the triggers can be unexpected. Littlechild described waiting in line at a breakfast buffet during a meeting of survivors. He noted there was toast available and remarked that during his school days students received toast once a week on Sundays; it was a big treat. A man overhearing his remarks said, "We had the same treatment."

Littlechild's voice broke with emotion as he described the power of spirituality and resilience in recovery work. "Our spirits cannot be broken. That has been the reoccurring message I've heard during this work," he said. "We must take the essential step of returning to our spirituality in order to heal. That first step starts with me. I must make myself right with the Creator."

I recall the sharp corners of my mother's arms during her infrequent hugs. She wanted to show us affection, but it must have been terribly risky for her, an invitation for more hurt. When Larry was dying from lung cancer in 2004, I could see she was nearly beside herself with fear and grief. Larry was never able to break free from her and live independently. After many failed relationships and fathering several children, he would inevitably circle back to her, finally living with her in her tiny retirement home in south Florida. It was here at age fifty-seven that he found himself dying. Even though he was the focal point of her lost love and traumatic life, she didn't know how to comfort him. He languished in the intensive care unit at a hospital in Fort Myers, slowly suffocating from the growing cancer in his lungs. Thankfully, a nurse in the unit contacted me. *You need to come down here and help your mother; she can't handle this by herself,* she told me over the phone. I was shocked at Larry's thin and frail appearance. If not for his prison tattoos on his now-gray skin, I wouldn't have recognized him. We arranged for him to be moved to hospice care, where we kept our final watch. She paced the room frantically.

Finally, at my insistence, she sat on the bed next to him and stroked his hair. *I think he's scared, Mom. Why don't you sit down close to him?* I said. More vulnerable than I'd ever seen her, she whispered to him, *It's okay, my boy.* He'd lain restlessly in bed all that day, but at her touch he quieted. In that way, he passed away. I leaned over and closed his eyes. Later, back at her condo, she told me, *You know, it would be okay if you wanted to get a bottle.* Her suggestion would have outraged me earlier in my recovery, but I was able to see that it was the only solace she knew to offer me. *No thanks, Mom,* I replied. *I'm an alcoholic; I can't drink.*

My mother's behavior and that of many other boarding school survivors reflect the insidious nature of oppression, how it shames us into believing that we are fundamentally unfit, even deserving of poverty. Joe Gone describes this concept neatly. Gone, whose family name was originally Gone-to-War, is one of my favorite interviews. He has the enviable ability to weave together complex psychological and social concepts in a way that nails the real reasons behind health disparities in Indian country. I'm a little intimidated by his brain, however, as I struggle to keep up with his conversation. I find myself plodding along, still sorting through the meaning of one complicated concept as he's already moved on to two more while conducting comparisons as well. But he's a patient, kindhearted man. He wears a pleasantly sardonic smile in his cover photo for Mad in America website. In 2021, *American Psychologist,* the journal for the American Psychological Association (APA), announced that Gone had won the award for Distinguished Professional Contributions to Applied Research for his "extraordinary contributions to the application of psychological knowledge for American Indian peoples."

Gone, a citizen of the Aaniiih–Gros Ventre tribal nation of Montana, says that the problems of Indian country will never be solved by more and better mental health or even health services. "Health and mental health services are rehabilitative by and large," he told me. "They're meant to fix people who have gone off a pathway of ideal development at some point in their lives and are struggling and having trouble. Indians enduring mental health inequities, especially addiction, trauma, and suicide, are the consequences of colonization. These inequities didn't arise because our brains suddenly went bad or because we had bad genes. This came about in the process of conquest, colonization, and dispossession, living in poverty, facing racial discrimination in border towns, attending crappy schools," Gone said in his Mad in America interview. He expanded on that point in a later interview with me. "Indian country needs a radical change in access to good development for young people, access to resources and the quality of life that every American wants for their families. The unreliable nature of resources for many in Indian communities also adds to the challenges." Funding for the Indian Health Service, for instance, is discretionary, varying from administration to administration; in March 2024, however, President Joseph Biden sought to build on a previously enacted advance appropriation for the agency by including mandatory funding in his proposed federal budget bill. The historically underfunded agency typically spends about one-third of the Medicaid and Medicare budget allocated per patient. Many essential services such as law enforcement and social services are tied to onetime grants, which hampers development of infrastructure.

"You can never count on anything; it's always shifting. And then in the end you get blamed for not having your life together. It's not right," he said. "Anyone with a sense of history can understand that, but some people don't want a sense of history. They prefer to blame Indians for their own problems. It shouldn't be too surprising that health services alone aren't gonna undo centuries of colonial subjugation." But Gone, and others, are trying to see and say something new about the "Indian problem."

The concepts of unresolved generational or historical trauma and the role of epigenetics in explaining the maladaptive social ills among Indians, however, are controversial. Some people caution that the science of epigenetics is too new and unproven. Others complain that using historical trauma to explain all that's wrong in Indian country ignores the role of personal agency and responsibility, setting the stage for a renewed form of eugenics, offering proof that Indians are fundamentally inferior. Worse, pathologizing our high rates of social ills may play a role in internalizing our oppression, feeding resignation and hopelessness that we are biologically destined for mental and physical illness. The popular polyvagal theory that frames our response to trauma based on the vagus nerve has also come under fire from researchers in the fields of neuroscience and trauma science. Critics claim that polyvagal theory is experimental and not sufficiently supported by research to be used in clinical settings. Even critics, however, admit that for trauma survivors, explanations of how our neuroanatomy responds to threat can help in gaining understanding and ultimately assist in creating healing strategies. Humans, after all, long for order over chaos and inexplicable horrific events. Indeed, my published writing regarding trauma among Indians has been among the most popular of my career. Interrogating my family's history in terms of science rather than personal failure and inferiority has opened a window to understanding and forgiveness that has enriched my mind and opened my heart to a new path forward. I often recall my mother's inexplicable, vexing behavior in response to occurrences in our lives together. She could come completely unglued over seemingly innocuous events; a quality of light, an odor, a sound could trigger visceral reactions, causing her to relive the horrors of her past. I can see her now, shaking her head, frantically trying to keep memories from intruding, or shaking her hands, still trying to rid them of an invisible, to us, clinging substance. Her fear of abandonment and deformed search for love and safety ruled her life. I recall explaining to a non-Indian friend complaining about my mother's challenging behavior that her boarding school experience damaged her in ways we don't understand. *What about Nelson Mandela?* the woman asked. *He had a tough life, but look at all the good things he did.*

Well, not everyone can be like Nelson Mandela, I responded. *Some of us are just ordinary.* For the ordinary people among us, the cost of the trauma and survival can be nearly too much to bear. I wish I had understood more during her lifetime and offered her the comfort she so desperately needed.

Since the news in 2021 of the discovery of unmarked graves of children at residential schools in Canada hit the media, many journalists have been asking Indians about the healing process from this painful historical past. The healing question places the burden on individuals and the Indian community alone, glossing over the broader nature of oppression and the structures that created hardship in the first place. Framing resilience as reliant only on personal agency, the bootstrap American exceptionalism myth, ignores the institutionalized violence created by U.S. government and white settler social infrastructures.

Effective healing in Indian country will first require several giant steps upstream. Trauma experts agree that healing and the prospect of opening up about trauma, perhaps for the first time, are risky, especially for folks who may not have access to safe, reliable food, health care, or housing. According to a study by the Prevention Institute, economic and social processes that concentrate poverty in communities create structural violence that not only traumatizes people but is a barrier to healing from past traumatic experiences.

Most available mental health and addiction services are based on evidence-based practices, or EBP, but they haven't been very successful among Indians. EBP is a process used to review, analyze, and translate the latest scientific evidence and integrate that knowledge into medical practice. The EBP model is the driver and gold standard of successful health interventions, but structural racism is deeply baked into its measures.

I decided it would be a good idea to look into practices that were actually working in Indian country and planned a visit to the Yukon Kuskokwim delta in Alaska, where Yup'ik folks had created a rapid-response trauma intervention program based on traditional teachings and culture.

They were building the young man's coffin in the front yard when we arrived. Portable construction lights illuminated the scene as men worked in the shadowy dawn that lasts almost until noon out here on the tundra. The men worked steadily and quietly in a manner that suggested front-yard coffin construction was a routine task. I soon learned that it was. We arrived about thirty minutes earlier via a shaky nine-seat bush plane, the only way in and out of most villages here on the Yukon Kuskokwim delta east of Bethel, Alaska. There are more than fifty Yup'ik villages on this great frozen sponge of a place, where the flat expanse of land leading to the Bering Sea is actually permafrost and thus constantly shifting.

Ray Daw, Navajo, the then-director of behavioral health for the tribally owned Yukon-Kuskokwim Health Corporation (YKHC), and Rose Domnick, Yup'ik, director of the corporation's Behavioral Health Prevention Department and leader of Calricaraq, invited me along to observe this unique rapid-response trauma intervention in action. Calricaraq means Healthy Living in Yup'ik and is unlike any other mental health professional intervention team. In addition to those trained in traditional Western behavioral health, it includes a group of Yup'ik elders with extensive knowledge of their language and culture. Daw, the first Indian director for behavioral health, describes the expertise of the Calricaraq team as heart skills that can't be learned from books.

"Western interventions are built primarily from books and depend on certification and a system that manages individual behavior by relying on an expert," he said. "That system is shunned by our elders and seen as a way to mask issues that individuals may have, issues that need to be addressed and cared for."

The entire Calricaraq team is Yup'ik and although much of what took place during this intervention was conducted in the Yup'ik language, I was able to follow the flow of events and human drama as it played out. English-speaking team members translated for me when they could. A man seated on a four-wheeler was waiting for us as our plane bounced down onto the barren airstrip. Wordlessly, he threw his arms around the first member of our group to emerge from the plane, Sophie Jenkins, Yup'ik, of the Calricaraq team. The man was the father of the young man who had recently been stabbed to death by another relative, the victim's niece. Both were nineteen years old. The murder was senseless. A now-forgotten argument, fueled by alcohol and maybe drugs, escalated into blind rage, and the young woman stabbed her uncle to death. They had grown up together, the niece often staying at the B. family home.

It was around eight degrees that day, and although I was raised in Wisconsin, a state with harsh winters, there was something different about this cold. It was serious cold. The light was crystalline and almost unbearably clear; the super-dry air made the world brittle and sharp. We made our way over the warren of narrow wooden boardwalks that serve as sidewalks out in the village and finally stomped the snow from our boots before entering the B. home. Like all homes here, it was a modest wooden structure on stilts to protect it from the shifting permafrost. It was filled to bursting with extended family and friends who had come to pay their respects at the boy's wake. We entered the main room, where an elder, the victim's grandma, pulled hopelessly mismatched socks onto the feet of a wriggling little girl. I learned later that she was the victim's daughter. The grandma appeared to be in her late seventies or early eighties and like the other adults in the room looked exhausted, dazed. Children periodically wandered into the room, confused by the weight of the gathering. A sleepy teenager stumbled in from some deep corner of the home and made a beeline for a huge box of donuts on the kitchen table. The Calricaraq team member Mardy Hanson, Yup'ik, sat between the grandma and another elder woman of about the same age. There was some tension between the two elders, and I watched them closely. The second elder woman drew my attention. She said nothing, but there was something about her presence, something calm about it, but unsettling. I would learn more about her later. We sat in a circle, and the team began their work. They spoke of their similar experiences. Sometimes crying, they shared painfully personal details of their struggles to survive trauma. The team's elders spoke of the guiding principles of the Yup'ik systems of living that include the medicine of *qaruyan* (healing) and of *kaholian* (unconditional love and understanding).

"Our ancestors gave us tools to understand our minds and name our feelings," Hanson told the group. "Our subsistence way of life, the very act of surviving and providing food for our families, is also an important means for healing. We say that true healing can be found on the tundra," said Hanson. Eventually, family and others began to speak. Their words emerged slowly, the syllables burbling pleasantly from the deep recesses of their throats in the Yup'ik tongue. The victim's grandmother embraced the wriggling little girl on her lap and said, "We have lost two of our young people to this tragedy. Alcohol has created an imbalance in our lives." The room went silent. It was getting light now; the sun streamed in, making the crowded rooms feel close and hot. After a long pause, the boy's father spoke, a mix of English and Yup'ik. He spoke of his son. "Lately he was so interested in doing subsistence hunting and fishing. He kept pushing me to get our tools ready. I think he must have known," he said, trailing off. Later, I learned that the father had made a public commitment (in Yup'ik) to remain sober and to follow the subsistence living ways, eschewing the food-stamp-dependent life he and his family had led in recent years. He described this as a gift to his grandchildren, a legacy from his son. He stopped talking and went out onto the back porch, returning proudly holding a torn cardboard box of raw frozen whitefish. He caught this fish, a Yup'ik delicacy, in his newly set nets, the nets he had planned to set with his son. He held them out to us like a sacrament, inviting us to feast. A huge crowd of people had filled the home by now, many bearing big pots of rich, dark moose meat stew, large platters of oily dried fish, and jars of viscous seal oil; we feasted at the kitchen table in shifts, dipping the raw frozen fish in salted seal oil. It was a Yup'ik orgy of omega-3 fatty acids; everyone smacked their lips appreciatively.

As our turn at the table waned, I looked out the big front window and saw a Russian Orthodox priest putter up on his four-wheeler. He set up his little altar for Mass in the crowded main room, a sign for the intervention team to slip away. I followed the team outside into the now-brilliant daylight as we made our way across the village to the home of the perpetrator. The atmosphere here was decidedly different. Her father sat alone on an old couch in his well-worn but clean and tidy house. Although other family members were clearly there, they were conspicuously absent from the darkened room where the father sat chain-smoking cigarettes. The Calricaraq team again began their work, sharing their stories with him. The father listened silently with his head down for a long time. An elder woman entered the front door of the house, holding the hand of a young girl I learned later was the perpetrator's daughter. The woman was the silent elder whom I had seen earlier sitting next to Hanson and the victim's grandmother at the feast. With a shock, I realized this was the perpetrator's grandmother. She took off her coat and sat down. A tiny woman in her eighties, she was clearly the matriarch of the family. As Jenkins later translated, she said to her son, "I have prepared you, I have taught you our ways that can help you go through tough times; I have taught you *kaholian*. There is health and wellness in our ways." Her son began to cry, a dark, jagged wail, like the sound a wounded animal might make. His thin shoulders heaved with the effort. A teenager who had just entered the room abruptly turned on his heels and left when he saw his uncle crying. Although Grandma followed and reassured him that everything was all right, he soon left the house with a group of boys. Grandma returned to the meeting with her son and the Calricaraq team. She sat nimbly on the arm of the couch. "It's safe to express your feelings and your pain here. We will not belittle you or talk behind your back," she told him. He stopped crying. As he lifted his head a bit to look her in the eye, he appeared to be exhausted, completely drained of energy. After a time, the grandma smiled patiently and invited us into the kitchen to eat. A feast of dried king salmon, pilot bread, and hot tea was already spread out on the oilcloth-covered table. Later she proudly showed us her collection of old-style Yup'ik tools, a fish trap, an ulu (woman's knife), and her ivory story knife covered with notches for each story from her girlhood. In the center was a faded photograph of her father as he worked his nets. He was a vigorous, mature man with a full head of white hair and a smile on his weathered face.

I recalled a personal anecdote that Mark Anaruk, Iñupiaq and Yup'ik, a tribal behavioral health consultant working with YKHC, had shared earlier with me. It seemed to sum up the tenacity of the Yup'ik people. "My wife is Yup'ik. When she was pregnant with our first child she had this (to me) odd habit of walking directly out of our front door immediately after waking in the morning. My mother-in-law explained that this is how they pass along their values and ability to survive even when the child is in utero."

All of this pride and capability seemed at odds with the negative data I'd learned about the population in this region. For the past fifty years or more, horrific levels of suicide, violence, sexual violence, and substance abuse have plagued these tiny villages. According to the FBI and a report by CNN, Alaska leads the nation in number of reported rapes, with almost 134 incidences of rape per 100,000 people. Nationally the rate is 40 per 100,000. Ron Perkins, former director of the Alaska Injury Prevention Center, told the *Juneau Empire* that rural Alaska has some of the highest suicide rates in the entire world. And data supports the *Juneau Empire* reporter Paul Berg's observation that "a major health and social crisis is spreading throughout regions of Alaska."

Throughout the twentieth century, the Alaska Native population was brutalized by waves of diseases like measles, influenza, diphtheria, and pneumonia. The 1918 flu epidemic, or Great Death, wiped out entire villages. Later came polio, tuberculosis, and more that were nearly as devastating. According to information from the Alaska History and Cultural Studies of the state's education department, the 1932 death rate for Alaska Natives in southeast Alaska from tuberculosis was 1,302 per 100,000; the rate among non-Indians in the United States during the same period was 56 per 100,000. Thousands of Alaska Native children who survived the initial onslaught of disease were orphaned.

"Out of necessity, missionary groups and the federal government began establishing orphanages for these children. In many ways, the Great Death jump-started boarding schools in Alaska," said Jim LaBelle, Iñupiaq. He is retired professor of Native American studies at the University of Alaska Anchorage and is past president of the National Native American Boarding School Healing Coalition. Beginning in the 1930s and 1940s these orphanages were transformed into large government- and church-run boarding schools. The schools, according to LaBelle, signaled the then-popular assimilation process of Alaska Natives into the dominant U.S. culture. "Authorities told most parents that they had no choice but to give their children over to boarding schools so that they could get a proper education. Parents who resisted were sometimes threatened with jail," he said. At the schools, children were taught that their traditional ways, spirituality, and language were inferior and even evil, according to boarding school survivors like LaBelle. Alaska Native communities grew to become ground zero for social "dis-ease" and nothing seemed to help. "Chaos from unresolved trauma is recycled in families here," said Rose Domnick.

"In the Kass'aq (white person) way we were taught to stuff our feelings and isolate ourselves from our Yup'ik traditions," Domnick said.

Anaruk noted that many mental health approaches have been used over the years in the region to address the cycle of trauma. "Money has been spent, various western-style interventions have been attempted. Mental health professionals have logged hours and hours in these efforts but to no avail. All the programs, clinics and interventions simply didn't work, people just kept getting sicker." The best efforts of such Western-based mental health intervention models didn't work for a simple, basic reason, according to Anaruk. "People in the villages didn't embrace them." Calricaraq, however, is different, he says. "Although we don't yet have any precise data, Calricaraq is by far the most requested behavioral health service that YKHC has ever offered," Anaruk reports. The significant difference between Calricaraq and past intervention methods is that behavioral health staffs don't deliver the service until community members request that they come to the villages.

"The healing process is rooted in Yup'ik culture," Domnick explained. "We are our own resource experts; we have it within us to transform ourselves and our communities into healthy, thriving places. We can do this by reinforcing what we already know as Yup'ik people."

Stacy Rasmus, Lummi, director at the University of Alaska Fairbanks's Center for Alaska Native Health Research, was the lead author of a 2014 study about the role of Yup'ik culture in social change and health. Two of her coauthors were the Yup'ik elders Charles Moses and James Charlie Sr., who wrote, "The social framework within which our ancestors once lived came out of an adaptive process, consisting of trial and error and testing. . . . This is how the Yup'ik society was created. Contact and contemporary processes have led the modern Yup'ik peoples away from something that has been developed, tried, and proven over many centuries, and much of the suffering in our communities today is related to this movement away from our traditional core values, subsistence strategies, and families."

Domnick helped found Calricaraq after years of working in behavioral health in her community in Bethel. Inspired by an elder's wisdom that helped her heal from her own trauma after being molested as a child, she realized that there are powerful tools in Yup'ik culture that speak to mental health. Traditionally, Yup'ik people openly discussed their feelings, often turning to elders to help sort out difficult situations and problems. A structured system provided guidance for behavior and working out conflict with others. In the unforgiving climate of the tundra, survival depends on cooperation, effective conflict resolution, and good mental and physical health. Health and healing were found in the everyday actions of subsistence living. Extreme measures, such as banishment, were used, essentially a death sentence on the tundra, as a last resort when all other efforts had failed, according to Domnick. Instead, people turned to the essential guiding principle for traditional Yup'ik behavior, *kaholian*.

Calricaraq defies description using traditional behavioral health language. For instance, Calricaraq would be unlikely to win the behavioral health intervention stamp of approval as an EBP. Typically, U.S. government agencies fund only EBPs. However, the Substance Abuse and Mental Health Services Administration and the Indian Health Service among others have begun to fund projects and protocols that they describe as promising, programs like Calricaraq.

There is little published information assessing such interventions. Joe Gone and several fellow researchers published a study examining what is known about culturally based mental health programs. The researchers note that the complex and holistic approaches often used in cultural interventions complicate efforts to isolate and study specific components. The typical Western research method of generalizing such interventions among varied tribes fails to capture important details about their effectiveness.

"Ironically, despite the holistic and balanced nature of wellness to Indigenous people, few studies collected a holistic set of wellness outcomes. While most studies evaluated physical outcomes, such as sobriety, few studies explored spiritual outcomes such as feeling connected or having a sense of belonging," the researchers wrote.

Gone likes to share an anecdote from his early research and consulting days. In 2009, he approached leadership of the traditional Crazy Dog Society for help in designing addiction treatment centering Blackfeet therapeutic traditions. Gone shared the importance of formal evaluation with society members because mental health researchers didn't yet know if participation in ceremonial practices could effectively treat addiction. At that point, Gone said, the gathering erupted into raucous laughter. "The leader explained that every participant in the ceremony was living proof that cultural traditions can remedy substance abuse problems," he said.

So far participant evaluations of Calricaraq programs are very good, according to Anaruk. "We have heard comments from people who were contemplating suicide or stuck in alcohol or drug abuse that had control over their lives. They have said that after hearing the Calricaraq teachings they have begun to change and reexamine their lives using the wisdom of the Yup'ik elders," he said. The healing process, however, will take time. Domnick noted, "Who we came to be today has a lot to do with what happened to us over the last 150 plus years." Jenkins said of the victim's father, "We saw the father's spirit wake up. He's ready to use this awakening to remind him of what his son started. He set his nets for the first time. It's not simple to maintain the nets in this season, the ice gets thicker and thicker and the nets get heavier and heavier. You have to remain vigilant to ensure they don't freeze; and so it is with our ways of Calricaraq and *kaholian*." Gone said:

> The interventions that people need may not be the latest scientifically driven, empirically supported treatments, but rather a return to tradition and the revitalization of Indigenous healing. The evaluation of whether these interventions work is less about scientific efficacy and more about Indigenous ways of knowing, sometimes called Indigenous epistemologies. I'm not saying that these claims should be widely accepted necessarily at this point. I'm describing what we see and hear in Indian country and what scholars should know. One must recognize that Indigenous communities, prior to the arrival of biomedicine, had doctoring practices. Today, in Indigenous communities, what we talk about as an alternative to mental health discourse is transformative healing, which is more about transforming the self into what is more conducive to well-being. In Indian country, it's about spirituality and ceremonial participation, and many people advocate for it: Indigenous ceremony, ceremonial participation, sweat lodge ceremony, sun dance ceremonies, et cetera. One can be skeptical about this, as scientists often are, but it is very difficult to design the kinds of studies to test this. What we do have are thousands and thousands of Indian people who will attest to the fact that they've contended with these serious issues and been helped by culture and tradition, even those whose problems were quite severe. Local communities of people don't only have beliefs.

They also know things that are true and can be important col-
laborators if we are to understand their experience.

Holly Echo-Hawk summarizes this principle with a simple play
on words. She suggests using the term "practice-based evidence" as
a means to measure the effectiveness of treatment. Echo-Hawk of
the Pawnee Nation is on the faculty of Reclaiming Native Psychological Brilliance, an online learning environment for mental health
professionals in Indian country that highlights the innate wisdom
and strengths in traditional ways. For Echo-Hawk, Western health-
care systems need to be destroyed and rebuilt in order to successfully
serve Native people.

"It's a gigantic challenge; the current mental health care system
is not designed for us," she said. "One of the biggest challenges is
convincing Western clinicians that although they are talented and
skilled, they may not have the knowledge needed to serve Indian
communities. It takes a lot of ego strength for them to admit this."
But the mainstream mental health world is beginning to take notice.
Echo-Hawk noted that the American Psychological Association conducted an internal investigative study and made a public apology
to Native Americans and other people of color in 2021 for all the
harm that their Western psychology has done. It reads in part, "Psychologists also provided ideological support for, and failed to speak
out against, the colonial framework of the government-sponsored
industrial (boarding) and day school systems for Indigenous youth."
The APA apology details examples of how "the discipline was complicit in contributing to systemic inequities, and hurt many through
racism, racial discrimination, and denigration of people of color,
thereby falling short on its mission to benefit society and improve
lives. APA is profoundly sorry, accepts responsibility for, and owns
the actions and inactions of APA itself, the discipline of psychology,
and individual psychologists who stood as leaders for the organization and field." The apology also includes a course of action with
analysis of psychology's history and a commitment to gain awareness

of other healing approaches emanating from Indigenous and other non-Western and healing traditions, advocate for funding for scholars of color, and engage communities of color in research. It could be that the discipline of Western mental health science has much to learn from Indians.

For instance, rather than focusing the study of epigenetic transmission of historical psychological characteristics solely on harm and damage, researchers might also find markers for resilience and hardiness. Surely, Indians' ability to preserve our ways to the degree we have in spite of the concerted efforts of U.S. government and organized religion to destroy them may paint us as one of the greatest examples of cultural and physical survival in human history.

NINE

ACCOUNTABILITY BEFORE
RECONCILIATION

n June 2015, I traveled to Ottawa to cover the closing events of
Canada's Truth and Reconciliation Commission (TRC), the cul-
mination of six years of work digging into the country's history
of Indian residential schools. In 2007, as part of the Indian Residential Schools Settlement Agreement, the Canadian government
approved a nearly $2 billion compensation package for residential
survivors and created the TRC in order to investigate abuse at the
schools, collect statements and stories from survivors, create a list
of recommendations for changes in government policies, and establish ways to support Indigenous peoples' mental health and healing
process. Part of the TRC's work included holding listening sessions
for survivors as well as delving into records and research about the
schools. That day in 2015, the TRC presented its final report to the
public, which included ninety-four recommendations or calls to
action for Canada's leadership, churches, and schools to begin repair-
ing their relationship to Indigenous peoples. The CBC, Canadian
Broadcasting Corporation, published an abbreviated version of the
recommendations:

- **HEALTH:** An acknowledgement that the current state of
  aboriginal health is a direct result of previous government poli-

cies and the implementation of health-care rights for aboriginal people.

- **EDUCATION:** The creation and funding for new aboriginal education legislation, which protects languages and cultures and closes the education gap for aboriginal people.

- **JUSTICE:** A commitment to eliminate the overrepresentation of aboriginal people in custody and in trouble with the law, along with the collection and publication of data on criminal victimization of aboriginal people.

- **PUBLIC INQUIRY:** The creation of a public inquiry into missing and murdered aboriginal women and girls.

- **MONITORING:** The creation of a national council for reconciliation, which would monitor and report on reconciliation progress, as well as the introduction of an annual State of Aboriginal Peoples report delivered by the prime minister.

- **LANGUAGE:** The government is asked to implement an Indigenous Languages Act and appoint a language commissioner in order to preserve and promote it.

- **FUNDING:** The report calls for $10 million over seven years from the federal government for the National Centre for Truth and Reconciliation.

- **COMMEMORATION:** The creation of a statutory holiday to honour survivors, their families, and communities—and to ensure "public commemoration of the history and legacy of residential schools remains a vital component of the reconciliation process."

- **MEMORIALS:** The report asks for funding for memorials, community events and museums, including a museum reconciliation commemoration program, to be launched in time for Canada's 150th anniversary in 2017.

It was raining on that June morning as I arrived at Rideau Hall—also known as Government House—where more than seven thousand residential school survivors and supporters prepared to march three miles to Parliament Hill, site of the country's capitol building, where the report would be delivered. The crowd included Indian men wearing eagle feather headdresses, Indian women in regalia, several groups of traditional hand drum players, hundreds of schoolchildren and many, many Indian residential school survivors, and their families. As the sun broke through the clouds, one of the three TRC commissioners, Marie Wilson, spoke to the crowd. She described the pain of hearing survivors share their stories during the TRC's work. "We heard survivors tell us, 'I didn't know what home meant, where home was, or who I was. I spend my lifetime trying to find my way home, to reclaim a sense of home,'" Wilson said. "We are all here on earth to accompany each other home. We as commissioners have had the honor of accompanying you on your journey homeward to reclaim a sense of self. We hope that this is also an opportunity for Canada to reclaim its dignity as a country. Today is just a stopover as we catch our breath on this six-year journey. We have a long road ahead; this march today is symbolic of a movement that cannot end."

A huge crowd of hand drum singers, many dressed in colorful ribbon shirts, stood ready to begin the march. A lone singer, his voice high and plaintive in traditional Ojibwe style, began a celebration song. Others joined him as they all began to walk together; heads held high, they sang loudly and triumphantly. Spectators lined the streets, clapping and cheering as the march wound its way toward Parliament. I spotted a tiny Indian elder in a wheelchair among the marchers. The expression on her face was a mixture of pride, anguish, and gratitude. I asked if she ever thought such a day would come. "Never in all my life did I think I'd see this day," she said. "I feel so mixed, happy, and hurt. I hurt for the little girl I was at residential school. I can't talk about myself—it hurts too much—but I can talk about that little girl and what she went through." The little girl was named Lorna Standingready of the Peepeekisis Cree Nation. She attended the Birtle Residential School in Manitoba. According to Standingready, friends helped her make the two-day drive from her home to Ottawa for the march.

"People here give me the strength to carry on no matter what happened to me."

The bells of Notre-Dame Cathedral Basilica pealed in celebration as marchers made their way past. A priest stood outside the heavy wooden doors, his arms opened wide.

Prior to the 2007 settlement and subsequent work of the commission, less than 5 percent of Canadians claimed to have any knowledge of residential school history, according to TRC commissioner Littlechild. "By the time we finished our work at the TRC, we conducted another poll and found that 59 percent of Canadians now have knowledge of Indian residential school history," said Littlechild. Now retired, Littlechild is a survivor of the Ermineskin residential school; a gifted athlete, he excelled at hockey and other sports and founded the National Indian Athletic Association. Littlechild earned a law degree from the University of New Mexico, became the first member of Parliament with treaty status in Canada in 1988, and has worked as an advocate for Indigenous rights and rights of residential school survivors throughout his career.

Looking back, the 2015 march represented a tangible crack in white innocence surrounding residential school history. No longer could non-Indians remain conveniently ignorant of Canada's sordid past. The TRC's final report, a result of eight years of work and research, documents the widespread physical and sexual abuses at government- and church-run Indian residential schools from 1883 to 1998. After the march, participants crowded into the ballroom of the Delta hotel in downtown Ottawa for a closing ceremony and remarks by TRC commissioners. Justice Murray Sinclair, Ojibwe, chairman of the commission, spoke to the audience. The first Indigenous judge to be appointed to serve in a Canadian province, Sinclair epitomizes the great oratory tradition of Ojibwe leaders. Sinclair is a large man with a booming voice and singular presence. He described the experience of listening to survivors tell their stories during hearings held by the commission. "This is a commission like no other," Sinclair said. "It was not set up by the government but by parties to the Indian Residential Settlement Agreement seeking to repair harm caused by residential schools." The ballroom overflowed with press and attendees, many sitting on the floor or standing against the walls. Healing for survivors came in simply allowing them to speak about what happened to them, Sinclair said. "They were not subject to cross examination as if on trial. They were invited to share what they had to share, no more, no less. Their stories were recorded into history and at the end of the day they were acknowledged." Members of the audience alternatively broke into tears or cheered aloud. Sinclair answered a reporter's question asking if commissioners considered scaling back the list of ninety-four recommendations contained in their final report as too much for the government to understand. "You have to remember that we are writing for the future, not just the current government," Sinclair responded. "This report will tell the test of time." Hundreds of people leaped to their feet at Sinclair's response, shouting and clapping loudly.

The closing events concluded later that day at an outdoor celebration of music and food. Suzanne Nottaway, a French-speaking Algonquin and residential school survivor, danced alone in the middle of the crowd, smiling broadly. "First Nation's people are as the fleur sauvage [weeds]; we survive everything they try to do to us," she said. In 2008, Prime Minister Stephen Harper made a statement of apology to students of Indian residential schools on behalf of the government of Canada. Several Christian denominations that ran residential schools have also apologized for their roles. In 2019, the Canadian federal court approved a nationwide class-action settlement for Indigenous people who were forced to attend federal Indian day schools. The settlement represents the largest class-action suit in Canadian history. The government began processing claims in January 2020, with survivors set to receive compensation of at least $10,000 each. Ottawa is also investing $50 million in the Day Scholars Revitalization Fund. The government also promised to quickly distribute about $22 million to help in locating and commemorating unmarked graves of children who died at the schools. But Indigenous peoples in Canada complain that the government has run out of steam in addressing the TRC's calls to action. In 2023, the

Indigenous-led think tank Yellowhead Institute of Toronto issued a statement that the organization will stop publishing its annual report tracking the government's progress. "At first, the project invoked hope and determination. If only the Canadian public knew about their government's lack of action, we believed, perhaps things would change," leaders of the organization wrote in its annual report. "That hope, as those who have followed us on this journey may have noticed, has begun to diminish." They complain that the government has failed to address racism embedded in institutions related to child welfare and education. "There are limits to how many times you can write a report about how Canada, once again, has failed to make any meaningful progress."

In 2022, Pope Francis traveled to Canada to deliver an apology for the Catholic Church's role in that country's residential school system. An apology from the pope was one of the TRC's calls to action demanded in its final report in 2015. The government of Canada and denominations of other Christian missionaries that operated the schools issued apologies years earlier. In addition to saying he was sorry several times, the pope said, "I ask forgiveness, in particular, for the ways in which many members of the church and of religious communities cooperated, not least through their indifference, in projects of cultural destruction and forced assimilation promoted by the governments of that time, which culminated in the system of residential schools."

Sandi Harper, who traveled with her sister to Maskwacis, Alberta, from the province of Saskatchewan to hear the apology, told the Associated Press, "It's something that is needed, not only for people to hear but for the church to be accountable. He recognizes this road to reconciliation is going to take time, but he is really on board with us," she said, calling the apology "genuine." The AP writer also noted that while the pope acknowledged blame, he also made clear that Catholic missionaries were merely cooperating with and implementing the government policy, which he termed the "colonizing mentality of the powers." This dodge of institutional responsibility was not lost on many Indians. Murray Sinclair issued a written statement in response regarding the pope's visit and apology. It reads in part, "Despite the historic apology, the Holy Father's statement has left a deep hole in the acknowledgment of the full role of the church in the residential school system by placing blame on individual members of the church. It is important to underscore that the Church was not just an agent of the state, nor simply a participant in government policy, but was a lead co-author of the darkest chapters in the history of this land. It was more than the work of a few bad actors—this was a concerted institutional effort to remove children from their families and cultures, all in the name of Christian supremacy. Reconciliation requires action, not passiveness." After the pope's visit, the Canadian Conference of Catholic Bishops declared a plan to raise $30 million for healing, culture, language revitalization, and other programs. It's unclear if this money would be in addition to paying the remainder of the church's promised share of the Indian Residential Schools Settlement Agreement.

To date, the Catholic Church has paid only $1.2 million of its agreed-upon $25 million in reparations to residential school survivors. The bulk of the $4.7 billion reparations promised as part of the Indian Residential Schools Settlement Agreement was paid by the Canadian government and other Christian churches such as Protestant churches, which paid about $9.2 million. According to *The New York Times*, the Catholic Church was able to raise only $3.9 million and paid about $1.3 million to a private fundraiser. "What happened to the remaining funds is unclear," the *Times* reporter wrote. A federal judge allowed the church to walk away from future reparation payments, even though the Catholic Church operated nearly half of Indian residential schools. This was especially disconcerting since the pope's historic visit cost the Canadian government more than $55 million, according to documents obtained by the Canadian press under freedom of information laws. Details of the Catholic Church's vast wealth, which includes money, assets such as priceless antiquities and art, including items stolen from Indigenous peoples, and land, is shrouded in secrecy. But clearly the accumulation of that wealth is built, in part, on the backs of Indigenous peoples' sacrifice of lives, land, and resources to colonization, a system both supported and orchestrated by the church. In 2023, the pope alluded to the church's role in supporting colonialism by formally repudiating the doctrine of discovery, statements backed by fifteenth-century papal bulls or laws that legitimized seizure of Indian lands and resources, and centuries of oppressive assimilationist policies. In the United States, the doctrine helped form the basis of some property laws today. But like his apology for Canada's residential schools, the repudiation is largely performative and continues to distance the church from culpability. Catholic entities, despite promises to allow access to residential school records, continue to resist opening up these records. And in another example of brazen deniability, the church continues to overlook its role in creating government Indian policy and operating Indian boarding schools in the United States. The church operated about one hundred schools on this side of the border versus sixty-four in Canada. Overall, there were far more Indian people affected by boarding school policies in the United States than in Canada.

CANADA	UNITED STATES
139 residential schools	More than 500 boarding schools
669 day schools	Number of day schools unknown
64 Catholic-operated residential schools	About 100 Catholic-operated boarding schools
2011 Indian population 1.4M	2011 Indian population 2.8M
2020 Indian population 5 percent of total	2020 Indian population 2.9 percent of total

The church continues to block access to boarding and day school records in both the United States and Canada with the claim of protecting individual privacy. Although several U.S. Catholic archives and entities claim to be conducting internal investigations of their

holdings and history, many survivors and researchers complain that
the work is opaque and conducted by church personnel rather than
independent researchers. The Raynor Library at Marquette University is now barring access to Bureau of Catholic Indian Missions
(BCIM) school enrollment records. In 1996, the Oglala Sioux Tribe
restricted the tribe's enrollment records for Holy Rosary Mission
held by the Raynor Library. According to Amy Cary, head of archival collections and institutional repository, a decision was recently
made by BCIM leaders to restrict all school enrollment records until
blood quantum information can be redacted, a process that could
take years. In several cases, unredacted copies of the same Catholic
school enrollment forms are available to the public in the National
Archives, but the bureau's collection is larger and more complete.
The bureau and other Catholic entities also bar access to sacramental
records, claiming they are protecting people's privacy. These records
include names of those who have received any of the church's sacra-
ments such as the three rites for dying Catholics. The data contained
in these records could help enumerate the number of children who
died from diseases contracted at boarding schools. The bureau was
the national administrative agency overseeing Catholic Indian missions in the United States and holds copies of school enrollment
forms as well as other documents. The bureau was a lobbying organization founded in 1874 to promote Catholic Indian mission interests
and played a dominant role in influencing the government's Indian
policies. The bureau still exists today and occupies a town house in
Washington, D.C., near the White House.

Deborah Parker, Tulalip, CEO of the National Native American
Boarding School Healing Coalition, wrote a statement in response
to the pope's repudiation of the doctrine and also demanding access
to Catholic school documents:

While the Vatican's decision to renounce the Doctrine of Discovery is the right one, it downplays the Church's role and accountability for the harm it has caused to Native peoples. It does not
change the fact that the Church's views gave permission to colo-

nizers to take Native lands and assimilate Native peoples. This doctrine imposed itself into U.S. policies and played a crucial role in justifying the genocide of Native peoples. This led to a series of atrocities, including the forced enrollment of Native children into Indian boarding schools, and gave colonizers the license to steal lands and commit acts of violence against Native children and families for centuries. We demand more from the Catholic Church. We demand more transparency, including access to Indian boarding school documents, which they have refused to provide. We demand that the Church returns lands to the Tribal Nations in which it operated Indian boarding schools. We demand that the Church supports the Truth and Healing Bill, which would establish a federal commission and conduct a full inquiry into the assimilative policies of U.S. Indian boarding schools. And we demand that the Church respects Tribal sovereignty and Indigenous ways of being. We believe these are ways in which the Church can begin to take accountability for their actions.

While searching for my mother's records in the BCIM archives, I found documentation showing that U.S. Catholic leadership received free title to Indian lands as well as trust and treaty funds to operate mission schools, actions that today could be viewed as clear violations of the U.S. Constitution's establishment clause in the First Amendment, "Congress shall make no law respecting an establishment of religion." The establishment of religion was described by a three-part test set forth by the U.S. Supreme Court in *Lemon v. Kurtzman.* Under the *Lemon* test, government can assist religion only if the primary purpose of the assistance is secular; the assistance must neither promote nor inhibit religion; and there must be no excessive entanglement between church and state. The passage of the 1887 Dawes Act made tribal lands available free of charge to Christian missionaries. According to the Raynor Library website regarding Indian lands given to churches and schools, "After 1887, the federal government would eventually allot most reservations.

In many instances with the assistance from the Bureau of Catholic Indian Missions. Catholic missions and schools were able to secure allotments on the lands so used." Unlike Indians, whose allotted lands were kept in trust by the government, churches were often given full allotments of tribal lands in fee simple, meaning they could use them or sell them freely. I found documentation that the BCIM received 10,578.37 acres of allotted Indian lands to be used for schools. In the 1960s and 1970s, however, the bureau divested itself of these lands, giving them via quitclaim to various Catholic dioceses and entities. In a shared investigation with *Indian Country Today* and *Reveal* News, the Center for Investigative Reporting, we found that much of this land is still in the hands of these organizations. Operating Indian schools played several important roles for the Catholic Church. Mission work with Native Americans elevated the church in the eyes of the general public; Catholic missions came to be seen as integral to the American project of "civilizing" the American wilderness. Boarding schools began a partnership early with the government that solidified the Catholic Church's political connections. In the nineteenth century, Catholics and other Christian missionaries directly received government funding to operate Indian boarding and day schools. But after Ulysses S. Grant's 1869 Peace Policy, Catholic missionaries found themselves excluded from federal funding as a result of rising anti-Catholic sentiment in the United States at that time. They regained their status and access to federal funding after a 1908 Supreme Court decision, *Quick Bear v. Leupp*, ruled that Native people could pay for tuition at Catholic schools by surrendering their treaty and trust fund money. By the beginning of the twentieth century, the federal government operated about two-thirds of U.S. Indian boarding schools. Most of the Christian boarding and day schools, however, were operated by the Catholic Church with about a hundred schools. According to the Court, allowing Indians to use their trust and treaty funds to pay for tuition in denominational schools would not violate the Constitution's commitment to the separation of church and state. The funds, they reasoned, belonged to tribes and individual Indians. Catholics devised a scheme in which Indians could sign petitions allowing the federal government to pay a portion of their trust and treaty funds over directly to the BCIM, which in turn paid the individual schools. The court held that the trust and treaty funds did not constitute public funds but rather belonged to the Indians, so allowing them to use the money to pay for tuition at Catholic schools would not violate the Constitution. "The president declared it to be the moral right of the Indians to have this trust fund applied to the Indians schools of their choice," reads the opinion. "The government is necessarily undenominational as it cannot make any law respecting an establishment of religion or prohibiting the free exercise thereof."

Incongruously, the 1908 court describes the plaintiffs, Indians of the Rosebud Sioux, as "citizens of the United States." The majority of Native Americans were not granted U.S. citizenship in South Dakota until the passage of the 1924 Indian Citizenship Act. The court also made much of the Lakota's freedom of choice in its *Quick Bear v. Leupp* decision, conveniently ignoring the fact that at that time Indians were prohibited from freely practicing their religion under penalty of law, as well as from selling their lands or freely spending their trust and treaty funds on items like food and supplies. Entrenched racism kept many Indian children out of public schools. Extreme poverty, especially during the Great Depression, forced many to send their children to Christian boarding schools. Mission schools were often located closer to reservations. Unlike at distant federal boarding schools, mission schools afforded parents some opportunities to connect with their children. For many parents, some of whom were barely literate, the approval to send their children to these religious boarding schools took the form of thumbprints. Pressed on government forms, signed and witnessed by church and government officials, these thumbprints authorized the mission schools to take portions of treaty and trust funds—owed to Indian families by the federal government in exchange for their land—to pay tuition. Catholic school leaders coerced Native parents to sign over their treaty funds; in many cases, families had no choice. Indians who chose to send their children to the federal school in Pine Ridge and keep their treaty and trust funds soon learned that Catholic charity had its limits. "One of the Indians who would not sign [form relinquishing treaty and trust funds] came to get something to eat and clothing so we told him to go to those to whom he had trusted his children. He now saw his mistake and wrote to Washington to have his name signed to the list but they would not pay attention to him and told him to send his children to the government school," wrote the sister secretary at Holy Rosary school on the Pine Ridge reservation. In total, Catholics operated about a hundred contract schools in which they received $108 or more per Indian student in trust and treaty funds. These schools, however, did not operate concurrently. Bureau archives at Marquette are filled with correspondence among Catholic leaders urging action in order to secure dominance on reservations with large trust funds such as the Osage and Chippewa tribes. In an earlier investigation, I found that, according to available records at Marquette University and the National Archives collections in Kansas City and Chicago, over a period of nine years—1910, 1933, 1935, 1939–43, and 1954—Indian people signed over some $30.4 million of their trust and treaty funds, adjusted for inflation, to pay for tuition at Catholic schools. In effect, we were paying for our own forced assimilation. According to a report from the Raynor Library at Marquette, the practice of using trust and treaty money stopped in the 1970s—because the funds had been siphoned to depletion.

Using the same sources, I found that at a very conservative estimate of two hundred students per year over a period of thirty-seven years at the government-stated rate of $108 per student, Holy Rosary school on the Pine Ridge reservation, alone, received more than $18 million in Indian trust and treaty funds, adjusted for inflation.

Many Catholic contract schools also directly received children's portions of their family's federal rations over several years. Beginning in 1900, Catholic schools received children's rations in the amount of $25,000 per year, payments paused briefly but reinstated after the *Quick Bear v. Leupp* decision. According to a confidential memo between the BCIM and the Department of the Interior in 1935, "Out of friendship for the Bureau, the Indian office got the appropriations

committee for the house of representatives to substitute $92k as a gra-
tuity to be paid for care of Indian children." The Catholic Church's
work in Indian education was an effective means to gain political
and social influence in the United States. "The political weight of the
Catholics in the nation and their successful lobbying for their interests in the Indian school question gave them a more widely accepted
role in national affairs," wrote the Jesuit scholar Francis Paul Prucha.
"It was no longer possible to think of management of Indian affairs
without some consideration of Catholic views."

Although not well documented, Christian and federal boarding
schools in the United States also played a role in child welfare, as
they did in Canada. I found documents in the BCIM archives indicating that some schools were paid by local child welfare agencies to
house and care for homeless children or those removed from their
homes. A number of survivors, including Kate Sanchez, citizen of
the Colville Confederated Tribes, told me about being placed at an
Indian boarding school by local child welfare authorities. Sanchez
attended St. Mary's Mission boarding school in Omak, Washington,
in the 1960s and 1970s from age five to thirteen. It was here that she
was sexually abused by a priest; Sanchez also recalls sneaking into
the kitchen one night to steal bread and stumbling across one of the
prefects raping a classmate.

"I remember sleeping under the bed at night so Morse [the priest
John Morse] wouldn't find me," she said. "Some of the kids just walked
around like zombies because of the abuse." For a long time, Sanchez
didn't think she had the right to live and attempted suicide several
times as a child and an adult. "We never talked to each other about
the abuse, and it wasn't something we could take to our parents," she
said. "They wouldn't have believed us anyway." "They picked on the
ones whose parents weren't involved at the school," she continued. "I
think they figured that those of us in foster care were lost anyway;
they seemed to know our families wouldn't say anything."

By the early years of the twenty-first century, hundreds of lawsuits had been filed against the Oregon Jesuit province, naming
scores of sexually abusive priests, predominantly in Indian commu-

nities in Alaska, Washington, and Oregon. In 2011, after the province declared bankruptcy, about five hundred victims, including sixteen who attended St. Mary's Mission in Washington, settled with the Oregon province for $166 million. In 2017, the Jesuits West Province of the Society of Jesus took over both the Oregon and the California provinces with churches and missions in Alaska, Arizona, California, Hawaii, Idaho, Montana, Nevada, Oregon, Utah, and Washington. As part of the settlement agreement, Jesuits West sent letters in 2018 to everyone who worked at or attended one of the churches or schools at the former California and Oregon provinces, notifying them of the settlement and including a list of all those who were charged with crimes or had credible claims of abuse against them. The list included the names of 132 priests and clergy, some of whom are now deceased. Sixteen of those on the list were assigned to St. Mary's from the 1950s to the late 1980s. Sanchez participated in the lawsuit. "I was really angry when people first began talking about the abuse at St. Mary's; I told them, 'You're not supposed to talk about this,'" Sanchez said. She has since realized that the abuse she suffered at St. Mary's is part of her story. "It took years of intense counseling for me to believe I had a right to live," she said. Although now retired, Sanchez went to college and got her bachelor's in social work, working for the tribe and the county public health department. "Creator gave me this experience in order for me to understand the hurt others are facing," she said.

For years the church covered up information about sexually abusive priests throughout the United States, often moving them from one location to another without informing people. Journalists began covering this story in the 1990s, but little has yet been uncovered publicly about the extent of the abuse at Indian boarding schools or the possibility that the church used the schools as dumping grounds for "problem" priests. In 2022, however, I wrote about a database created by the academics Kathleen Holscher and Jack Downey, Desolate Country, which shows that nearly half of the Jesuit priests and clergy credibly accused of sexual abuse in the western United States spent time working in Indian boarding schools and missions.

In the last couple of years of my mother's life, she would allude to sexual abuse she suffered at St. Mary's in Odanah. Dementia kept her memories vague and ill-defined. She would lean in closely and lower her voice, *I probably shouldn't tell you this, but . . .* Her rambling memories included reference to a man who would chase her down and throw a blanket over her head. He carried her to a table where he held her down while *he did things* to her. Shaking her head, she looked away.

There are many anecdotal stories of sexual abuse at U.S. boarding schools, but unlike in Canada, few survivors have successfully brought lawsuits against churches or the government. Most victims of sexual abuse at the schools have never found justice. In 2010, the State of South Dakota enacted a law barring victims of sexual abuse aged forty and older from filing lawsuits against institutions. This law was mostly aimed at protecting organizations that ran Catholic Indian boarding schools in the state. Eight of the thirty boarding schools in South Dakota were operated by Catholic entities. Since 2003, 108 former students have sued the Catholic Diocese of Sioux Falls, which oversaw the eastern half of South Dakota, where St. Paul's school was located. The lawsuits include the infamous, in Indian country, case of the Nine Little Girls, siblings from the Charbonneau family who allege they were all sexually abused at St. Paul's between the 1950s and the 1970s. Their case was dismissed by a circuit court in 2011, never advancing to trial. The court cited South Dakota's legislation limiting civil actions by sexual abuse victims. In 2004 a federal judge dismissed a $25 billion class action filed against the federal government by thousands of Indian victims claiming sexual abuse at boarding schools. Plaintiffs claimed the federal government violated the 1868 Treaty of Fort Laramie by allowing "bad men" to abuse them. Judge Diane Gilbert Sypolt, however, found that plaintiffs failed to follow an esoteric procedure requiring them to ask the Bureau of Indian Affairs to first hear the case.

I found two 1921 letters in the BCIM archives that offers a window into the opaque nature of Indian boarding schools. Sister Henrietta, principal of St. Agnes Mission School in Antlers, Oklahoma, wrote to the director of the bureau. She described how a former student, now a runaway girl, was seeking to "fasten scandal" on the school by complaining that Father Charles was behaving "improperly" to girls in the dormitory. Sister Henrietta describes the girl's story as "too absurd to be believed," and is primarily concerned that anti-Catholics might hear the story, believe it, and attach scandal to the school. There were no follow-up letters about the incident.

Perhaps owing to some mysterious placement or internet algorithm present in the news cycle in 2021, the world was awakened to Indian residential and boarding school history in the United States and Canada. The awareness was driven by the discovery of unmarked graves of 215 children at the Kamloops Indian Residential School in British Columbia, Canada. For Indians, the most shocking element of the story was not the discovery of graves but the fact it's taken so long for non-Indians to acknowledge the grim details of this long-ignored history, especially in the United States. In a rare synchronicity of good luck, U.S. Indians were well positioned to seize the day on this development; a Native woman, Deb Haaland, had recently been appointed leader of the Department of the Interior. Like most Indians, Haaland's family bears the generational effects of boarding schools, and she was eager to draw attention to the long-ignored fallout from those assimilationist policies. In June 2021, she announced the Federal Indian Boarding School Initiative. Several months later the first volume of an investigative report was released; it includes preliminary data examining the scope of the boarding school system as an express policy by the federal government and Christian churches to dispossess Indians of land and resources and destroy language and culture. The report includes information about numbers of schools, locations, and associated burial sites and calls for a continued full investigation including a comprehensive records review and digitization, a determination of the amount of Indian trust and treaty funds used to support the system, identification of religious organizations that received federal funding, Native language revitalization, and access to mental health resources for survivors and descendants. Haaland also launched "The Road to Healing" tour, in

which she and government representatives traveled to twelve locations throughout the United States giving survivors the opportunity
to share their stories and be connected with trauma-informed supports. The National Endowment for the Humanities committed $4
million through the Bureau of Indian Affairs to be used to create a
permanent collection of the oral histories gathered during the tour
as well as a digital archive of federal boarding school records. The
National Native American Boarding School Healing Coalition is
undertaking the work. It's important to note, however, that there is
no enforcement mechanism or federal funding allocated for any of
the recommendations made in the initiative report. When Haaland
served as congresswoman for New Mexico in 2020, she and Senator
Elizabeth Warren introduced the Truth and Healing Commission
on Indian Boarding School Policy Act. It failed but was reintroduced
in 2023 and passed the Senate but is awaiting reintroduction in the
House. The act would authorize creation of a commission to formally
investigate, document, and acknowledge the country's boarding
school past and make recommendations on moving forward. One of
the big stumbling blocks so far is giving the commission subpoena
power for accessing records from churches. It seems unlikely that the
United States would agree to a course of reckoning akin to the efforts
in Canada, where the country settled the largest class-action lawsuit
in its history, $1.9 billion, in 2006 for survivors' reparations. Most
U.S. citizens have dodged this history by default; it has never been
presented to them. But Indians don't have the luxury of ignorance.
History flows through us; it is embedded in us. And it is something
with which we must all contend. Vestiges of historic trauma intrude
on our thoughts, minds, and lives; this is the nature of oppression.
Settlers dismiss our insistence on the truth; they've disdained our
calls for justice as misguided grousing over the inevitable loss of our
lands, lives, and cultures to superior Western worldview and society.

Not long after the discoveries of graves of children who died at Canada's Indian residential schools hit the news, I met a woman in Cin-

cinnati who worked at a Catholic Indian boarding school shortly
after she graduated from college in 1966. She was shocked to the core
over the news from Canada and wanted to reexamine her memories
of her months at St. Mary's Mission boarding school on Confederated Tribes lands in Omak, Washington. Jodine, known as Jodi,
Grundy agreed to an interview.

Grundy was twenty, an idealistic, newly minted graduate from
the Jesuits' Santa Clara University in California interested in art and
social justice. Energized by the church's involvement in civil rights
issues, she jumped at a priest's invitation to teach at the remote
boarding school as a means to live out her Catholic faith and help
improve the world. It was a romantic adventure that turned sour in
less than a year, forever tainting her relationship with the tenets of
Catholic mission work. Today, decades later, vague misgivings and
a sense of half-hidden evil linger on. Did she serve a higher calling,
even during her brief time at the school? Or had she been duped
into accepting a narrative that didn't exist? She's still trying to answer
those questions. "What is important to me is the verification of what
actually happened," she said.

The nagging uncertainties grew after Grundy received a letter in
2018 from the Jesuits West Province of the Society of Jesus informing
her of credible claims of sexual abuse of minors by clergy stationed
at churches and schools in the California and Oregon Jesuit prov-
inces. St. Mary's was a part of the Oregon province. One name in
the letter immediately stood out: Joseph Obersinner, the priest with
the magnetic personality who took her under his wing at St. Mary's.
Grundy had admired Obersinner. The gregarious priest seemed genuinely passionate about preserving the Indigenous students' culture
and language. He sometimes took her along when he visited homes
on the tribal lands. Could he really have abused the children? she
wondered. A self-described "cradle Catholic," Grundy was raised to
trust the clergy. For a time, she even considered becoming a nun.

"I was Catholic all the way, Catholic elementary, high school and
college," she said. Recalling that Obersinner had died in 2018, and
emotionally unprepared to dig further into the unpleasant findings,

Grundy put the letter aside. She returned to the comfort of her carefully curated and orderly retirement life in a spacious high-rise apartment. Here she could gaze down at the tree-covered city or out into
an endless sky. A lot has transpired since she abruptly fled the school
in 1967 to live in a commune in the Haight-Ashbury neighborhood
of San Francisco. Her remarkable life has been filled with marriage,
social justice work among California farmworkers, children, farming
and organizing local farmers markets, a second degree and career in
psychotherapy, a heart attack, and grandchildren. It was all a long
time ago, but there's something about those months at St. Mary's
that won't leave her alone. Although her time teaching art and other
classes in the long, thin building on the school's campus was short,
she still thinks of it. Clearly uncertain about her tenure there, unwill-
ing to entirely believe the terrible allegations against Obersinner, she
clings to her positive memories of the children.

She had long red hair in those days. "The kids were all over me,
touching and braiding my hair," she said. "I loved being with them
and they loved being with me." That red hair has now turned wispy
white. Cut in a tidy bob, it frames her sharp blue eyes as she spreads
the contents of a file folder out onto her coffee table. The folder
holds drawings, paintings, and written essays on construction paper
created by her students at St. Mary's. She's saved them all these years
as a touchstone, a reminder of the children she loved. There was one
girl—a large, outgoing girl who was held back several grades due to
her "failure to progress"—who described a fantasy world of clowns
in an essay written in a small, tortured script. "[She] really struggled
with school but she wanted to please me," Grundy said. Abandoning
the school's curriculum, Grundy encouraged the children to express
themselves. "I had an entire wall covered with pictures from current
magazines," she said. "My class was a lively, open place; it was a good
place for them."

Another of her students, Charlie Marchand, kept his artwork, but
she often thinks of the boy. He was obviously a gifted artist, and she
wonders what became of him. She left him all her art supplies when
she departed. Grundy recalls the beautiful, rugged landscape and

clear blue sky, collecting apples in a nearby orchard with the children, and watching with a combination of delight and fear as they jumped from high cliffs into the Okanogan River. She loved their exuberance over basketball and dancing on Friday nights to a jukebox in the gym. "They were crazy over basketball and they were good," she said. She remembers the touching generosity of the people, the time she was measured for moccasins during one of her excursions with Obersinner, and the way women hung their babies in handmade cradleboards along the back wall of the church. Although she was saddened to know the children were removed from their families, she told herself they were better off at the mission. Obersinner and others at the school told her the students came from dysfunctional living conditions, with a lot of abuse and alcoholism in their homes. She believed them. At least, she reasoned, they were fed and received an education.

Every day began with the same breakfast for the children—a bowl of oatmeal, a cup of milk, and a single apple. Many of the children, however, were filled with rage, she found. Sometimes they ran away or acted out; there were times they were taken away by Obersinner for discipline. She assumed their anger came from toxic home lives. "I never witnessed any abuse," Grundy said. "But then I was 100 percent busy with the students. I taught art, remedial reading, and writing, and even religion." But as time went on, she grew uneasy over the school's mission. "My sense grew that the whole thing was rotten," she said. "It was an impossible journey for these kids. They were being systematically removed from their culture by this education and Christianization." She wrote to former classmates at Santa Clara, trying to process her sense of unease. What was going on at St. Mary's flew in the face of the vision she and her friends had of Catholic social justice. It was months before the Summer of Love in 1967, and her boyfriend and college friends were preparing to join the 100,000 young people who converged on San Francisco's Haight-Ashbury neighborhood to create a new society, rejecting consumerist values and the war in Vietnam. But there was something else wrong at the school, something she couldn't identify. It was a dream that confirmed her misgivings and persuaded her to leave. Even now, the dream is vivid, she said. "I'm a strong dreamer; I remember dreams from my childhood," she said. "There was this incredible blackness. It was like a huge, black wave coming off Osoyoos Lake, a black moving thing coming over me, over this mission. And then a message, 'This place is the Devil.'" She told school administrators she was leaving in the middle of the spring term, and strangely, they failed to question her decision or the reasons behind it. She remembers one other thing, too. Obersinner suddenly went missing, reassigned elsewhere after being at St. Mary's for several years. Staff wasn't given any explanation for his departure. "Maybe they were afraid I'd seen something," she said. "I don't know."

I reached out to Grundy's former students via social media at her request. A handful responded. Others who answered were family members of students who had already died. Most asked to have their loved ones' artwork sent to them and declined to be interviewed. Grundy is arranging to mail the artwork and essays to those who requested it. The younger sister of the girl who wrote about clowns agreed to speak with Grundy via Zoom. But the sister asked that neither her name nor her sister's be included in the story. The elder sister died a few years ago but not before taking part in the lawsuit against the Oregon diocese over abuse she suffered at St. Mary's. The younger sister also attended St. Mary's in the 1970s, before it was taken over by the Colville Confederated Tribes and renamed Paschal Sherman Indian School in 1973. She has good memories of her time there as a teen. Many people in Colville liked Father Obersinner, she said.

The former St. Mary's student Kate Sanchez remembers things differently. Although she said Obersinner frequently protected her from sexual abuse by another priest, John Morse, also named in the Jesuits' list, her friends reported that Obersinner sometimes fondled them. Morse died in 2015. Sanchez has no memories of Grundy. Hunger is among her most vivid memories during her time at the school. "I hated picking up those windfall apples, [but] sometimes that was the only food we got," she said. "Everything else was donated. We had rice and a cup of milk every day for breakfast except Sundays, when we got cereal." Thankfully, she recalls, a local dairy donated milk to fill the morning cups. The staff at the school ate much better food than the students, according to Sanchez. "They would deny us dinner as punishment," she said.

No longer a practicing Catholic, Grundy is now rethinking and recalibrating her experience at the school and the mission of the Jesuits she so loved and respected. "What do I do with this new knowledge?" she asked. Grundy is glad that the Jesuits are coming forward and admitting the abuse happened, even if they were forced to do so. "It's kind of cold comfort, I guess," she said. "Ultimately I feel betrayed and abused by everything I was brought up in."

The U.S. Catholic Church has mostly remained silent regarding its role in operating schools and carrying forward assimilationist policies. I sent repeated telephone and email requests to the U.S. Conference of Catholic Bishops (USCCB) asking if they had any plans for an organized apology or reparations for the Catholic Church's role. The USCCB is the highest-ranking Catholic authority in the United States. I received an email from their director of public affairs, Chieko Noguchi:

> We are deeply saddened by the information coming out of two former residential boarding school sites in Canada. We cannot even begin to imagine the deep sorrow these discoveries are causing in Native communities across North America. It is also important to understand what might have occurred here in the United States, and therefore, we are following closely the announcement last week by the Department of the Interior of a formal inquiry into residential boarding schools. The United States Conference of Catholic Bishops will look for ways to be of assistance. By bringing this painful story to light, may it bring some measure of peace to the victims and a heightened awareness so that this disturbing history is never repeated.

In November 2023, USCCB leadership withdrew a document created by the organization's subcommittee on Native American affairs that included an apology for the church's involvement in or failure to oppose institutional discrimination and abuse of Native peoples. Although approved in July 2023 by the subcommittee and National Advisory Committee—the conference's consultative body made up of laity, religious, and diocesan priests—several bishops expressed concern that the document would create potential legal liability. But on June 14, 2024, the day after the boarding school healing bill made it out of committee in the U.S. House of Representatives, USCCB leaders issued their most formal apology to date for the role of the U.S. Catholic Church in operating boarding schools. "We apologize for the failure to nurture, strengthen, honor, recognize, and appreciate those entrusted to our pastoral care," reads the introduction. Some Native people thought the apology was an important step forward. Jim LaBelle called it "powerful" and said he was "elated the church would start naming the harm" that was done to Native communities. As is their habit, however, church leaders minimized the institution's role in legitimizing centuries of colonialism in the United States. Bishops refuted the doctrine of discovery in the document, for instance, but claimed that it was European and Eurocentric world powers that exploited well-intentioned laws to justify enslaving and mistreating and removing Indigenous peoples from their lands. "If you're going to give an apology, just apologize," said Nick Tilsen, chief executive of NDN Collective, an Indigenous rights advocacy nonprofit organization. "How many times have people taught their children: 'Don't say sorry and then say, but . . . ,'" said Tilsen of the Oglala Lakota Tribe. He noted that the bishops' document sets acknowledgments of harm done to Native children alongside claims about the positive impacts of missionizing such as sheltering children orphaned by epidemics and poverty.

The language in the fifty-six-page document, however, suggested that the church may consider allowing access to sacramental records for boarding school survivors and descendants, a major step that would run counter to Catholic canon law, which prevents "outsiders" from viewing such records. "Fostering dialogue and engaging in other efforts to reconcile involvement remains an important priority of the USCCB on the issue of boarding school accountability as we walk with the impacted communities on their path towards healing," said the spokesperson, Noguchi, in a statement released to the media. But the bishops declined to address growing public allegations of sexual abuse by church officials, including a May 2024 investigative report by *The Washington Post* that revealed "a portrait of pervasive sexual abuse endured by Native American children at Catholic-run schools in remote regions of the Midwest and Pacific Northwest, including Alaska."

Deb Parker of the National Native American Boarding School Healing Coalition, who has worked for years lobbying Congress in support of the boarding school bill, told me that the bishops' statement and apology show that the church can no longer dodge its troubled history and years of inaction. "They're coming forward because they know that our bill is going to pass," she said.

Some Catholic entities are conducting what they describe as reconciliation work with Indians. The Sisters of Perpetual Adoration, the nuns who served at St. Mary's in Bad River, for instance, have donated $250,000 toward establishment of the Culture Revitalization and Youth Center in Bad River and have returned some cultural items to the tribe such as paintings created by Peter Whitebird during the WPA project. When I visited the sisters' motherhouse in La Crosse, Wisconsin, in 2021, they were still reeling from the public attention generated by my 2019 article "Death by Civilization" in *The Atlantic* about the order's role in operating the school my mother attended, St. Mary's boarding school. Sister Eileen McKenzie, the order's president, told me they were in the process of determining, which they describe as "discerning," how to respond. "This is all new to us," she said. Unlike Indians, the nuns had forgotten about the nearly ninety years they spent on Bad River as part of the assimilationist agenda to Christianize and civilize us. "As we hear stories about how the institutional nature of boarding schools was abusive, we are realizing we were part of that larger system. We are learning that our church is colonial and how we've been complicit in these things," McKenzie said. Many people have asked why the nuns didn't know about their history supporting Indian boarding schools and why it's taken so long for them to confront it, according to McKenzie. Why indeed, I wondered. For me, the answer is simple: Catholic leadership has ignored this past because they could. In a later interview with reporter Dan Stockman of Global Sisters Report, McKenzie said, "There was an effective erasure. In my world, that policy worked, but my world is one of white supremacy. This history has been erased in my culture." Overall, that erasure has worked out pretty well for the Catholics and the Sisters of Perpetual Adoration.

During my visit, Sister Mary Ann Gschwind gave me a tour of the St. Rose Convent, where the mostly elderly sisters reside, and the Mary of the Angels Chapel, where they worship.

There is a small, seldom visited museum in the basement of the convent where the order's archives and vast collection of retired religious gear are kept. Sister Gschwind flicked on the lights of a large, darkened room containing scores of statues of angels, all facing inward to an empty open space in the center of the room. Sister explained that sometimes people request their caskets be placed there before their funeral Mass. We walked through a long cave-like tunnel, its boulder-like walls painted with shiny cream-colored paint, connecting the convent to the Mary of the Angels Chapel. This is where the perpetual adoration after which the nuns are named takes place. The Society of Architectural Historians describes the chapel, which was consecrated in 1906, as "one of Wisconsin's most lavish church interiors." Its six thousand square feet contain pillars veined with gold, numerous stained-glass windows, and vaults decorated with gold filigree and statues of angels and saints, lots of statues. The altars, of which there are several, are made of Carrara marble imported from Italy and inlaid with mother-of-pearl. "The total cost of the church is unknown," Sister said. The chapel is nearly empty when we enter except for an elderly nun who is playing a huge golden harp, a gift from a parishioner long ago. The harp's music is almost swallowed up by the empty space with its vast lofted ceiling. I hear a low humming sound coming from the rear of the church. The humming gets louder as we approach; this is where the perpetual adoration happens in a smaller chapel behind the main altar. In 1878, at the instruction of Mother Antonia, the nuns began to pray for a church. She promised, according to the order's history, that if they prayed continuously, their prayers would be answered and Mother would see to it that a church "as beautiful as our means would allow would be built." The round-the-clock prayer continued after the church was built until the COVID pandemic hit in 2020. Today the prayer goes on in shifts except during the hours from 10:00 p.m. to 6:00 a.m. Laity and non-Catholics help with prayer. The sisters offer a call-in prayer service as well in which people can phone in and make prayer requests.

Later Sister McKenzie apologized to me personally on behalf of the order for the pain my mother experienced. For me, her apology, genuine and well intentioned, spoke volumes about the disconnect and delusion under which Catholic leadership operates. Maybe because of my Catholic upbringing, I smiled and said nothing, still mindful and protective of white fragility. The Catholic Church is still dodging its wrongdoing. Its leadership continues tending its great hoards of wealth in the form of buildings and sacred objects amid a dying membership while desperately clinging to a moral ascendancy that for that institution simply doesn't exist.

Settlers have long dismissed our calls for justice. But if the United States simply honored the deliverables promised in the more than three hundred treaties signed with Indian nations and passage of subsequent legislation, which addressed education, health care, economic development, and access to ceded lands, Indian country would not be where it is now. "We'd like to have the resources to resurrect and stop the degradation of our languages that was discouraged at the schools; when you lose your language, you lose who you are as an Indigenous person," Jim LaBelle told me. "And in the course of losing who you are, you start losing out on traditions, singing, praying, dancing, and how to survive in the environment." LaBelle recalled that after being beaten and humiliated for speaking his language at the Wrangell Institute, he was embarrassed to be seen in public with his mother, a citizen of the Iñupiaq tribe. "If I saw my mother in town, I'd cross the street to avoid her; although she spoke English, she still spoke Iñupiaq, and I was ashamed of her," he said. "That's how effective the indoctrination was at Wrangell."

LaBelle hopes that passage of the boarding school bill, which, at the time of this writing, is awaiting vote in both the Senate and the House, and the Catholic apology may address some of the harm of forced acculturation in the form of healing centers throughout Indian country. Healing will take a while. It will take longer than one generation to undo more than five hundred years of colonization. But before any sort of meaningful work toward justice begins, for the federal government or churches, we require a thorough accounting of what happened from the perspective of those who were harmed.

TEN

JINGLE DRESS HEALING

f I sometimes had doubts about my quest, events such as verifying the Sister Catherine story drove me onward; dreams and visions filled my irresistible mission, part journalistic research, part spiritual pilgrimage. I dreamed about relatives, some I'd never met and some I'd known only briefly. In one dream I drove an enormous old gas-guzzling car filled with *mindimooyenyag* (elder Ojibwe women) toward an unknown destination. Tiny and wrinkled, the *mindimooyenyag* wore old-fashioned flowered cotton dresses like ones I've seen in family photographs. They were sunk down low, nearly swallowed by the soft bench seats of the car, and barely able to see over the dashboard. They sat erect, however, gazing ahead placidly, oblivious to the sound of the roaring tattered muffler as I comically wrestled with the loose steering wheel, struggling to keep the vehicle with its blown-out shocks on the road.

Later in the dream, we passed by my uncle Hashy's house. His real name was Hudson. In my childhood, I knew Hashy as an irreverent comedian, forever poking fun at the white man's vision of Ojibwe. As a young woman, I was a frequent chauffeur for my mother and other elders during visits to the reservation. When I'd drive to Hashy's house to pick him up for bingo, he would be waiting outside, posed like an Indian from one of the "noble savage" sculptures and paintings popular in the early twentieth century. Sometimes he'd be the "End of the Trail Indian" slumped over his horse in defeat but minus the horse, or the "Prayer to the Great Spirit Indian" with arms outstretched and gazing heavenward or shielding his eyes as he looked toward a long trail, and sometimes he'd hold an old rake aloft like a lance as he charged us on his imaginary horse. He'd hold the pose long after we stopped, finally emitting a loud, drawn-out *aye!* My mother would say, *Oh, for Chrissakes, get in the car!* In my dream, however, Hashy was uncharacteristically serious when we arrived; he greeted us by singing a one-word hand drum song. The word, unfamiliar to me, was *Waabanang.* Later I learn that *Waabanang* means "to the east," as in a directive to journey east. Those *mindimooyenyag* were placing their trust in me, reminding me that this quest includes an obligation to see the journey all the way through.

My mother's mental capacities began to decline and her driving skills deteriorated. She worked part time as an in-home care provider for the elderly. As part of training for the job, she took a four-week class offered and paid for by the company providing the care. She began telling people she was a nurse, even in our family's presence. The uniform gave her a new identity and authority. *I know, because I'm a nurse!* she often said. In 2008 she ran a stop sign in south Florida and was hit by a cement truck. For a time, it seemed she might not make it, but she survived. Since Bill and his wife, Donna, were living near St. Augustine, we had her moved to a nursing facility there for her rehabilitation. Unaccountably, she grew angry and verbally abusive to Bill and Donna. She refused their help and support and moved alone, against doctor's orders, back to her little condo near Fort Myers. When we expressed concern, she declared we'd never loved her and only wanted to control her and steal her money. By this time, her collection of the U.S. Mint's state quarters were the extent of her ready cash. She displayed all fifty of them proudly in a cardboard frame. Maddeningly, she lowered the steel wall in her mind, stubbornly refusing to speak to us. We were frosted. Her dementia grew worse; she constantly frightened and surprised us with her actions. Announcing she was driving to Wisconsin, she'd get hopelessly lost, disappearing for days. Sometimes a cop or Good Samaritan would call us, and we'd try to guide her over the phone. She sold her condo and moved into a shabby rental apartment in Janesville. Occasionally she would join the family for meals or holidays, but inevitably she would leave in a fit of anger over imagined critical comments or slights. Sometimes she inquired about my work. Once, I showed her my portfolio, but it seemed to irritate her. Pursing her lips, she muttered sharply, *Hmmm, hmmm,* as she quickly flipped through the pages of photographs and newspaper tear sheets as though put upon to admire the work of a bothersome gasbag. She grew especially angry hearing me speak with colleagues on the phone about my work. *Oh, you just know everything, don't you?* she huffed.

During this time, I was also investigating both my mother's and America's Indian boarding school history as well as its impact on generations of Indian people's mental and physical health. In the process I uncovered her long-hidden secrets and gained an understanding of the trauma that helped create her and our family's subsequent disease. I began to get over myself a bit and understand her pathological behavior wasn't only about me and my pain and hurt. Her life and story were part of a larger picture and the traumatic impact of misguided U.S. assimilationist policies on generations of Indian people. In learning about the neuroscience of trauma and the devastating role it played in damaging her psyche, I gained some control—not over her, but over how I saw her. My daily prayers for her, ordered by my AA sponsor, began to pay off. One day I noticed, as though by magic, I was no longer angry with her. This, and things like it (not a change in her behavior), helped me heal. The recirculating power of the shame and rage of her childhood, the Sister School message that Indians are unfit, was turned inward and took the form of the enormous chip she carried on her shoulder. She could never allow herself to delve into the real circumstances that drove her mother, Cele, to leave her and her siblings at the Sister School. The risk of forgiveness was too great. But determining my mother's history has been like putting together a puzzle, its pieces events that initially appeared unrelated but became essential to completing the whole. If I were ever to truly understand her, I needed to take a deep dive into her personal past. I began with Auntie Pat.

It was nearly midnight in 2009 by the time I reached the most deserted part of the journey to Bad River, far past Wisconsin's tourist towns, where the dense curtain of trees welcome me home. I am in Ojibwe country at last, where the land, uncluttered and raw, stretches out before me. I've made this drive many times. Ordinarily, I'm relieved to finally escape the sea of T-shirt shops and garish miniature golf courses that dot northern Wisconsin's white man's vacation paradise. Tonight, however, an eerie mist rises from the cedar swamps as the cool night air advances. More tired than I'd realized, my eyes begin to close. It was the end of a very long day; I'd been up since dawn, outside in the heat and humidity for a photography assignment, taking photos of Indian people conducting traditional food preparation and craft demonstrations during Milwaukee's annual Summerfest. Now, as I traveled north, the bogs, low and fecund, lay between the towering stands of pine. After the muggy heat of the day, they were aglow with swamp gas, shining like slow-moving ghosts. Although I've heard of this phenomenon of methane and hydrogen sulfide, this was my first sighting; the glowing lights appeared alive, disturbed by my presence. For the first time, the normally welcoming landscape seemed inhabited by forewarning spirits.

I drove for miles without seeing any other cars and began to nod off. Startled and spooked, I shook myself to wakefulness, finally seeing the tribe's casino and lodge sign blinking through the fog.

My mother was still alive at this time. Auntie Pat was waiting for me when I arrived at her house the next morning. Her hair was freshly permed. Dressed neatly in her Kateri Society blazer, she reminded me of a plump little partridge serenely ensconced in her recliner in her crowded reservation living room. Over breakfast at a local restaurant she said, *I'm going to tell you about your mother, but you gotta promise not to tell her I was the one.* She asked what I knew about my grandparents, Cele and Joe. I didn't know much.

My mother seldom spoke of Cele, the mother who abandoned her and her siblings and was to blame for the children ending up in the Sister School. She blamed Cele for her harshness toward Joe and for breaking up the family. Joe was always the savior, the hero, in her stories: the father who loved them despite all the odds against him. My mother would sometimes describe the last terrible fight between her parents, a mental scar she carried for a lifetime: *Pa came home drunk, but he was singing; he was always one of those happy-go-lucky drunks. Ma got mad and hit him on the head with a beer bottle; he sank right down on the floor,* she said. *I thought she'd killed him, so I began to scream and scream.*

My mother clenched her fists, closing her eyes tightly during this story, shaking her head from side to side. She flapped her hands violently as though trying to shake something from them. She ended each telling with the words *I never did like my mother!*

But on that steamy summer morning, Auntie Pat told me a very different story.

Joe was from the Red Cliff reservation, but he met Cele during a visit to Bad River; he was still wearing his World War I army uniform when they met, giving him a worldly, sophisticated air. He'd spent time in France and Germany fighting for his country; now back on the reservation he intended to claim the equal opportunity due all Americans. Although he was quite a bit older than Cele, they seemed a good match, both forward thinkers, looking to challenge the old backward, racist standards that permeated the reservation. But during the war, Joe fought in the Meuse-Argonne offensive, the deadliest campaign in American history. The fight took place in France and Belgium and was the final battle of World War I; it was one of the largest battles of that deadly war. Joe served in the infantry as a runner and was severely gassed during the battle but "refused to be evacuated until he completed his mission." Although the Meuse-Argonne offensive took place from September to November 1918, it wasn't until February 1919 that he "was forced to seek treatments." He spent several months in various army hospitals in Europe and the United States until his discharge in June 1919.

Phosgene and mustard were the primary gases used during the Meuse-Argonne offensive. Mustard, dubbed the king of battle gases, caused painful blisters internally and externally and could lead to permanent blindness. Phosgene, a colorless gas, was stealthy and could be deadly, often killing days after exposure as victims slowly suffocated to death. Gas also had a profoundly damaging psychological effect on soldiers; it was horrifying to be gassed. "First wonder, then fear, as the first fringes of the cloud enveloped them and left them choking and agonized in the fight for breath-panic," wrote S. J. M. Auld, a member of the British Military Mission to the United States. According to the World Health Organization, soldiers exposed to mustard gas could experience mental disturbances and heightened anxiety. "In more chronic cases, these symptoms could persist for some time." When the gas alert gongs sounded, soldiers already weighed down with weapons and packs struggled to find their gas masks; the masks were unwieldy and made breathing difficult, and training in their use was limited. Joe had no tools for dealing with the fallout from the terrible trauma he'd experienced, so he turned to the only antidote he knew, alcohol. He began to drink heavily and beat Cele. He had what they called back then shell shock, for which there was little recognition or help. Soldiers were left to deal with the pain of what we now know as post-traumatic stress disorder as best they could, if at all.

More Native Americans per capita have served in the U.S. armed forces than any other group of Americans. Indian soldiers were among the first U.S. combat units to reach France in 1917 and fought in every critical battle that ended World War I. According to the National Museum of the American Indian, "They fought to demonstrate their patriotism, prove themselves in battle and defend democracy in Europe." Like Indian involvement in sports, they were also, I think, pushing back against the eugenics-supported notion that Indians were inherently inferior. Many also expected to gain U.S. citizenship as a reward. Although Congress granted them citizenship in 1924, many states did not recognize them as citizens. About 5 percent of Indian soldiers were killed in World War I versus 1 percent of U.S. forces as a whole. In a poignant gesture to prove their bravery and humanity, many Indian soldiers embraced the warrior myth.

But back at home, the white settler enterprises in the Great Lakes region simply left after devouring their chosen resources; like the windigo, their greed was insatiable, with little regard for humanity. And the Indians who had been forced to buy into the economic agenda were left with little means to feed their families. Civilization had been a monstrous lie. Tricked into betraying their world of balance and reciprocity, they grew vulnerable. When the Great Depression arrived, life on Bad River was desperate. Joe couldn't find, much less keep, a job; he would get drunk and disappear. No longer the brave, inspiring soldier, Joe was just another Indian trying to feed his family. *Times was tough,* Auntie Pat said. Overwhelmed, Cele grew angry; she unleashed her famous rage against Joe, bawling him out when he showed up drunk and empty-handed after going missing for several days.

He was so drunk the day of their final fight that he was barely able to stand when he wordlessly shuffled into the kitchen. Cele was furious; there was no food for the children, and Joe had once again spent what little they had on alcohol. She raged at him, his incompetence, fecklessness, uselessness. My mother and Rags retreated to the farthest corner of the kitchen, wedging themselves defensively under a table, making themselves as small as possible. Their older siblings, Don, Lucille, and Geraldine, were away. Suddenly, seemingly transformed by Cele's outburst, Joe found his footing and leaped on Cele. The normally gentle, soft-spoken man seemed possessed as he attacked his young wife. He began to beat her with his fists as the children watched in horror; he punched her and ripped at her clothing. At first Cele bellowed angrily as they fought, but soon her power vanished, replaced by terror. Joe meant to kill her. She screamed for her life as Joe began biting into her body like a wild beast, chewing off most of one of her breasts. Kicking, punching, and screaming wildly, she somehow knocked Joe backward. Stumbling to her feet, she grabbed a beer bottle and smashed it over his head, knocking him unconscious. As he fell to the floor, her eyes met those of her children still watching silently from their places under the table. *There was so much blood,* Auntie Pat said. *Your mom must have been about four years old and Rags barely two.*

Cele gestured to the children to come out, but they remained frozen. *Come on,* she commanded hoarsely. Cele grabbed them by their hands, pulling them forward as they emerged slowly. Standing up, Bernice looked down at her hands, now covered with her mother's blood. She began to scream uncontrollably as she literally tried to shake it off. She would unwittingly repeat that gesture her entire life, never able to recognize its truth nor free herself from her mother's blood. From that moment onward, Bernice labored to keep the images of Joe's attack firmly buried in her mind, desperately swatting the memories away whenever they threatened to reemerge. *Cele dragged herself and the kids over to our house; Ma, Mary Moore, your great-grandmother, was a midwife, and she doctored her.*

Cele eventually recovered but stayed at Grandma Moore's house, too frightened to return home. *Ma told her, even a bitch dog stays with its pups,* Auntie said. But Cele had had enough; she left Bad River and married a white man. Although she visited occasionally, she would never live there again. Grandma Moore tried to raise Cele and Joe's children, but her resources were too thin; she still had several of her own children at home. *Ma would say to Joe, for Chrissakes, give me a little money and I'll take care of the kids.* But Joe would cuss her, insisting he'd raise his own goddamned kids. That's how my mother and her siblings came to live at the Sister School. Occasionally Joe would take the children out of school and try to care for them himself. His only income came from the homemade whiskey he made and sold out of a shack, but the authorities closed him down due to an outbreak of smallpox.

It didn't matter, though, even without the authorities, Auntie said, *he'd go off on another toot, and the kids would end up back at the Sister School.*

Although Auntie Pat's family was poor, both parents were present at home. Auntie Pat and her siblings didn't have to board at the Sister School; they were "day scholars" and lived at home. As she continued to talk, she drew herself up in that uniquely Moore family way. Seeing her straighten herself all around, I mentally prepared myself for more.

Auntie Pat also told me about George C., my brother Larry's father. And she told me there was another son, a boy named Bobby.

"Was George also Bobby's father?" I asked.

Of course! She never loved no one else but George. Your auntie Lucille and uncle Donald were living near Janesville. They came up to look for her and found her living with George's people; her face was all bruised up and they tried to take her and the boys away with them. George wasn't there; he was in jail, but his people wouldn't let her take Bobby, who was around two years old. Since Larry was nursing, they let her take him. She and Larry went to live with Lucille and Donald in Janesville; that's where she met your dad. She left Bobby behind. But what happened to Bobby? I wanted to know.

He died in Chicago in the 1980s. Your aunt Lucille and uncle Donald found him there in the 1960s; he was homeless. They tried to connect him and your mom, but she didn't take to him. I think he looked too Indian for her and her new life with a white man. As I drove Auntie Pat home from the restaurant where we had breakfast, she pointed to a house. *If you want to know more about your grandpa Joe, you need to go to that house.* I thanked Auntie and said goodbye. My mind was numb, a blank. The prospect of hearing more, of going to the house she'd shown me, was out of the question. My mind reeling, I began the long drive south, with the plan to stop in Madison and see my fellow journalists and good friends Mark Anthony Rolo and Shiela Reaves.

Shiela was a journalism professor at the University of Wisconsin–Madison; she'd been my mentor since I got my first newspaper internship in the early 1980s. Mark was a journalist and playwright. His mother, Corrine, was also from Odanah, where she'd attended the Sister School a few years after my mother. Mark was one of nine kids, eight boys and one girl, all born one right after another to Corrine and her husband, Don, a white man of French and Irish descent. His father was a drunk and veteran of World War II or, as he called it, *the second world fuck.* Don moved his family to an isolated, decrepit farm outside Big Falls, Minnesota, where he expected them to live off the land. According to Don, northern Minnesota winters were ancient. For Mark and his siblings, those winters seemed to live to a thousand years.

Mark's family grew up dreadfully poor without even the small reservation subsidies like commodities or knowledge of Ojibwe culture and ways that might have sustained them. Corrine died suddenly when Mark was around ten years old; he became the de facto leader and protector of the family. He described his life in his last book, *My Mother Is Now Earth*. Known for his wicked, dark humor, he depicts the shame and racism of being Indian in rural 1960s America while dodging his brutal alcoholic father, whose words *You guys are no goddamned good!* were a frequent refrain. Mark and Shiela were my bookend touchstones, offering literary support and brutal honesty.

It was nearly the Fourth of July and the highway was crowded with holiday travelers as I drove south toward Madison. The radio had no reception; so I retreated deep into my own thoughts in the silence, thinking about Uncle Rags and how he'd been nailed to the table at the Sister School. Certainly, I reasoned, he could have wiggled free if the nuns had nailed him to the table through his clothing, unless they used lots of nails. Anticipating the next thought, my brain recoiled like a jellyfish seeking shelter from an attacker. Surely those nuns couldn't have nailed his hand or another part of his body to the table, could they? What about the decision to leave him there overnight? Rags is gone now. I reached out later to my cousins about the incident. Although they never heard him tell this story, they recall his generalized references to the nuns' cruelty.

I think he didn't want to hurt us with details of those bad memories; he just wanted to move on and make a life for himself and his family, his daughter-in-law Gloria told me over the phone. *He told us he ran away from the Sister School when he was fifteen,* she said. *And, you know, he always hated onions.* I wondered if his brain recorded the event or if mercifully his limbic system went off-line, sparing him that future pain. Or did the memory intrude occasionally, triggered by certain sounds, smells, or quality of light? Either way, Rags must have been terrified. My mother and her siblings would have lain in bed listening to his cries. And the other students too, silently waiting for it to stop. According to Auntie Pat, Grandma Moore couldn't leave her own children alone on the night Uncle Don escaped from the Sister School to tell her about the incident. She had to wait until morning. Although she must have been horrified over her little grandson's treatment, she didn't have enough resources to take him and the others home. She left them there.

I recalled some of the many stories told to me by survivors of their days at boarding schools. Now as adults, looking back at the behavior of the Catholic nuns who served at many of the schools, some people wonder if the women might have experienced nervous breakdowns or mental collapse. Many survivors have described an unhealthy culture among staff that often translated into brutality toward students. "Those sisters and priests were locked up with students 24/7; it wasn't a healthy situation," said Bryan Brewer, Lakota, former student at Holy Rosary Catholic Indian mission on the Pine Ridge reservation. "They took out their frustrations on us kids in the form of harsh discipline," he recalled.

My mother often described Sister Catherine, the Mother Superior, and some other nuns at St. Mary's as paranoid and defensive, especially regarding outsiders who might threaten ongoing Catholic leadership at the school. Indeed, I found several of Sister Catherine's letters to leadership at the BCIM in the archives at Marquette University. They are filled with seemingly unfounded accusations and concerns about state and county welfare workers as well as public school efforts to "meddle" in the school's affairs.

"You know, I think some of those sisters kind of went crazy," said Tom Deragon, former student at St. Mary's in Odanah. Catholic nuns were discouraged by their orders from leaving or transferring their postings at schools until directed by leadership. According to the house diary kept by the nuns serving at Holy Rosary school, several sisters died during their service and are buried in the cemetery next to the school. Unlike the simple wooden plaques marking the graves of children who died there, which have since weathered away, the tall stone monuments marking the nuns' graves still stand today next to the now renamed Red Cloud Indian School. Teachers at the federal Indian boarding schools, however, could leave their postings at any time. And many did; the staff turnover rates were notoriously high. Teachers cited harsh conditions, isolation, and low pay as reasons for leaving.

According to the Franciscan Sisters of Perpetual Adoration congregational history book, Sister Catherine remained at St. Mary's for nearly forty years. Other nuns were posted at the school for thirty or forty years. Carie Novitzke, a former nun with the Sisters of Perpetual Adoration, told me it is unusual for nuns to remain at mission postings for such long periods. Novitzke speculated there was something unhealthy about those long tenures. Nuns were also discouraged from speaking out about abuse toward students at the schools, or anything else for that matter. The vow of obedience taken by Catholic nuns includes not only compliance with directions from superiors but also maintaining confidentiality.

"As a nun, I was taught that confidentiality is one of the biggest aspects of obedience; it's a code that says nobody talks," said Novitzke. Would we ever learn the full story of the pathological environments in which our relatives and ancestors lived? I wondered as I drove along silently.

Suddenly I was jolted from my reverie—a beat-up sedan veered off onto the shoulder as it sped past me. Police cars, their sirens blaring, raced by in pursuit. I caught a glimpse of the front-seat passenger in the fleeing car. The man was shirtless; his sunburned arms were thin and rangy. The wind forced his thick bushy hair back away from his face; his arm was outside the window as he held on to the car's door frame. His wire-rimmed glasses lent him a scholarly appearance as he looked straight ahead, sitting bolt upright, braced for impact. This was no carefree joyride; the driver drove as though he and the passengers were fleeing a serious crime. Soon, traffic came almost to a stop. A woman on a motorcycle sped past, weaving through cars. *"That's the car!"* she screamed.

We stopped for what seemed like hours. I gazed out at the expanse of cornfields, buzzing hotly in the July sun. At last we began to move again. The fleeing car had crashed; its crumpled body was now surrounded by police and rescue vehicles. The passenger's naked arms were extended as he lay back in his seat; it looked as though the entire engine had been forced into his lap, trapping him, its wires and metal parts smoldering. It was nearly dark when I pulled up to Shiela's house. She and Mark were seated outside on her patio, lazily drinking wine and savoring the evening air. Nick, Mark's ten-year-old nephew, lit a huge handful of sparklers. The red-hot wires were too hot to hold, and he dropped them in the grass with a yelp.

Still dazed from the events of the day, I poured out the details of all that had happened, my terrible anticipation driving to Odanah, my aunt's stories, and finally the accident I'd just passed. They both remained speechless for several moments, blindsided and a little trod upon at having their pleasant evening disrupted. At last, Mark quipped dryly, "Ah, good times."

I jumped to my feet. *"You fucker!"* I shrieked at him.

It was then that we started to laugh. Wave after wave of gravelly laughter, scouring out our craws until we could gain our balance.

Just then, Nick emerged from Shiela's kitchen, wearing oven mitts. Triumphantly, he ignited dozens of blazing sparklers, holding them easily in each hand. It looked as though he were juggling twin fireballs as he ran wildly across the darkened yard.

Later, during the pandemic, Mark blew his brains out with a gazillion little bottles of cheap, cinnamon-flavored whiskey, the kind bought on impulse in the checkout line at convenience stores. He lay in hospice alone, waiting to die as his liver began to fail. His brothers and nephew had to shout at him through the closed window to his room during their visits. I wept during our final telephone calls, which seemed to soothe and reassure him. Soon, he was gone. I made and sent him a pair of plain moccasins for his final journey; the nurse promised to put them on his feet before cremation. God, I miss him.

I'd returned to Cincinnati, where summer gave way to fall. Auntie Pat called me with some news. My cousin John, Pat's son, worked as a security guard at the tribal casino and had chatted up a young woman wearing a jacket embroidered with the word "Petoskey," a town in Michigan near the Little Traverse Bay Bands of Odawa Indians. *Oh, so you're from Petoskey, aye?* John asked. *Yes,* she said. *But my grandma is supposed to be from here in Bad River; her name is Bernice Pember.* John said, *Wait right here.* He introduced her to Auntie Pat; her name was Pam. I got to know Pam over the next several months, learning about Bobby, her father, and my half brother, whose existence I'd learned of only recently. As I talked with Pam, I recalled an indistinct yet strangely lasting childhood memory. I had met Bobby before, briefly in Chicago. My mother's brother Don and sister Lucille found Bobby on Chicago's North Side, where so many Indians had settled as part of the relocation program. He was virtually homeless. They tried to arrange a reunion with my mother.

I was around seven years old in that troubling recollection; my mother and I took the train to Chicago to visit my auntie Lucille, who met us at the station. As always, I was enthralled with the grandeur of the great Union Station, mostly ignoring the furtive adult conversation. At some point I found myself sitting in the backseat of my auntie's borrowed car with a young man. I saw his upturned face as he gazed out the car window bathed in that unique skyscraper-reflected light that defined my childhood experiences of the great city. He was clearly nervous, anxiously talking to no one in particular about his future life plans: he was taking welding classes; one day he hoped to be a pilot. *I want to fly,* he said. Looking at that delicate Ojibwe face, one could sense his insecurity, apparent even to a seven-year-old. I remember feeling embarrassed for him. Having tried to win my mother's attention myself, I knew the humiliation of those efforts all too well. My gaze turned to the tall buildings once again as I wondered at their canyons of windows and concrete. When I looked back, the young man was gone, and I was alone in the backseat. I caught bits of adult conversation. Aunt Lucille was telling my mother that the young man attended a vocational school for welding. Auntie said, *They say his welds don't hold.*

I never saw him again. As was so often the case, people floated in and out of our family, and I knew better than to ask questions. According to Pam, Bobby's daughter, he died of complications from asthma when she was about ten years old, in the early 1980s. Bobby lived with Pam, her younger sister, Michelle, and their mother, Marilyn, in an apartment in Chicago. My mother and father attended Bobby's funeral. *Hi, I'm your grandma,* my mother said to Pam, bending down to her height at the funeral home. Hearing they had no money to pay for the funeral, my mother wrote a check and promised to pay for a headstone. They never heard from her again. Bobby was buried in a potter's field; his grave remains unmarked. I related the story to my brother Bill and his wife, Donna; it turned out to be a revelation that shed light on a long-ago, painful event that happened when they lived outside Chicago during that time.

One Saturday afternoon, my parents showed up at their door unannounced; they explained they had been out for a drive and ended up there. It seemed implausible at the time since they lived nearly three hours away and they appeared to be unusually well dressed for a simple Saturday drive. Donna's relatives were visiting too, so they decided to make a party of it; they broke out the booze and my mother quickly got drunk, arguing with the other guests. Out of nowhere, she flew into a rage, accusing Donna's relatives (inaccurately) of making racist comments about Indians. *An Indian's an Indian,* she declared as she stormed out, my father following after her. Donna was hurt and devastated; for years she tried to understand what had happened. Although delayed, the final piece of the story offered an explanation and a bit of cold comfort. A year or so before my mother died, I introduced her to Pam. *Mom, this is your granddaughter, Bobby's daughter,* I told her. I watched her impassive face closely; if she understood the entirety of this development, she didn't let on. We'd learned one of her most closely guarded secrets; she had abandoned her child, just as her mother had. Cautiously, I questioned her later about Bobby. She explained she'd tried to get her firstborn son back with the legal help of Leon Feingold, whose office she cleaned years ago. But George would have none of it; he refused to give her custody of Bobby. Relatives and folks in the community, however, had no recollection of this. According to community memory, Bobby was homeless in Odanah, even as a little boy. I tracked down an elder from Bad River, Flavia, who took Bobby in and raised him for some time. Flavia had no recollection of my mother ever coming to Odanah to look for Bobby. According to Marilyn, Bobby's wife, he contacted my mother once during their marriage, asking her for financial help. She turned him down; afterward, he refused to speak of her again. I was stunned. I'm nearly certain my father would have accepted Bobby into our family. All those years of secrets, denial, rationalization, and guilt—how had she carried it all? I wondered. Although much had been explained, she remained a mystery.

I was shocked and stunned to discover that her behavior was nearly an identical reenactment of Cele's actions, actions over which she ruminated, a wound she nursed her entire life, forever blaming Cele for the entirety of the family's suffering. Like her mother before her, she was tragically placed in an impossible situation with an impossible choice. And like her mother she chose her own physical survival. Still stuck in the freeze response of a four-year-old's brain witnessing the attack on Cele, she really had no choice when she abandoned Bobby. She had no emotional or mental tools with which to process the trauma of witnessing her mother's attack and subsequent abandonment, the brutality and racism of the Sister School, her relationship with George, or her leaving Bobby.

In 2010 my mother had a stroke, and we moved her to a nursing home in Janesville, which pissed her off. Within a few weeks, she'd buffaloed the staff at the home, accusing them of stealing. She was a tiny woman, about five feet tall, and never weighed more than 105 pounds, but the director of the facility called me regularly, clearly shaken up by Mom's behavior. She screamed at staff, threw stuff at them, and completely alienated Bill and his family. I eventually had her transferred to a facility in Cincinnati closer to my home. She died on September 19, 2011. Bill and his family joined me by her side as she lay dying, her breath growing more and more shallow as the night wore on. She lay there quietly on her bed, her eyes closed as though asleep. She raised her eyebrows in question as I called to her; my voice seemed to be calling her back from a faraway place. During her lifetime, it seemed we could never get a good look at her face. Although we'd never spoken of it before, after her death Bill and I almost simultaneously expressed this to each other. In life, her eyes were obscured by her large, framed glasses; her thick helmet of short hair created an impenetrable barrier between herself and the world. Her white lady disguise melted away and we could see her at last for what she truly was, an Ojibwe woman. Before death was so close and she was still awake, she told me about a visit from Auntie Pat. *Honey,* I said, *Auntie passed away last summer, don't you remember?* She looked annoyed. *She most certainly did not,* she responded indignantly. *She was just sitting right there in that chair!* Foolishly, I'd thought I was all squared away about our lives together and her impending death. But something so momentous is never so simple. She died quietly. Gently blowing out her last breaths, until there were no more and she was still. My heart narrowed and for a moment the pain was almost unbearable.

She'd always insisted on being cremated. I'm not sure how she arrived at this wish since both the Catholic faith and traditional Ojibwe spirituality call for burial. *Cremation is clean,* she'd said. So we respected her wishes. We held a Mass in her honor, followed by a simple family gathering. My brother Bill was the first to speak at the gathering. Bill is a big man, and although he'd recently had a stroke, he made his way to his feet with the dignity that has sustained him his entire life, a dignity that imbued him with the strength to endure the withering, skinny love our mother doled out. *My mother wasn't an easy person to love,* he said. He stopped, overcome, but continued, *But I loved her.* And he and his family, wife and two fine sons, were there. They didn't allow her confusing, broken ways to break that bond. Although she'd often stated she'd like her ashes scattered in Lake Superior, our cousin Annie, a boss lady for the Medicine Lodge, told us it would be more respectful and appropriate to bury them. Graciously, the folks at Bad River dug a shallow hole in her father's grave, and I placed her ashes there, safe in her father's lap.

Ojibwe people believe that we may not be recognized in the

spirit world if we don't know our traditional Indian names. It's always pained me that the sisters made my mother forget hers. I had intended to have another naming ceremony for her. Unfortunately, time and circumstances didn't allow for this to happen. But Dora, an elder from Balsam Lake, Wisconsin, gave her a name that is used for babies who die before their naming and for people like my mother. The name is Zagima, child of love. Not long after her death, I sat at my desk thinking of her and our family's life. I spotted a stray piece of her loomed beadwork, a bit that survived my destructive scissors so long ago. *Why did you let me cut up all your beautiful beadwork?* I asked her as an adult. *Oh, why do we do the things we do?* she responded dreamily. The fragment of her work was meticulous, and like all good loom work it lay flat and strong. Her ambivalence about the beadwork and its connection to her heritage and the Sister School still haunted me. I thought of these things as I laid the pretty little scrap over my wrist and admired, once again, its strength and intricate design, a bit frayed on the ends but still durable after all these years. I noted that I had inadvertently placed the beads over that old jailhouse "squaw" tattoo made years ago during my month-long stint in the detention center. It was my defiant declaration of ethnic pride in the face of a racist world. My swagger wasn't very tough even back then, and the tattoo, barely legible, still gave me a twinge of embarrassment.

Seemingly out of nowhere, the idea of having the beadwork design tattooed over the "squaw" tattoo came to me. I'm not sure if Mom would have approved of me getting a tattoo at this stage in my life, but for some reason I was able to put her picture up afterward. Her framed image, the one we displayed at her funeral, lay facedown in my house for months after her death. I couldn't bring myself to look at it. Now I pass it every day; I don't have any woulda, coulda, shouldas about her death or our relationship. But all her fear and angst about her unexamined life still hangs in the air. She was never able to admit and know, while she was alive, that she had it all wrong. But now, having forgiven her and reconciled myself, I owed it to her to tell the whole story. My own ongoing healing is a part of that story.

Since she died, I've made several trips to Bad River in search of my own path forward. One journey in the fall after her death stands out in my memory. The rain that day began in the early morning and faded to a drizzle. As I walked over the wet grounds where my mother, grandmother, aunts, and uncles lived at St. Mary's, I couldn't get a bit of verse by Dylan Thomas out of my head: "And I rose / In rainy autumn / And walked abroad in a shower of all my days." Life here was harsh, and the day's rain seemed still filled with the bitter shower of my relatives' days with the sisters. I came here to grieve and understand their lost childhood days for them, something they were never permitted to do. Before I could begin to grieve for them, though, I got back in my car and drove through a snarl of tall weeds and bushes covering the old driveway leading to the crumbling remains of St. Mary's. The brush snapped back so that my rental car couldn't be seen from the road; it was quiet here. I could just see the steeple and bells of the pretty little church, freshly painted white and blue, above the trees. My mother often spoke of fights among the children over who would have the privilege of ringing the daily Angelus. The forest air worked on those prim Catholic bells, I imagined, transforming their song into something wild and beautiful, the sound flowing over the landscape. Although they lived on the reservation, the children dwelled light-years apart from their community and culture; hearing those bells was one of the few experiences they shared with their families.

So there, on that rainy day, I offered up prayers and smoked my demure old lady's pipe. My mother's trauma spirit is durable and resistant to many of my intellectual efforts to heal myself from the confusing anger and fear she passed on to me. It's a spirit that relentlessly demands my energy and attention. All I have to give it is ceremony. I've heard elders say that everything we need to heal ourselves is already here in our old ways if only we ask the Creator for help. When my little ceremony was complete, I got back in my rental car and began the rounds of visiting.

My cousin Marylu put me up in the spare room of her little rez home in Bad River. We talked about the impact of historical trauma on Native peoples. Marylu is a devout Catholic and alum of St. Mary's (the Sister School) and seemed a bit skeptical. The school had stopped boarding students when she attended, and overall her experience there was good. She described the school as a safe place, unlike the public school in Ashland. Her parents were strong, hardworking folks who never, in her words, "allowed me to blame who I was for what happened to me."

She understood, however, that not everyone was so lucky and she agreed to help me find out more about my family's history. Marylu is fiercely committed to her community, known throughout the reservation for her caring and hard work. She introduced me to elders who might remember something about my family. A distant cousin described the extreme poverty of my mother's childhood. "All of us were poor but your mom, Bernice, had it really bad; they lived in a shack with a dirt floor." Generally elders shared no fond memories of my mother; it seems she could never shake that "throwaway kid" jacket.

While staying with Marylu in Bad River, I attended a gathering of residents and employees of the tribe's social services department. According to the employees, the department is operating in "crisis mode" as they struggle to help the growing number of drug-affected babies born to tribal members. "In the past year, one-third of our babies on the reservation were born affected by drugs. Half of those infants were addicted to narcotics at birth," noted Esie Leoso, the now-retired director of Bad River Social Services. The problem, she explained, is not confined to the Bad River reservation. According to Leoso, at one point in 2013 all of the babies born addicted to narcotics that were being served by the neonatal unit at the hospital in Duluth were Indian. The Minnesota Department of Health reports that between 2012 and 2016 there was an eightfold higher rate of neonatal abstinence syndrome among infants born to Native American mothers compared to those born to white mothers. At the time of my visit Marylu worked part time in the social services administration office; seated with me during the gathering, she was visibly worried. "What will become of our people in the future? Who will care for all these children when they grow into adults with special needs?" she asked to no one in particular. The gathering was part of the department's efforts to reach out to the community for answers to this growing epidemic. I asked if learning about history such as that of my grandma's experience at the Sister School would help in such a crisis. "Addressing historic trauma is a big piece in recovery [from addiction]," Leoso said. "It would help give them a sense of the bigger scheme of things. Many of our young people are hopeless and think this is just the way it is supposed to be. Knowing the history would help them realize that powerlessness and low self-esteem are not part of our identity as Native people."

Later that evening I joined several ladies in a community sweat. My ancestors did not have this luxury. If they did, it would have been done in secret. It felt good to pray for them there. Before entering the lodge, we danced and briefly faced the darkness, acknowledging the spirits that dwelled there. This was not surrender; it was an understanding of the forces, good and bad, that govern us all. I was no longer just researching and studying the healing qualities of my Ojibwe ancestors; I'm now a participant in the traditions and ceremonies I've inherited.

But I had to keep pulling that thread of my mother's life. I couldn't let go of the notion that if I uncovered all her secrets, I would know what motivated her cruelty and inexplicable behavior. Why, for instance, didn't she reunite with Bobby? It was a chance to vindicate two generations of abandonment. And what about Cele?

Cele is remembered for her loud, profane mouth and voice that could be heard from a great distance. I learned that occasionally Cele would return to the reservation to pick medicines but never to visit her children. She would shove into a bed with one of our many cousins; Marylu recalled she would keep others awake as she prayed the entire rosary every night in bed. As a teenager before she married Grandpa Joe, Cele gave birth to a girl she named Geraldine, known to everyone as Bum. After marrying her last husband, Herschel, she brought the then-teenage Bum to live with them. When Bum became pregnant, however, Cele ordered her out of the house, declaring her actions sinful. Bum was later incarcerated as "incorrigible," and her child was adopted away. Cele's actions were the beginning of a cycle of abandonment. Did Cele come to believe that she and Indians were unfit to parent their own children? I wondered if she hoped her nightly prayers whispered into the darkness might somehow redeem her. Cele's sole remaining child, my uncle Russ, lives on the Nez Perce reservation in Idaho, where Cele and her husband, Herschel, settled after leaving Wisconsin. I'd met Russ only once before and decided I needed to speak with him about the book and his mother's history, so I made a trip to visit him in 2023.

The Palouse region of eastern Washington state where it borders Idaho appears to be one enormous contiguous wheat field in which a few isolated bits of land have been begrudgingly surrendered to a narrow road and a few solitary buildings. Nearly devoid of trees, the low hills roll endlessly into the horizon. The effect is unsettling. I began to wonder if my flight had landed me in the right place. Trucks and agricultural vehicles were the only signs of life. Where were the creatures of this unlikely world? I wondered uneasily. At last, the road began to descend steeply for a very long time. The narrow shoulders were dotted with upwardly aimed truck slopes filled with deep sand; the ends of the slopes were piled high with dirt and gravel. They were intended to stop runaway big rigs operated by drivers who foolishly choose to rely on brakes rather than transmissions to slow down. The slopes offered me little reassurance. Gratefully, I arrived at the bottom in Lewiston, Idaho, where the Clearwater and Snake Rivers meet.

Russ was a young teenager when his parents left the Great Lakes region. After joining his family in Idaho, he graduated from high school, married a Nez Perce girl named Juanita, and raised two sons, Shawn and JR. Uncle Russ remained in Idaho close to his sons and many grandchildren. We arranged to meet at one of his favorite haunts, a little roadside diner where Indian veterans gathered to tell about their years in the service to no one in particular. But being Indians, the customers all stopped and listened.

Russ is a tall man like his father, Herschel, with an open, pleasant face. Age, however, has diminished him. At eighty-six he's a bit unsteady, but he still has the bearing, a sort of natural authority, from his days as a lawman with the Bureau of Indian Affairs on the Nez Perce reservation. During my newspaper days, I often worked the cops beat. Russ is what cops would describe as "natural police." He confessed that he often missed the job, the human contact and connection with community. I have a feeling Russ was a really good cop. Today he lives with his adult son, JR, and their border collie, Hazel, in their family home, where he and Juanita raised the boys. Juanita is gone now; she passed away a few years ago after a long struggle with kidney disease. Faithfully, Russ drove her to dialysis treatments twice a week at the clinic in Lewiston, about half an hour from home, a trip that still ate up most of the day for them. Remnants of her garden roses poke through the weeds in front of their house. Seeing me filled Russ with emotion as he recalled his youth in and around Bad River. Later we sat on the deck of my rented cabin as he gazed out over the Clearwater River that wound its way through the valley below. We ate the fresh apricots I'd bought at the farmers market, spitting the pits far away into the tall grass so Hazel wouldn't try to eat them. I was surprised to learn that Cele made no secret of her marriage to Grandpa Joe, his drunkenness, and his treatment of her. Although she didn't tell Russ directly about that final awful attack, he learned about it as an adult from relatives. "Mom wasn't one to dwell on the past," Russ said. Once in Idaho she grew famous for her cooking and hard work; soon she was in demand at the best restaurants in that region. Russ remembers Cele as quick-tempered but affectionate and utterly intolerant of drunkenness. He recalled that she once threw a butcher knife at him in anger, but realizing he'd been hit, she cried out, "Let me see, my boy! Are you hurt?" Russ had only a scratch.

Cele's undiagnosed stomach cancer caused her great pain in her final two years of life, but she seldom complained. She worked until she could no longer stand. In the only photo we have of her, she wears pants and stands in the Idaho woods with Herschel and her two sons. She smiles easily at the camera; her comfort and happiness are palpable. She insisted on being buried in the little town of Presque Isle in Wisconsin, where the Upper Peninsula begins, near the boardinghouse she and Herschel ran when they were first married. "Don't take me back to Bad River," she insisted on her deathbed. Later I found her grave in Herschel's family plot just outside town. Herschel transported her body back to Presque Isle himself. He died a few years later from emphysema and is buried next to her. Cele was fifty-six years old when she died. For a long time I thought of Cele mainly in terms of Joe's attack, which I envisioned as a windigo that he passed on to her, poisoning her life. I see now she was so much more than that. In the end, she'd appeased that windigo and wrestled love and safety from life in her years with Herschel and their family.

I would never explain Cele's and my mother's behavior with my endless journalist's poking. This is not that kind of story. Despite my mother's ambivalence about pursuing the white man's dream of family and success, she stayed. She ensured we were housed, clothed, and fed, something she could never have dreamed of as a child. In the end, however, she and Cele couldn't help being the people they were, mysterious mixtures of cruelty and love. And as I move forward, I see that both these women left their marks on me in ways that continue to surprise and sometimes unsettle me. All three of us turned to white men for survival and safety, the best choices available to us at the time. Cele's and Bernice's choices were far more fraught than mine, but in the end all of us found love, a measure of acceptance, and even happiness. Our marriages reflect a bittersweet allegory for U.S. Indian history in general and Indian women in particular. We all found out the hard way that proximity to whiteness didn't make us white, especially in the settler world. But we survived and protected our culture as best we could, passing it along to our children whenever possible. I am the luckiest, of course. John and I continue to work our way through the disease of alcoholism, my drinking, and his enabling. We use the tools of recovery and Ojibwe culture to live more healthy lives. For me, the enigmatic yet simple gifts of Ojibwe spirituality nurture and sustain me and my family.

But there is seldom a radiant vision or dream filled with instructions from the ancestors. For instance, not long ago, I simply found myself guiding material through the sewing machine; I'd been at work for a couple of hours before I noticed I was building a jingle dress, my jingle dress. I can't say for sure when I began to accumulate the huge pile of 365 jingles made from snuff can lids shaped into cones that comprise the *zibaaska'iganagoode,* the dress of exploding sound in the Ojibwe language. As is so often the case with matters relating to my Ojibwe culture and spirituality, I found myself engaged in a complex project without any conscious memory of deciding to begin. From experience, I know that although my importance and agenda loom large in my own mind, it was likely that the jingle dress project was part of a larger undisclosed plan.

So I went along with this vague directive from the universe, confident that the greater purpose would emerge later.

The origins of the jingle dress and dance are passed down through Ojibwe oral history. Like most Indigenous languages, Ojibwe is not a written language. According to the teachings, a dream came to an Ojibwe father whose daughter was sick with the Spanish flu sometime between 1918 and 1920. Indians were especially hard hit during the great pandemic; entire populations of some Native Alaskan villages were wiped out. In the dream, the father saw a woman dancing in springlike steps but always keeping one foot on the earth. The dancer in his vision wore a dress covered in bits of metal that created explosive sounds. He built the dress for his daughter as the spirits had instructed. The daughter put on the dress and began to dance like the woman in her father's vision. As she danced, she began to feel better, eventually making a full recovery. Soon, the dress and dance gained a reputation for healing and spread to communities throughout Ojibwe country.

Today, Indian women from many tribes make and dance in the jingle dress. Although they may include elements unique to their cul-

tures in the design, the spirit of the jingle dress reflects women's healing power over life; recognizing this great responsibility, the dancer
conducts herself with dignity and humility and the knowledge that
she is a symbol of this power. In contemporary Indian communities, women are utilizing this traditional tool of empowerment to
draw attention to environmental concerns, high rates of missing and
murdered Indigenous women, and other issues. Scores of women in
jingle dresses, for instance, danced for the water protectors opposing
the Dakota Access Pipeline camped near the Standing Rock reservation in North Dakota.

As the daughter of an Ojibwe woman and a white father, however, I am often torn by paradoxical desires to at once order and clas-
sify life while accepting and celebrating its great mystery. Regardless,
I continued building my jingle dress, soothed by the faith that more
details would make themselves known. Sometimes I streamed old
movies, like those my mother and I watched together, during my
hours at the sewing machine. We loved films with dark and inscru-
table themes and characters as well as those featuring the triumph
of underdogs or villainous greed and injustice receiving their come-
uppance. In the safety of our darkened living room seated before
the television, she would often describe her own underdog story of
surviving life at the Sister School. We also bonded over our famous
bouts of incapacitating laughter and a deep appreciation for the
absurd. Once we began laughing over an idiotic remark while carrying a heavy couch up a flight of stairs. *Goddamn it, stop laughing,*
my mother begged as she collapsed into laughter, her knees rubbery
beneath her. My dad found us prostrate mid-carry, still laughing
while the couch rested on our laps. *What the hell's the matter with you
damned women?* he'd demanded, which only made us laugh more. I
thought of all these things as I built my dress, carefully attaching the
365 jingles, one at a time, one for each day of the year.

The dress's meaning was coming into focus. I was sewing our
story as well as our salvation into its seams. After finishing, I feasted
the dress with traditional foods including manoomin (wild rice),
venison, and strawberries. Finally, in August of that year, I traveled

to the annual Bad River Manoomin Harvest festival and powwow, where my *niiyawen'enh*, Dennis and Cleo White, the couple who gave me my Ojibwe name, which is Babaa-anikwad, blessed my dress of exploding sound. My name roughly translates to "changing clouds" or "changing sky."

I watched the men at the powwow as they gathered around their drums and prepared their dance regalia. I marveled at their society, their tenderness with each other, and their uninhibited joy in seeing friends. How they laughed! I was reminded of the observations written so long ago in *The Jesuit Relations* describing how Indian men took such delight in greeting their friends and spending time visiting. It's gratifying to see that our joy in being human together has survived the white man's efforts to extinguish this essential part of Ojibwe nature. It continues to nurture and sustain us.

The powwow grounds at Bad River where the manoomin festival is held are within sight of St. Mary's boarding school. Although the building was razed long ago, its cement foundation was still visible among the weeds. Like its overgrown basement, the legacy of the school and its influence on our lives are still with us. Although my mother died in 2011 at the age of eighty-six, I felt her presence with me as I waited with the other dancers to enter the powwow circle. During her lifetime she could never have dreamed of wearing the jingle dress or dancing its healing dance. So I danced for her. My aging knees didn't allow me to dance with the springlike steps envisioned by the Ojibwe father who dreamed the ceremony, but I moved briskly nonetheless. I danced. More than vindication, my dance was a celebration of being an *Anishinaabekwe:* an Ojibwe woman. Surrounded by friends and family, we laughed and celebrated together. Not only have we survived, but we have flourished. This was the message of my jingle dress. I looked at the people, *my* people, as I danced. I saw the care they had put into their regalia, and the care they had put in themselves and their relationships. The drum was loud and the arbor well shaded, beyond which I could see the birch and poplar trees that had survived their own genocide and grew straight and tall. The drumbeats—like the trees, the arbor, like us—rose from the ground, too. Not rising, and certainly not stand-ing, but felt nonetheless, were the ruins of the Sister School. Just a whisper of the foundation, murmuring among the hazel brush and scrub that will soon overwhelm it. It's still there. I can see it. But barely, among the growth that dwarfs it.

ACKNOWLEDGMENTS

This book began for me even before I learned to write, when I sat on the floor, using a black crayon to record symbols on the underside of my family's kitchen table. Although I didn't know it then, I'd already embarked on the quest my mother set out for me. It's been an irresistible, challenging pilgrimage to a place not often accessible to Native people. Were it not for the encouragement, generosity, help, and support of others, I would not have made it. It's difficult to know where to start in thanking and acknowledging them all. I begin by offering a *Chi-migwech* (big thank-you) to David Treuer, writer and editor at Pantheon Books, for believing in me and helping me in ways that continue to humble and amaze. His dedication and patience as I struggled with technical and life challenges along the way have been phenomenal and give me hope for the future of Native American writers. Adam Eaglin and Isabel Mendía of the Cheney Agency walked me patiently and expertly through the whole challenging proposal and book-writing process, an undertaking that put them to the test. Remarkably, they showed me only support and kindness.

As always, my husband, John Metz, gave so many gifts that they are difficult to enumerate. His unconditional love, forgiveness, and acceptance and help with family and child-care duties gave me the time, courage, and faith to finish a life's work. His endless grace when the words woke me up at night, clamoring to be written down, has been remarkable. To my children, Rosa and Danny, dearest hearts, I am grateful for the love, patience, and joy you gave me along the way. My brother Bill has been an inspiration in dignity and kindness as he endured my endless questions about our family and history, questions I know brought up difficult memories at times. I'm grateful for my many cousins in Bad River, Delphine Hurd, Marylu Salawater, Lynn Bigboy, Faye, Annie, and Melvin Maday, and so many others who have been open and welcoming, always willing to share their bounty of memory, humor, and tradition. Truly, you and the Bad River community embody the spirit of home, Mashkiiziibii, Medicine River, that place that feeds Ojibwe body and spirit. *Chi-migwech* to Dennis and Cleo White for loving me through my tumultuous college years to the present, selflessly guiding me along in ceremony and healing. I'd also like to thank Jane Isay, a wise guide and mentor; Julia Rymut, good friend; James Simon (Mishibinijima), who helped in my early sobriety, directing me to where I needed to be; and my colleagues at *Indian Country Today,* now called ICT News. The editor at large, Mark Trahant of the Shoshone Bannock Tribes, longtime friend, mentor, and colleague, has helped me in innumerable ways, always reminding me that Native people can do this thing called journalism and to do so is to be a part of something truly important and greater than oneself. It's gratifying to share in bringing out our stories, nudging the needle toward if not justice and reckoning, at least truth, which always needs to come first. I'm forever grateful to the many survivors of Indian boarding schools, such as Tom Deragon, Frank Dickenson, Lorna Keepsready, Bryan Brewer, Tim Giago, Willie Littlechild, Basil Braveheart, Emma Jean Brown, and so many others throughout Indian country, who let me into their lives, bravely and generously sharing their stories. I also want to acknowledge the work of the National Native American Boarding School Healing Coalition and its leaders Deb Parker, Denise Lajimodiere, Jim LaBelle, and others who began championing boarding school awareness and justice decades ago, helping to get us to where we are now. I'm grateful for their ongoing generosity in sharing their time and resources. Thanks also to my uncle Russell Spencer for his kindness and openness. My great hope and prayer is that this book helps shine some light on this important history and moves us all a few steps closer toward truth, healing, and reconciliation. This book was written and edited by Ojibwe people; the cover design and author's photo were created by the Ojibwe artists Sarah Agaton Howes and Nedahness Rose Greene. *Migwiich.* We've always known we belong here. I am grateful to my father, Charles Gordon Pember, who gave me perhaps the greatest, most important gift of all, unconditional love—the knowledge it exists and is deserved. Bernice, my mother, here is your story at last; I hope I've done it justice.

NOTE ON SOURCES

Some quotations are from conversations with my mother and relatives long before I began recording and writing down this information. Fortunately, my mother repeated her stories often throughout our lives together, which helped cement them in my memory. From 2000 onward, I began writing down our talks and discussions in anticipation of this book. I corroborated this information whenever possible with relatives who are still living, but in the interest of full disclosure I reflect this by using italics for their quotations. In all other cases, all quotations and information are taken from my interviews with sources, written or recorded, archival documents in the National Archives and Records Administration, the Catholic Bureau of Indian Missions, the Carlisle Indian School Digital Resource Center hosted by Dickinson College, the Jesuit Relations archives hosted by Creighton University, U.S. government archives, and many others in addition to numerous academic journals, books, and news articles that are listed in the endnotes.

NOTES

Introduction

5 **For 150 years:** *Federal Indian Boarding School Initiative Investigative Report, Vol. 1*, Bureau of Indian Affairs, May 2022, 93, bia.gov.

6 **Oklahoma contained seventy-six:** Ibid., 83.

6 **A large proportion of the cost:** Ibid., 48.

6 **The government directly provided:** Chapter 119 of the 49th Congress, Indian General Allotment Act, Feb. 8, 1887, 3.

6 **Missionaries went on to play:** Catherine O'Donnell, "Jesuits in the North American Colonies and the United States: Faith, Conflict, Adaptation," *Brill Research Perspectives in Jesuit Studies,* April 17, 2020, brill.com.

6 **From the very beginning:** Ibid.

6 **Indigenous or pagan people living:** "Doctrine of Discovery," Upstander Project, 2024.

7 **"Many [families] refuse all aid":** Martin Marty, "The Indian Problem and the Catholic Church," *Catholic World,* Feb. 1889.

7 **Some still board Indians:** *Federal Indian Boarding School Initiative Investigative Report, Vol. 1,* 8.

7 **federal Indian education policy:** Special Subcommittee on Indian Education, *Indian Education: A National Tragedy, a National Challenge* (Washington, D.C.: U.S. Government Printing Office, 1969), 143.

8 **"Let it be spread abroad":** George Washington, "President of United States General George Washington Speech to the Five Nations Delegation at Philadelphia," April 25, 1792, Papers of the War Department, 1784–1800, wardepartmentpapers.org.

8 **"extirpate the savage in order":** William B. Cairns, ed., *Benjamin Franklin's Autobiography* (New York: Longmans, Green, 1909), 134.

8 **"wear civilized clothes":** "Indian Land Under the Dawes Act of 1887," nebraskastudies.org.

8 **"whites used the land":** Thomas Hart Benton, Congressional Globe, 29:1, 1846, 917–18.

8 **"Let a philosophic observer":** Jefferson to William Ludlow, Sept. 6, 1824, National Archives.

9 **In 1819, Congress enacted:** "An Act Making Provision for the Civilization of the Indian Tribes Adjoining the Frontier Settlements," 15th U.S. Cong., 2nd Sess., March 3, 1819.

9 **This was a deep irony:** Elizabeth Prine Pauls, "Native American: Indigenous Peoples of Canada and United States," in *Britannica*, March 28, 2024.

9 **In 1891, Congress authorized:** Erin Blakemore, "A Century of Trauma at U.S. Boarding Schools for Native American Children," *National Geographic*, July 9, 2021.

9 **"The Secretary of the Interior, may":** "Regulations for Withholding Rations for Nonattendance at Schools," 25 U.S.C. § 283, March 3, 1893.

10 **"all traits of Indian culture":** Brenda Child, *Boarding School Seasons: American Indian Families, 1900–1940* (Lincoln: University of Nebraska Press, 1998), 5.

10 **"The kids would end up":** David Wallace Adams, *Education for Extinction: American Indians and the Boarding School Experience, 1875–1928* (Lawrence: University Press of Kansas, 1995), 134.

10 **"I can remember when I":** Ibid., 110.

10 **"I just hate to get the checks":** Child, *Boarding School Seasons*, 29.

11 **"It would be pretty bad":** Ibid., 47.

11 **"It seems it would be easier":** Ibid., 50.

11 **The heyday of the off-reservation:** Brett Lee Shelton and Michael Johnson, "Trigger Points: Current State of Research on History, Impacts, and Healing Related to the United States' Indian Industrial/Boarding School Policy," Native American Rights Fund, Nov. 2019, 23.

11 **By the 1920s about 76 percent:** Jenna Kunze, "Q&A: Darren Lone Fight, Founding Director, Center for the Futures of Native Peoples at Dickinson College," *Native News Online*, Feb. 25, 2023.

11 **"The labor of [Indian] children":** Lewis Meriam et al., *The Problem of Indian Administration: Report of a Survey Made at the Request of Hubert Work, Secretary of the Interior, and Submitted to Him, February 21, 1928* (Baltimore: Johns Hopkins Press, 1928), 13.

11 **Many children died from communicable diseases:** Mary Annette Pember, "Sending Them Home to Die," ICT News, Jan. 29, 2024, ictnews.org.

11 **the Department of the Interior has identified:** *Federal Indian Boarding School Initiative Investigative Report, Vol. 2,* Bureau of Indian Affairs, July 2024, 15 and 16, bia.gov.

12 **Canada operated 139 federal schools:** "Your Questions Answered About Canada's Residential School System," *CBC News*, June 4, 2021, cbc.ca.

12 **Canadian authorities have detected:** Carina Xue Luo, "Missing Children of Indian Residential Schools," StoryMaps, Feb. 24, 2024.

12 **U.S. boarding school policies:** Mary Annette Pember, "Canada, US Differ on Boarding Schools," ICT News, July 18, 2021, ictnews.org.

12 **It wasn't until the discovery:** Courtney Dickson and Bridgette Watson, "Remains of 215 Children Found Buried at Former B.C. Residential School, First Nation Says," *CBC News,* May 28, 2021, cbc.ca.

12 **In June 2021, Secretary of the Interior:** U.S. Department of the Interior, June 6, 2021, doi.gov.

12 **The agency issued a report in 2022:** *Federal Indian Boarding School Initiative Investigative Report, Vol. 1,* Bureau of Indian Affairs, May 2022, bia.gov.

12 **"Indian boarding school policies":** Kalle Benallie, "A Look at the Nearly Two-Year 'Road to Healing,'" ICT News, Nov. 13, 2023.

13 **cultural and familial disruption:** *Federal Indian Boarding School Initiative Investigative Report, Vol. 1,* 89.

13 **The school closed in 1969:** Dan Stockman, "US Congregations Face Their Complicity in Trauma of Native Boarding Schools," Global Sisters Report, July 21, 2022, globalsistersreport.org.

13 **The Bad River reservation is located:** Sister Mileta Ludwig, *A Chapter of Franciscan History: The Sisters of the Order of Saint Francis of Perpetual Adoration, 1849–1949* (New York: Bookman Associates, 1950), 234–84.

13 **Bad River lands are on a continental divide:** Elizabeth Borneman, "North American Continental Divide," *Geography Realm,* March 29, 2021, geographyrealm.com; "Continental Divide," Travel Wisconsin, travelwisconsin.com.

13 **the Everglades of the North:** "Kakagon and Bad River Sloughs Recognized as a Wetland of International Importance," Bad River Tribe, April 5, 2012, badriver-nsn.gov.

13 **Jesuit missionaries accompanied:** Jane C. Busch, "People and Places: A Human History of the Apostle Islands," Midwest Regional Office, National Park Service, U.S. Department of the Interior, 2008, 83.

13 **Wisconsin was, for the most part:** Ludwig, *Chapter of Franciscan History,* 235–49.

14 **Indigenous peoples were present:** Amorin Mello, "Early Settlement of the Bad River Indian Reservation," Chequamegon History, March 9, 2016.

14 **Ojibwe first lived in the east:** Busch, "People and Places," 32–72.

14 **People fished year-round:** Michelle M. Steen-Adams, Nancy E. Langston, David J. Mladenoff, "Logging the Great Lakes Indian Reservations: The Case of the Bad River Band of Ojibwe," *American Indian Culture and Research Journal* 34, no. 1 (2010): 41–66, nancylangston.net.

14 **When the winter hunting season:** Busch, "People and Places," 10.

14 **"There is one thing":** Steen-Adams, Langston, and Mladenoff, "Logging the Great Lakes Indian Reservations."

14 **Ojibwe occupied more than twenty-two million acres:** Ibid.

14 **The population of the seven bands:** Commissioner of Indian Affairs, *Fifty-Eighth Annual Report* (Washington, D.C.: U.S. Government Printing Office, 1889), 302–6.

15 **By the early twentieth century, approximately:** Busch, "People and Places," 65.

15 **Despite timber company promises:** Steen-Adams, Langston, and Mla-
    denoff, "Logging the Great Lakes Indian Reservations."

Chapter 1: Poking

19 **The bureau was founded in 1874:** "Bureau of Catholic Indian Missions,"
    Raynor Memorial Libraries, Marquette University.
22 **"By the time these lines":** Sister Macaria Murphy to Ketcham, Jan. 3,
    1934, St. Mary's, Odanah, Wis., Bureau of Catholic Indian Missions
    Archives, Raynor Memorial Libraries.

Chapter 2: Life at the Sister School

25 **discipline in Ojibwe households:** Margaret Connell Szasz, *Indian Educa-
    tion in the American Colonies, 1607–1783* (Lincoln: University of Nebraska
    Press, 1988), 17–19.
25 **called a ghost leg:** Frances Densmore, *Chippewa Customs* (St. Paul: Min-
    nesota Historical Society Press, 1979), 58, 59.
27 **Although it was new and frightening:** Adams, *Education for Extinction*,
    8–9.
27 **Through force or poverty-fueled necessity:** "Boarding School Body
    Count," *Sahan Journal*, July 26, 2021, sahanjournal.com.
27 **"invade, search out, capture":** Nicholas V, "Romanus Pontifex," Papal
    Encyclicals Online, papalencyclicals.net.
28 **In a stunning example:** Ivan Luvier Garcia, "Historical Perspectives
    on Bartolomé de las Casas" (master's thesis, California State University,
    Dominguez Hills, 2017), 8.
28 **Spain in the fifteenth century:** Paola Tartakoff, "Expelled from Spain:
    July 31, 1492," *Exploring Hate*, PBS, July 26, 2022, pbs.org.
28 **Long before 1492, Jews and Muslims:** David M. Gitlitz, "Conversos and
    the Spanish Inquisition," *Secret Files of the Inquisition*, PBS, 2007, pbs.org.
28 **Ferdinand and Isabella established:** Joan-Lluis Palos, "To Seize Power
    in Spain, Queen Isabella Had to Play It Smart," *National Geographic*,
    March 28, 2019, nationalgeographic.org.
28 **Indigenous people were there:** Gillian Brockell, "Here Are the Indige-
    nous People Christopher Columbus and His Men Could Not Annihilate,"
    Washington Post, Oct. 14, 2019.
29 **"These people are very simple":** Christopher Columbus, *Journal of Chris-
    topher Columbus (During His First Voyage, 1492–93): And Documents Relat-
    ing the Voyages of John Cabot and Gaspar Corte Real*, ed. Clements Markham
    (Cambridge University Press, 2010).
29 **Columbus established a fort:** Brockell, "Here Are the Indigenous People
    Christopher Columbus and His Men Could Not Annihilate."
29 **"They slaughtered anyone and everyone":** Bartolomé de las Casas, *A
    Short Account of the Destruction of the Indies* (New York: Penguin Classics,
    1999).
29 **Casas won limited support:** Ibid.
30 **Squanto's kidnapping is seldom included:** Tony Tekaroniake Evans,

"Who Was Squanto, and What Was His Role in the First Thanksgiving?," History.com, Nov. 21, 2022.

30 **Baron Justinian von Welz:** Wolfgang Bruel, *Theological Tenets and Motives of the Mission* (Amsterdam: Rodopi, 2012), 42.

30 **Pope Paul III's 1537 declaration:** Pope Paul III, "Sublimis Deus: On the Enslavement and Evangelization of Indians 1537," Papal Encyclicals Online.

30 **Thus, Christian conversion, civilization, and assimilation:** "First Encounters: Native Americans and Christians," Pluralism Project, Harvard University, pluralism.org.

31 **Children were forcibly educated:** Carey McWilliams, *The Indian in the Closet* (New York: Duell, Sloan and Pearce, 1946).

31 **In 2015, Serra was canonized:** Carly Severn, " 'How Do We Heal': Toppling the Myth of Junípero Serra," KQED, July 7, 2020.

31 **Unlike other Christian missionaries:** *The Jesuit Relations and Allied Documents: Travels and Explorations of the Jesuit Missionaries in New France, 1610–1791,* vol. 3, *Acadia, 1611–1616* (Cleveland: Burrows Brothers, 1897).

32 **"Their religion consists only in superstitions":** Alan Ziajka, "The Jesuits and Native Communities," *Pierless Bridges,* Sept. 29, 2022; *Jesuit Relations and Allied Documents,* vol. 3, *Acadia, 1611–1616;* Joseph Jouvency, *Concerning the Country and Manners of the Canadians or Savages of New France* (Rome: printed from the history of the Society of Jesus, book 15, part 5, Printing house of Giorgion Placko, 1710).

32 **Ojibwe kept extensive accounts:** Densmore, *Chippewa Customs.*

32 **Jesuits began pressing the Indians:** Victoria Jackson, "Silent Diplomacy: Wendat Boys' Adoptions at the Jesuit Seminary, 1636–1642," *Journal of the Canadian Historical Association* 27, no. 1 (2016).

32 **In 1634, Andrew White established:** Edward Devitt, "Andrew White," in *The Catholic Encyclopedia* (New York: Robert Appleton, 1912).

33 **Marquette teamed up with:** "Jacques Marquette: Jesuit Explorer," in *Britannica,* March 25, 2024, britannica.com; "The Mississippi Voyage of Jolliet and Marquette," in *Early Narratives of the Northwest, 1634–1699,* ed. Louise Phelps Kellogg (New York: Charles Scribner's Sons, 1917).

33 **The Jesuits' texts were among:** Michael Swan, "The Jesuit Relations Opened Up the New World to Europe," *Catholic Register,* Sept. 15, 2011.

33 **"If all men are created free and equal":** Frank Thilly, *A History of Philosophy* (New York: Henry Holt and Company, 1914), 389–90; Donald A. Grinde and Bruce E. Johansen, *Exemplar of Liberty: Native America and the Evolution of Democracy* (Los Angeles: American Indian Studies Center, 1991).

34 **Indeed, this fantasy endures:** Helen Gardner, "Explainer: The Myth of the Noble Savage," *Conversation,* Feb. 24, 2016.

34 **greed or violence:** Michel de Montaigne: "Of Cannibals" (ca. 1580).

34 **Missionary efforts in the New World:** Nicholas P. Cushner, "The Jesuits in Colonial America: 1565–1767," Fundación Ignacio Larramendi, 12–27, larramendi.es.

34 **"Indians treat their children":** Pierre Biard, "Letter from Father Pierre Biard to the Reverend Father Provincial at Paris," in *Jesuit Relations and Allied Documents, 1610–1791*, vol. 4, *Quebec, 1612*.

35 **The relationship between mother and daughter:** Densmore, *Chippewa Customs*, 48–61; Johann Georg Kohl, *Life Among the Lake Superior Ojibway* (St. Paul: Minnesota Historical Society, 1985), chap. 1.

36 **"When they first heard":** Jouvency, *Concerning the Country and Manners of the Canadians or Savages of New France*.

36 **"those who hold things together":** Brenda Child, *Holding Our World Together: Ojibwe Women and the Survival of Community* (New York: Penguin Books, 2013), 63, 64.

36 **"Women continuously worked":** Ibid., xiv, xv.

36 **"Ojibwe ideas about property":** Ibid., 23–30.

36 **"When early travelers and settlers":** Ibid., 63.

37 **The most important and essential element:** Mary Annette Pember, "The Power of Ojibwe Women," ICT News, Aug. 4, 2017, ictnews.org.

37 **Ojibwe women have survived:** Child, *Holding Our World Together*, 30, 63.

37 **"They are never in a hurry":** Jouvency, *Concerning the Country and Manners of the Canadians or Savages of New France*.

38 **Work and menial labor:** Herman J. Viola, *Thomas L. McKenney: Architect of America's Early Indian Policy, 1816–1830* (Chicago: Swallow Press, 1974), 186–87.

38 **In solving the country's Indian problem:** Special Subcommittee on Indian Education, *Indian Education*, 143.

38 **The weapon was aimed:** Viola, *Thomas L. McKenney*, 33–37.

Chapter 3: The Sister School Comes to Odanah

41 **The United States began paying:** Knox to Washington, July 7, 1789, Founders Online.

41 **"teaching them the great duties":** Nathan S. Chapman, "Forgotten Federal-Missionary Partnerships: New Light on the Establishment Clause," *Notre Dame Law Review* 92, no. 2 (2020).

41 **in 1886, Unitarians successfully created:** Francis Paul Prucha, *The Great Father* (Lincoln: University of Nebraska Press, 1984), 51; "A UU Action Network, Unitarian Indian Boarding School and WA Interfaith Response to Burials," JUUstice Washington, July 27, 2021.

42 **McKenney's work laid the groundwork:** Viola, *Thomas L. McKenney*, 1–92.

42 **The number of religious Indian boarding schools:** Adams, *Education for Extinction*, 64; Viola, *Thomas L. McKenney*, 186–97.

42 **"the habit of labor":** Viola, *Thomas L. McKenney*, 186–87.

42 **"Labor is painful":** Ibid., 187.

42 **He complained that once removed:** Ibid., 186–95.

42 **Indian people were not necessarily averse:** Matthew Fletcher and Wenona Singel, "Indian Children and the Federal Tribal Trust Relationship," *Nebraska Law Review* 95, no. 4 (2017).

43 **According to the U.S. census:** P. K. Whelpton, "A History of Population Growth in the United States," *Scientific Monthly,* Oct. 1948, 277–88.

43 **The government failed in its mission:** Jessica Keating, "The Assimilation, Removal, and Elimination of Native Americans," Teaching Human Dignity, University of Notre Dame, 2020, nd.edu.

43 **Congress passed the Dawes or Allotment Act:** "Land Tenure History," Indian Land Tenure Foundation, iltf.org.

43 **"The only alternative left":** Adams, *Education for Extinction,* 19.

43 **Manifest Destiny, a collective social decree:** John L. O'Sullivan, "Annexation," *United States Magazine and Democratic Review,* July 1845.

44 **thirteen million acres:** Elizabeth Stawicki, "Supreme Court Upholds Mille Lacs Treaty Rights," Minnesota Public Radio, March 24, 1999.

44 **Although Ojibwe understood:** Steen-Adams, Langston, and Mladenoff, "Logging the Great Lakes Indian Reservations."

44 **The anthropologist James Clifton:** James A. Clifton, "Wisconsin Death March: Explaining the Extremes in Old Northwest Indian Removal," in *Transactions of the Wisconsin Academy of Sciences, Arts and Letters,* Vol. 75, (1987): 1–40.

45 **The delegation secured a meeting:** "Buffalo and O-Sho-Ga Protest Forced Removal," Wisconsin Historical Society, wisconsinhistory.org; Benjamin C. Armstrong, *Early Life Among the Indians: Reminiscences from the Life of Benjamin C. Armstrong, 1892* (La Pointe, Wis.: Mad Island Communications, 2018), 7–17.

45 **The Bad River reservation was established:** Busch, "People and Places," 31.

45 **Ojibwe have always called it Mashkiiziibii:** "Hearings Before the Subcommittee on Roads of the Committee on Public Works," House of Representatives, 84th Cong. (Washington, D.C.: U.S. Government Printing Office, 1956), 55.

45 **Finally, at the mouth of the Bad River:** "Bad River Wisconsin, Fishing Reports and Conditions," upnorthfishing.com.

45 **By 1877 the rail to Chicago:** Amorin Mello, "Ashland, Wisconsin: Its Early Days," *Chequamegon History,* Nov. 29, 2016, chequamegonhistory .com.

46 **The events leading up to:** Steen-Adams, Langston, and Mladenoff, "Logging the Great Lakes Indian Reservations," 41.

46 **That problem was the barrier:** Prucha, *Great Father,* 50–55.

47 **They immediately began offering:** Ludwig, *Chapter of Franciscan History,* 235–49.

47 **In addition to reading and writing:** Commissioner of Indian Affairs, *Fifty-Eighth Annual Report* (Washington, D.C.: U.S. Government Printing Office, 1889), 301–2.

48 **The sisters traveled to Bad River:** "President Ulysses S. Grant and Federal Indian Policy," National Park Service, nps.gov.

48 **The cheapest solution to the Indian problem:** Adams, *Education for Extinction,* 263–69.

48   **"The greatest danger hanging over":** Carl Schurz, "Present Aspects of the Indian Problem," *North American Review,* July 1881.

48   **Reformers also called for:** Adams, *Education for Extinction,* 23.

49   **Custer was defeated:** "Treaty of Fort Laramie," National Archives, archives .gov.

49   **"The only good Indian":** Andrew G. Gardner, "The Indian War," *Colonial Williamsburg Journal* (Spring 2010), research.colonialwilliamsburg.org.

49   **Together the men embarked:** Erin Blakemore, "Native Americans Have General Sherman to Thank for Their Exile to Reservations," History.com, July 11, 2023.

49   **In October 1876:** "Fighting for the Black Hills: Understanding Indigenous Perspectives on the Great Sioux War of 1876–1877," National Park Service, nps.gov.

49   **the Supreme Court ruled in 1980:** *United States v. Sioux Nation of Indians,* 448 U.S. 371 (1980).

50   **Parker supported the reservation system:** "President Ulysses S. Grant and Federal Indian Policy."

50   **Tribes were forced to remain:** Mark Hirsch, "1871: The End of Indian Treaty-Making," *American Indian* 15, no. 2 (Summer/Fall 2014), american indianmagazine.org.

50   **Thereafter, the federal government:** "President Ulysses S. Grant and Federal Indian Policy"; J. Weston Phippen, "Kill Every Buffalo You Can! Every Buffalo Dead Is an Indian Gone," *Atlantic,* May 13, 2016; John Mark Hansen, "The Complicated History of Gen. Philip Sheridan," *Chicago Tribune,* Sept. 21, 2017; "The Biography of Ely Parker," pbs.org.

50   **Article 7 of the 1868 Fort Laramie Treaty:** "Treaty of Fort Laramie."

50   **"Defeat, imprisonment and exile":** Carlisle Indian School Digital Resource Center, carlisle.dickinson.edu.

51   **"In Indian civilization I am a Baptist":** Richard Henry Pratt, *Battlefield and Classroom: Four Decades with the American Indian, 1867–1904* (Norman: University of Oklahoma Press, 2003), 335.

51   **"Even wild turkeys":** Lindsay Peterson, " 'Kill the Indian, Save the Man': Americanization Through Education: Richard Henry Pratt's Legacy" (honors thesis, Colby College History Department, 2013), digitalcommons .colby.edu/honorstheses/696.

51   **In 1879, Pratt founded:** Carlisle Indian School Digital Resource Center; Adams, *Education for Extinction,* 41–64; Pratt, *Battlefield and Classroom,* 335.

51   **Ezra Hayt ordered Pratt:** Pratt, *Battlefield and Classroom,* 222.

51   **Pratt made the trip to the Dakotas:** Ibid., 220.

52   **the school was more like a military training camp:** Ibid., 221–29.

52   **"How lonesome the big boys and girls":** Luther Standing Bear, *My Indian Boyhood* (Lincoln: University of Nebraska Press, 1931).

52   **"would start the girls to crying":** Adams, *Education for Extinction,* 109–34.

53   **Many children died or ran away:** Adams, *Education for Extinction,* 174–83.

53   **"Pratt used the panopticon":** Landis, recorded interview by author, Sept. 15–16, 2023, Carlisle, Pa.; "The Panopticon," Bentham Project, ucl .ac.uk.

53 **It was from this vantage point:** *Indian Helper,* 1885–1900, Carlisle Indian School Digital Resource Center.

53 **The man had spies among students and staff:** Ibid.

54 **Rather than learning useful skills:** Jacqueline Fear-Segal, *Boarding School Blues: The Man on the Bandstand at Carlisle Indian Industrial School* (Lincoln: University of Nebraska Press, 2006), 99–126.

54 **"He claimed it was needed":** Landis, recorded interview by author, Sept. 15–16, 2023, Carlisle, Pa.

54 **The foundation of its four dank cells:** "The Guard House," Carlisle Indian School Digital Resource Center.

55 **White, associate professor of First Peoples studies:** Mary Annette Pember, "Professor Answers Call to Find Boarding School Children," ICT News, Sept. 30, 2021, ictnews.org.

55 **She is also a cofounder:** National Native American Boarding School Healing Coalition, boardingschoolhealing.org.

55 **Together they created a public digital archive:** Mary Annette Pember, "Deaths at Chemawa," ICT News, Oct. 14, 2021, ictnews.org.

55 **"Suddenly through the horrendous events":** Ibid.

55 **The archive includes a short 1907 article:** Ibid.

56 **"I have four children":** Ibid.

56 **"He's not a statistic":** Ashley Hiruko, "A 12-Year-Old Boy Was Shot Running from a Native Boarding School. His Tribe Mourns Him Today," KUOW, March 1, 2023.

56 **Thorpe was the first Indian Olympic gold medalist:** "Jim Thorpe," Carlisle Indian School Digital Resource Center.

57 **"In 1927, the U.S. literally tried":** Landis, recorded interview by author, Sept. 15–16, 2023, Carlisle, Pa.

57 **"Buried here are the Indians":** Office of Army Cemeteries, armycemeteries.army.mil.

57 **Nick Estes of the Lower Brule Sioux Tribe:** Nick Estes, "The U.S. Stole Generations of Indigenous Children to Open the West," *High Country News,* Oct. 14, 2019, hcn.org.

57 **To date, thirty-two children:** Email from Olivia Van Den Heuvel (public affairs specialist, Arlington National Cemetery), May 5, 2024.

58 **"White Thunder, let me have":** Adams, *Education for Extinction,* 135.

58 **wrote to his father:** Adams, *Education for Extinction,* 137.

58 **"When the children went to school":** White Thunder to Knocks Off, 1879, Carlisle Indian School Digital Resource Center.

59 **"White Thunder's son is very sick":** "Letters from Pratt to White Thunder About the Health of Ernest," 1879, Carlisle Indian School Digital Resource Center.

59 **"Your son died quietly":** "Letters from Pratt to White Thunder," 1879, Carlisle Indian School Digital Resource Center.

59 **"You, my friend, are a good man":** "Letters from Pratt to White Thunder," 1880, Carlisle Indian School Digital Resource Center.

59 **"Our hearts will grieve":** White Thunder to Pratt, 1880, Carlisle Indian School Digital Resource Center.

59 **There is no indication:** "Letters from Pratt to White Thunder About the Health of Ernest."

60 **"We put candy on each":** Brandi Morin, "These Indigenous Children Died Far Away More Than a Century Ago. Here's How They Finally Got Home," *National Geographic,* Aug. 6, 2021, nationalgeographic.org.

60 **"The experience of our people":** Ibid.

60 **Tribes continue to work:** Mary Annette Pember, "Obscure Government Agency at Center of Dispute of Carlisle Repatriation Dispute," ICT News, Aug. 29, 2024.

61 **"I went to [Carlisle] school":** Pember, "Sending Them Home to Die."

61 **In 1860, the Indian population:** James P. Collins, "Native Americans in the Census 1860 to 1890," *Prologue Magazine* 38, no. 2 (Summer 2006); David J. Hacker and Michael R. Haines, "American Indian Mortality in the Late Nineteenth Century: The Impact of Federal Assimilation Policies on a Vulnerable Population," *Annales de démographie historique* 110, no. 2 (2005).

61 **Not unlike the smallpox-infected:** Pember, "Sending Them Home to Die"; Patrick J. Kiger, "Did Colonists Give Infected Blankets to Native Americans as Biological Warfare?," History.com, July 6, 2023.

62 **The deadliest was tuberculosis:** Aleš Hrdlička, "Tuberculosis Among Certain Indian Tribes of the United States," *Bureau of American Ethnology Bulletin* 42 (1909).

62 **nearly one-fifth of the population:** Don Southern, "James R. Walker's Campaign Against Tuberculosis on the Pine Ridge Reservation," *South Dakota History* 34, no. 2 (2004), sdhspress.com.

62 **Pratt describes the process:** "Report of Returned Pine Ridge Students with Tuberculosis," Aug. 1916, Carlisle Indian School Digital Resource Center.

62 **"Occasionally students recover who are sent home":** Sick Children Sent Home to Die, 1880–1915, Carlisle Indian School Digital Resource Center.

62 **Although a total of sixteen children:** Preston S. McBride, "A Lethal Education: Institutionalized Negligence, Epidemiology, and Death in Native American Boarding Schools, 1879–1934" (PhD diss., University of California, Los Angeles, 2020), escholarship.org/uc/item/1bw51497.

63 **In 1897 the superintendent at Crow Creek:** *Report of Superintendent of Crow Creek School to Commissioner of Indian Affairs* (1897), 267–68, search .library.wisc.edu.

63 **"It is not sufficient":** Pine Ridge Agent to Commissioner of Indian Affairs, 1928, National Archives, Kansas City.

63 **By 1925, when the overall tuberculosis:** "1925: American Indian TB Deaths Outpace General Population," Native Voices, National Library of Medicine, nlm.nih.gov.

64 **"The prevailing disease among the Oglala":** W. H. Clapp to Commissioner of Indian Affairs, Oct. 31, 1899, search.library.wisc.edu.

64 **"Pulmonary tuberculosis is widespread":** Diane T. Putney, "Fighting

the Scourge: American Indian Morbidity and Federal Policy, 1887–1928"
(PhD diss., Marquette University, 1980).

64 **During the first year:** Pember, "Sending Them Home to Die"; Rahder,
recorded interview by author, July 2004, Haskell Indian Nations University, Lawrence, Kans.

64 **"The Indians complained to the government":** Chronicles of Sisters of
St. Francis, Holy Rosary Mission, Pine Ridge, South Dakota, 1888–1929,
Bureau of Catholic Indian Missions Archives.

65 **"One day," the sister secretary wrote:** "These Notes on Holy Rosary
Mission, Pine Ridge, South Dakota, Have Been Translated from the German Diary of the Sisters of St. Francis, Who Have Been in Charge Since
the Very Foundation: 1888–1929," Bureau of Catholic Indian Mission
Archives.

65 **Trachoma, often called "sore eyes":** "1912: Trachoma Poses Blindness
Risk in the West," Native Voices, National Library of Medicine, nlm.nih
.gov.

65 **She expressed annoyance:** "These Notes on Holy Rosary Mission, Pine
Ridge, South Dakota, Have Been Translated from the German Diary
of the Sisters of St. Francis, Who Have Been in Charge Since the Very
Foundation."

66 **Information on the number of Indian schools:** "The Carlisle Indian
Industrial School: Assimilation with Education After Indian Wars,"
National Park Service, nps.gov.

66 **more than five hundred federal or religious:** *Federal Indian Boarding
School Initiative Investigative Report,* Vol. 1, 87.

66 **It's estimated that nearly ten thousand:** Carlisle Indian School Digital
Resource Center.

66 **Preston McBride, an assistant professor:** McBride, "A Lethal Education."

66 **"Sending sick students back":** Ibid.

66 **He examined records from 1870:** Ibid.

66 **973 boarding school deaths:** *Federal Indian Boarding School Initiative
Investigative Report, Vol. 2,* 5.

67 **"I took all the archival material":** McBride, recorded telephone interviews by author, Dec. 2023 and Jan. 2024.

68 **"We did the best we could":** Newland, recorded telephone interview by
author, Aug. 20, 2024.

68 **"Children don't just die":** McBride, recorded telephone interviews by
author, Dec. 2023 and Jan. 2024.

68 **Although a number of treaties:** "Education of Indians," 25 U.S.C.,
chap. 7, house.gov.

69 **Although the men claimed:** Erin Blakemore, "Alcatraz Had Some Surprising Prisoners: Hopi Men," History.com, July 11, 2023.

69 **A tuberculosis diagnosis in those days:** "Early Research and Treatment
of Tuberculosis in the 19th Century," *American Lung Association Crusade,*
University of Virginia, exhibits.hsl.virginia.edu.

69 **This belief was driven:** Hannah Cornish, "How Tuberculosis Became a

Test Case for Eugenic Theory," Welcome Collection, Sept. 6, 2022, well comecollection.org.

70 **Although Robert Koch identified:** Tuberculosis in Europe and North America, 1800–1922, Curiosity Collections, curiosity.lib.harvard.edu.

70 **Many prominent Progressives:** Cornish, "How Tuberculosis Became a Test Case for Eugenic Theory."

70 **Hundreds of college courses:** "Chapter 19: The Progressive Era: Eugenics," Teaching American History.

70 **many religious groups were also supporters:** National Human Research Institute, National Institutes of Health, genome.gov.

70 **Conditions at Indian residential schools:** Christian McMillen, "Indigenous Peoples, Tuberculosis Research, and Changing Ideas About Race in the 1930s," *Canadian Medical Association Journal,* Nov. 2021.

70 **Davin recommended a similar system:** Nicholas Flood Davin, "Report on Industrial Schools for Indians and Half-breeds," Ottawa, March 14, 1879.

70 **Van Wagenen's report included:** Edwin Black, "Eugenics and the Nazis—the California Connection," SF Gate, Nov. 9, 2003, sfgate.com.

70 **In the 1927 case *Buck v. Bell:*** *Buck v. Bell,* 274 U.S. 200 (1927); Nithya Arun, "From Buck v. Bell to Roe v. Wade: A Legacy of Control," Women's Media Center, July 11, 2022, womensmediacenter.org.

71 **According to Bryce's 1907 and 1909 reports:** Crystal Fraser, Tricia Logan, and Neil Orford, "A Doctor's Century-Old Warning on Residential Schools Can Help Find Justice for Canada's Crimes," *Globe and Mail,* July 17, 2021, theglobeandmail.com.

71 **disgusted by government inaction:** Miles Morrisseau, "A National Crime: One Hundred Years Ago, Dr. Peter Henderson Bryce Exposed the Horrifying Death Toll Among Children in Residential Schools," *Canada History,* Sept. 7, 2022, canadahistory.ca.

71 **"It is readily acknowledged":** Bernie M. Farber, "The Troubling Legacy of Duncan Campbell Scott," *Ottawa Citizen,* Aug. 26, 2013.

72 **a unique, more virulent form:** Mary Logan McCallum, "Colonialism, Racism, and the Creation of Indian TB," Manitoba Indigenous Tuberculosis History Project, indigenoustbhistory.org.

72 **Adolf Hitler was greatly influenced:** Pember, "Sending Them Home to Die."

72 **were destined for extinction:** Zane Grey, *The Vanishing American* (New York: Harper & Brothers, 1925).

73 **The boarding school experience:** Doug Kiel, "Competing Visions of Empowerment: Oneida Progressive-Era Politics and Writing Tribal Histories," *Ethnohistory* 61, no. 3 (Summer 2014); Standing Bear, *My Indian Boyhood;* "Marie Louise Bottineau Baldwin," National Park Service, nps.gov; Adams, *Education for Extinction,* 329–41.

73 **The society went on to advocate:** "Pan-Indian Movements," in *The Encyclopedia of Oklahoma History and Culture,* okhistory.org.

73 **The Little Wound School:** Pember, "Sending Them Home to Die."

73 **Reformers such as Estelle Reel:** Estelle Meyer Reel, *Course of Study for the Indian Schools of the United States* (Washington, D.C.: U.S. Government Printing Office, 1901).

74 **Each motion—lining up, marching, sitting:** Denise K. Lajimodiere, "Native American Boarding Schools," Minnesota Historical Society, mnopedia.org.

78 *He painted scenes from Ojibwe life:* Peter Whitebird, *Shaping the Canoe*, Wisconsin Historical Society, wisconsinhistory.org.

Chapter 4: Rage for Survival

80 **psychologists have created a diagnosis:** Caelan Soma, "Oppositional Defiant Disorder or Trauma," STARR Commonwealth, April 7, 2011, starr .org.

82 **St. Mary's School didn't officially participate:** Adams, *Education for Extinction*, 174–83.

83 **Although many Indian people succumbed:** Kunze, "Q&A: Darren Lone Fight."

83 **In 1917, for the first time:** David Treuer, *The Heartbeat of Wounded Knee: Native America from 1890 to the Present* (New York: Riverhead Books, 2019), 198.

83 **"so monstrous and so un-Christian":** Wayne J. Urban, Jennings L. Wagoner, and Milton Gaither, *American Education: A History* (New York: Routledge, 2019), 245.

83 **she described the emotional pain:** Zitkala-Sa, "The School Days of an Indian Girl," *Atlantic*, Feb. 1900, theatlantic.com.

83 **primitive cultures' emphasis on family:** Matthew Lynch, "Educators: What the 20th Century Progressive Education Movement Did for You," Edvocate, Sept. 2, 2018, theedadvocate.org.

83 **Considered out of step:** Adams, *Education for Extinction*, 350–52.

83 **By 1909, after more than 4,000 students:** Ibid., 316.

84 **White reformers had also failed:** Ibid., 323–34.

84 **"We started drilling at five":** Margaret L. Archuleta, Brenda J. Child, and K. Tsianina Lomawaima, *Away from Home: American Indian Boarding School Experiences, 1879–2000* (Phoenix: Heard Museum, 2000), 27.

84 **They qualified for jobs:** Treuer, *Heartbeat of Wounded Knee*, 190–91.

84 **About 30 percent of the adult male:** Ibid., 189–90.

84 **Their casualty rates were five times:** Ibid., 189–93.

85 **Once considered the best model:** Adams, *Education for Extinction*, 352–54.

85 **"all Indian trails led to Lawrence":** Kim Warren, "All Indian Trails Lead to Lawrence, October 27 to 30, 1926," *Kansas History: A Journal of the Central Plains* 30, no. 1 (Nov. 2007): 2–19.

86 **"Knees bend grotesquely":** Ibid.

86 **In the process, they made Haskell their own:** Ibid.

87 **Billy Mills, who won an Olympic:** Levi Rickert, "Is It Time to Change Haskell Indian Nations University's Name?," *Native News Online*, June 4, 2023, nativenewsonline.net.

87 **could undeniably be violent:** David Wallace Adams, "Beyond Bleakness: The Brighter Side of Indian Boarding Schools, 1870–1940," in *Boarding School Blues: Revisiting American Indian Educational Experiences,* ed. Clifford E. Trafzer, Jean A. Keller, and Lorene Sisquoc (Lincoln: University of Nebraska Press, 2006), 35–36.

87 **"When they whip 'em":** Clyde Ellis, "We Had a Lot of Fun but of Course That Wasn't the School Part," in Trafzer, Keller, and Sisquoc, *Boarding School Blues,* 77.

87 **"Well, they whip you hard":** Ibid.

88 **"I recollect the impression":** Adams, "Beyond Bleakness," 46, 47.

88 **Indian Service jobs:** Ibid., 44–45.

88 **"I didn't learn my Indian ways":** Ibid., 59.

88 **"Kiowa remained the dominant language":** Ellis, "We Had a Lot of Fun but of Course That Wasn't the School Part," 73–89.

89 **"The Woman Who Makes You Scream":** Adams, "Beyond Bleakness," 57.

89 **"We did not wait to be ordered a second time":** Ibid., 57–60.

89 **He is best known:** Ibid.

89 **"I was so weak":** Denise Lajimodiere, *Stringing Rosaries: The History, the Unforgivable, and the Healing of Northern Plains American Indian Boarding School Survivors* (Fargo: North Dakota State University Press, 2019), 34, 35.

90 **congressional hearings dealing with misuse:** Proceedings and Debates of the Second Session of the Sixty-Ninth Congress, vol. 68, part 1, Nov. 10–Dec. 6, 1926, Cong. Rec., 1076.

90 **I was surprised to see:** Ibid.

90 **As part of the Code of Indian Offenses:** Code of Indian Offenses, "Rules Governing the Court of Indian Offenses," Department of the Interior, Office of Indian Affairs, March 30, 1883.

91 **One of the women was later found:** Proceedings and Debates of the Second Session of the Sixty-Ninth Congress, vol. 68, part 1, Nov. 10–Dec. 6, 1926, Cong. Rec., 1076.

91 **"permitted to escape":** Ibid.

91 **When the white government farmer:** Ibid.

91 **In civics class at the Sister School:** U.S. Constitution due process clause in Fifth and Fourteenth Amendments, Constitution Center, constitutioncenter.org.

92 **Not long afterward, in 1924:** Indian Citizenship Act, June 2, 1924, Library of Congress, loc.gov.

92 **"Most stirring to the imagination":** "Indian Women Organize," *Forward,* Oct. 1924, 10.

92 **"band of serious thoughtful women":** "Situation in Wisconsin," *Forward,* June 1929, 3.

92 **Wheeler-Howard Act:** Better known as the Indian Reorganization Act of 1934, National Archives, archives.gov.

93 **"The discovery that came to me":** Adams, *Education for Extinction,* 361–62.

93 **Yielding to pressure from reformers:** Meriam et al., *Problem of Indian Administration,* 3.

93 **The report was named after:** Adams, *Education for Extinction*, 360–64.

93 **Henry Roe Cloud:** "Henry Roe Cloud: Native American Educator and Activist," Willamette University, willamette.edu.

94 **"stinging reproach to a niggardly":** Donald T. Crichlow, "Lewis Meriam, Expertise, and Indian Reform," *The Historian* 43 (1981), 325–43.

94 **"An overwhelming majority of the Indians":** Meriam et al., *Problem of Indian Administration*, 3.

94 **"On the whole government practices":** Ibid., 347–429.

94 **"The labor of [Indian] children":** Ibid., 376.

94 **"solitary confinement and corporal punishment":** Ibid., 347–429.

94 **unsanitary conditions:** Ibid., 189–325.

95 **"quite possible for missionaries":** Ibid., 838.

95 **The Meriam Report drew great media attention:** "Federal Education Policy, Indian Treaties: Their Ongoing Importance to Michigan Residents Federal Education Policy and Off-Reservation Schools, 1870–1933," Clarke Historical Library, Central Michigan University, cmich.edu.

96 **Indian education continued to primarily focus:** Adams, *Education for Extinction*, 360–64; Shelton and Johnson, "Trigger Points"; Margaret Connell Szasz, *Education and the American Indian: The Road to Self-Determination Since 1928* (Albuquerque: University of New Mexico Press, 2003), 33–61.

96 **His recommendations surrounding religion:** Treuer, *Heartbeat of Wounded Knee*, 204–9.

97 **Collier's policies did not include:** Joseph Watras, "Progressive Education and Native American Schools, 1929–1950," *Journal of Educational Foundations* 18, no. 3 (Summer–Fall 2004): 81–104.

97 **Under the rules of the act:** Szasz, *Education and the American Indian*, 89–105.

97 **"it is doubtful":** Special Subcommittee on Indian Education, *Indian Education*, 30–40.

98 **By 1933, the number of children:** Szasz, *Education and the American Indian*, 31.

98 **According to Collier's 1936:** Watras, "Progressive Education and Native American Schools," 92.

98 **The town changed its name:** "Chronology," presqueisleheritage.org.

99 **no longer serving elementary students:** Bill Ellingson, "A History of Flandreau Indian School," South Dakota Public Broadcasting, Sept. 10, 2021, sdpb.org.

99 **At Flandreau she got a taste of life:** "Throwaway Kids: 40 Years Later," April 12, 2023, brokenthefilm.org.

100 **"The Bad River reservation of Chippewas":** Joyce Erdman, *Handbook on Wisconsin Indians* (Madison: University of Wisconsin Extension, 1966), 15.

100 **"a short little shit":** Delphine Hurd, written and recorded interviews by author, 2008–21, Odanah, Wis.

101 **glaciers failed to cover the area:** Jonah Beleckis, "Where Does the 'Driftless Area' Get Its Name?," Wisconsin Public Radio, Oct. 5, 2022, wpr.org.

101 **The lyrical names of his childhood homes:** Louise Phelps Kellogg, "The

Story of Wisconsin, 1634–1848," *Wisconsin Magazine of History* 3, no. 3 (1920): 314–26.

101 **kyphosis, severe curvature of the spine:** "Post Polio Syndrome," National Organization for Rare Diseases, April 8, 2009, rarediseases.org.

Chapter 5: Assimilation Revisited

108 **"'De-Indianizing the Indian' was back":** Szasz, *Education and the American Indian*, 110.

108 **"the final solution of the Indian problem":** Special Subcommittee on Indian Education, *Indian Education*, 13.

108 **trust land, and reservations would cease:** Watras, "Progressive Education and Native American Schools," 99.

108 **However, enrollment in boarding schools:** Szasz, *Education and the American Indian*, 106–22.

108 **The postwar economic bang:** "Hard Times and Racism," *Native Words, Native Warriors*, National Museum of the American Indian, americanindian.si.edu.

109 **During this era with its emphasis:** "The Wonder Years," Minnesota Libraries Publishing Project, mlpp.pressbooks.pub.

109 **Of an Indian population of approximately 400,000:** "Native Americans in the United States Armed Forces, World War II," National Museum of the American Indian, americanindian.si.edu.

109 **Indian veterans found themselves:** Quil Lawrence, "Native Americans Living on Tribal Land Have Struggled to Access Veteran Home Loans," *All Things Considered*, NPR, Aug. 10, 2022, npr.org.

109 **Between 1953 and 1968:** "1953 to 1969: Policy of Termination and Relocation," Stanford Medicine, Ethnogeriatrics, geriatrics.stanford.edu.

109 **the Menominee Indian Tribe of Wisconsin:** "Menominee Tribe of Wisconsin Restoration of Federal Supervision," Menominee Indian Tribe, menominee-nsn.gov; Donald L. Fixico, *Termination and Relocation: Federal Indian Policy, 1945–1960* (Albuquerque: University of New Mexico Press, 1968), 183–98.

109 **Under the voluntary program:** Fixico, *Termination and Relocation*, 134–57.

109 **"Our apartment was not":** Mary Annette Pember, "Indian Relocation: Sending Roots Under Pavement," *Daily Yonder*, Dec. 8, 2008, dailyyonder.com.

110 **It's estimated that around sixty thousand:** Melody L. McCoy, "Indian Education Support Project: Trivializing Indian Education," Native American Rights Fund, Jan. 2005, narf.org.

110 **In those days on the reservation:** Samantha M. Williams, "Native American Boarding Schools: Some Basic Facts and Statistics," May 8, 2020, samanthamwilliams.com.

110 **"Let's see, there was Dago Mary's":** Pember, "Indian Relocation."

111 **the relocation program was a failure:** Ibid.

111 **The stats back it up:** Fixico, *Termination and Relocation*, 148, 149.

111 **"Like many Native Americans":** Pember, "Indian Relocation."

111 **Several of the founders:** Russell Means, "Cleveland American Indian Center," in *Encyclopedia of Cleveland History*, case.edu.

111 **Others include Karen Diver:** Konnie Lemay, "Racial Equity and Tribal Sovereignty Champion Karen Diver Honored," ICT News, Sept. 13, 2018, ictnews.org.

111 **Wilma Mankiller of the Cherokee Nation:** Sarah Ramirez, "Wilma Mankiller Led as the First Woman Principal Chief of the Cherokee Nation," Smithsonian American Women's History Museum, June 6, 2022, womenshistory.si.edu.

119 **There was a singing bear:** Alex Tieberg, "From the Land of Sky-Blue Waters, a History of Hamm's Beer," MinnPost, Nov. 25, 2019, minnpost .com.

123 **Long ago, our ancestors understood:** Louis Cozolino and Ruth Buczynski, "The Neuroscience of Psychotherapy," National Institute for the Clinical Application of Behavioral Medicine, nicabm.com.

123 **There is a lock-and-key:** Ibid., 21.

124 **In the roster's preprinted column:** Franciscan Sisters of Perpetual Adoration Archives, Motherhouse, La Crosse, Wis.

124 **the multivolume report documents:** Chippewa Indian Historical Records, 1936–42, Works Progress Administration, microfilm, Wisconsin Historical Society, Madison.

124 **Roosevelt created the WPA:** "The Works Progress Administration," PBS, pbs.org.

125 **"In the early days":** WPA Indian Research Project, Chippewa Indian Historical Records, 1936–42, envelope 5.

125 **"Dreaming was the Indian method":** Bob Wilson, "Dreams—Their Significance," Chippewa Indian Historical Records, 1936–42, reel 1, envelope 6.

125 **"By means of a shake lodge":** WPA Indian Research Project, Chippewa Indian Historical Records, 1936–42, envelope 9.

125 **"The Indian knew about":** Angeline Cedaroot, "Indian Prophecies," Chippewa Indian Historical Records, 1936–42, reel 2, envelope 15.

126 **notes from "Missionary Labors":** Chrysostom Verwyst, *Missionary Labors of Fathers Marquette, Menard and Allouez: In the Lake Superior Region* (United States: Creative Media Partners LLC, 2016).

126 **1882 to 1912:** "Verwyst, Chrysostom Adrian, 1841–1925," Wisconsin Historical Society, wisconsinhistory.org.

126 **"They shrink not from suffering":** "Narrative and Operational Records," Chippewa Indian Historical Records, 1936–42, reel 1.

126 **I was disheartened:** WPA Indian Research Project, Chippewa Indian Historical Records, 1936–42, envelope 5.

126 **"There are still a few pagans":** WPA Indian Research Project, Chippewa Indian Historical Records, 1936–42, envelope 19.

127 **the Great Medicine Society:** Densmore, *Chippewa Customs*, 86–97.

127 **"In contrast to the project's official purpose":** Chantal Norrgard, "Beyond Folklore: Historical Writing and Treaty Rights Activism in the Bad River WPA," in *Tribal Worlds: Critical Studies in American Indian Nation*

Building, ed. Brian Hosmer and Larry Nesper (New York: State University of New York Press, 2013), chap. 7.

127 **"Many not-so-devout Christians":** Leoso, recorded interviews by author, 2018, 2021, 2023.

128 **Two of the nine rules:** "Rules Governing the Court of Indian Offenses," Office of Indian Affairs, Department of the Interior, Dec. 2, 1882.

128 **Although the code was amended:** " 'We Also Have a Religion': The American Indian Religious Freedom Act and the Religious Freedom Project of the Native American Rights Fund," *Native American Rights Fund Announcements* (Winter 1979), narf.org.

129 **During the late nineteenth:** Henry Wadsworth Longfellow, *The Song of Hiawatha,* Maine Historical Society, hwlongfellow.org.

129 **"Our ancestors risked their lives":** Mary Annette Pember, "Our Ancestors Risked Their Lives and Freedom," ICT News, April 18, 2022, ictnews .org.

129 **Mosay was born in a wigwam:** Anton Treuer, "Keeping Legends Alive: Nibaa-Giizhig and Anishinaabe-Bimmadiziwin," *Oshkaabewis Native Journal* 3, no. 2 (Fall 1996).

129 **The St. Croix Ojibwe are descended:** "Who We Are: A History of the St. Croix People," St. Croix Chippewa Indians of Wisconsin, stcroixojibwe -nsn.gov.

129 **"We lived with that constant threat":** All quotations from Dora Mosay Ammann were recorded by the author in 2023, Round Lake, Wis.

141 **Maryknoll Catholic seminary:** Maryknoll Fathers and Brothers, mary knollsociety.org.

141 **Maryknoll's liberation theology:** Kira Dault, "What Is Liberation Theology?," *U.S. Catholic,* Oct. 14, 2014, uscatholic.org.

Chapter 6: Inner-lectual

143 **the occupation of Alcatraz:** Paul Chaat Smith and Robert Allen Warrior, *Like a Hurricane: The Indian Movement from Alcatraz to Wounded Knee* (New York: New Press, 1969), 10–35.

143 **But many of the demands:** Ibid., 142–68.

143 **In 1973, Indian activists:** Ibid., 190–91, 201–28.

143 **Two Indian men:** Ibid., 249, 257.

143 **Two years later two FBI agents:** "RESMURS Case (Reservation Murders)," FBI, fbi.gov.

143 **He remains incarcerated:** Yvonne Bushyhead, "In the Spirit of Crazy Horse: The Case of Leonard Peltier," *Yale Journal of Law and Liberation* 2, no. 1 (1991).

144 **Ada Deer of the Menominee Indian Tribe:** "Ada Deer," Wisconsin Women Making History, womeninwisconsin.org.

144 **There was also Truman Lowe:** "Truman Lowe, Acclaimed Ho-Chunk Artist and Professor Emeritus, Dies at 75," Diversity, Equity, and Inclusion, University of Wisconsin–Madison, April 8, 2019, diversity.wisc.edu.

144 **And there was Dorothy Davids:** "Dorothy Davids," Wisconsin Women Making History, womeninwisconsin.org.

144 **Stockbridge-Munsee:** Stockbridge-Munsee Band of Mohican Indians, dpi.wi.gov.

144 **The women's rights movement:** *Trammel v. United States*, 445 U.S. 40 (1980).

144 **"a relentless focus on power":** "Gerda Lerner: Historian," gerdalerner .com.

145 **I joined Wunk Sheek:** "Student Organizations: Wunk Sheek," American Indian and Indigenous Studies, University of Wisconsin–Madison, am -indian-indigenous.wisc.edu.

145 **"I think I admired him":** Dean Chavers, "Richard Nixon's Indian Mentor," ICT News, April 10, 2016, ictnews.org.

145 **Menominee Restoration Act:** "Richard Nixon: Statement on Signing the Menominee Restoration Act," Dec. 22, 1973, American Presidency Project, presidency.ucsb.edu.

145 **Indian Education Act of 1972:** Treuer, *Heartbeat of Wounded Knee*, 333–34.

146 **"The time has come":** "Richard Nixon: Special Message to the Congress on Indian Affairs," July 8, 1970, American Presidency Project, presidency .ucsb.edu.

146 **Nixon appointed Louis Bruce:** "Louis Bruce Nominated Commissioner of Indian Affairs," Bureau of Indian Affairs, Aug. 7, 1969, bia.gov.

146 **In 1970, Nixon signed a bill:** "Remembering the Return of Blue Lake," Richard Nixon Foundation, July 13, 2022, nixonfoundation.org.

146 **Alaska Native Claims Settlement Act:** "Native Land Claims in Alaska," PBS, pbs.org.

146 **Although he resigned from the presidency:** Indian Self-Determination and Education Assistance Act, Public Law 93-638, Department of the Interior, Bureau of Indian Affairs, bia.gov.

146 **"the Abraham Lincoln of the Indian people":** "Setting Precedent for Native American Progress," Richard Nixon Foundation, July 31, 2013, nixonfoundation.org.

146 **Nixon eagerly supported family planning:** "History of the U.S. Population Issue," Clinton White House Archives, clintonwhitehouse3.archives .gov.

146 **Several thousand Native American women:** Mary Annette Pember, "'Amá' and the Legacy of Sterilization in Indian Country," Rewire News Group, March 15, 2018, rewirenewsgroup.com.

146 **Other life-changing policy:** "We Also Have a Religion."

147 **Tribal College Act:** "Chapter 20—Tribally Controlled Colleges and Universities Assistance," 25 U.S.C., chap. 20, uscode.house.gov.

147 **thirty-seven tribal colleges:** "Tribal Colleges Locations," American Indian Higher Education Consortium, aihec.org.

147 **In 2023 the U.S. Supreme Court:** "Indian Child Welfare Act (ICWA) (Haaland v. Brackeen)," Native American Rights Fund, narf.org.

148 **"I was born in an age":** "I Was Born 1,000 Years Ago: Open Letter from Chief Dan George of the Capilano Indians," *UNESCO Courier* 28, no. 1 (1975): 20.

Chapter 7: Drinking to Live

151 **Hemingway worked there as a reporter:** Kynala Phillips, "Which Book Did Ernest Hemingway Write in a Johnson County Bedroom? How KC Inspired the Author," *Kansas City Star,* July 8, 2022, kansascity.com.

152 **After my internship I joined:** Dhaulagiri, Himalaya, March 11, 2001, naturalhazards.nasa.gov.

152 **His research focused on tree species:** "Magar," Government of Nepal, Ministry of Culture, Tourism, and Civil Aviation, Chhauni, Kathmandu, Feb. 28, 2020, nationalmuseum.gov.np.

152 **I developed a taste:** Brian Udall, "Raksi Is an Iconic Nepalese Alcoholic Drink That's Often Brewed at Home," Tasting Table, Dec. 5, 2023, tasting table.com.

152 **red is the color of marriage:** Neha Tandon, "Why Do Indian Brides Wear Red?," *Brides,* Aug. 4, 2023, brides.com.

153 **a long slow train wreck:** Buddy T, "How to Tell if You're Enabling an Alcoholic and How to Stop," Very Well Mind, Sept. 30, 2023, verywell mind.com.

153 **I was supremely lucky:** Frederic B. Hill, *The Life of Kings: "The Baltimore Sun" and the Golden Age of the American Newspaper* (Lanham, Md.: Rowman & Littlefield, 2023).

155 **I found the help and support:** Caroline Knapp, *Drinking: A Love Story* (New York: Dell, 1997), 215.

155 **We recognized that denial:** Ibid., 149.

157 **My first assignment was photographing:** Jim Simon Mishibinijima art gallery, mishmountains.blogspot.com.

157 **Jim is a painter:** "Woodland Style of Painting," Da Vic Gallery, Native Canadian Arts, nativecanadianarts.com.

Chapter 8: Poking Trauma

158 **As part of the Rosalynn Carter Fellowship:** "The Rosalynn Carter Fellowships for Mental Health Journalism, 2014–2015," Carter Center, thecartercenter.org.

158 **other journalism awards:** University of Southern California Annenberg Award and the Dennis A. Hunt Fund for Health Journalism, 2014, annenberg.usc.edu.

158 **Epigenetics posits that we pass along:** Mary Annette Pember, "Trauma May Be Woven into DNA of Native Americans," ICT News, Oct. 2017, ictnews.org.

158 **I also met with Mary Vicario:** Mary Vicario, "Resilience Interventions Based on Neuroscience," Finding Hope Consulting, findinghopeconsulting.com.

158 **children tend to blame themselves:** Michal Tanzer et al., "Self-Blame Mediates the Link Between Childhood Neglect Experiences and Internalizing Symptoms in Low-Risk Adolescents," *Journal of Child and Adolescent Trauma* 14, no. 1 (2020).

158 **young children think they control:** Serhat Kurt, "Piaget's Preopera-

tional Stage of Cognitive Development," Education Library, Sept. 15, 2023, educationlibrary.org.

159 **In the moments of the fight:** Hisashi Hanazawa, "Polyvagal Theory and Its Clinical Potential: An Overview," *Brain and Nerve* 74, no. 8 (2022): 1011–16.

159 **The dorsal vagus governs:** Kasia Kozlowska et al., "Fear and the Defense Cascade: Clinical Implications and Management," *Harvard Review of Psychiatry* 23, no. 4 (2015): 263–87.

159 **The limbic system is a set:** Olivia Guy-Evans, "What Is the Limbic System? Definition, Parts, and Functions," Simply Psychology, Jan. 17, 2024, simplypsychology.org.

159 **"Our limbic system wants":** Vicario, recorded and written interviews by author, 2014, 2016, 2023, Cincinnati.

159 **The dorsal vagus nerve places:** Odelya Gertel Kraybill, "Fight-Flight-Freeze and Withdrawal," *Psychology Today*, April 30, 2021, psychology today.com.

159 **When the dorsal vagus nerve takes over:** Margaret C. McKinnon et al., "A Review of the Relation Between Dissociation, Memory, Executive Functioning, and Social Cognition in Military Members and Civilians with Neuropsychiatric Conditions," *Neuropsychologia* 90 (Sept. 2016): 210–34.

159 **frequently the abuser:** Rebecca Bailey et al., "Appeasement: Replacing Stockholm Syndrome as a Definition of a Survival Strategy," *European Journal of Psychotraumatology* 14, no. 1 (2023).

160 **"Experiencing physical or emotional":** Vicario, recorded and written interviews by author, 2014, 2016, 2023, Cincinnati; Çiğdem Dereboy et al., "The Relationship Between Childhood Traumas, Identity Development, Difficulties in Emotion Regulation, and Psychopathology," *Türk psikiyatri dergisi* 29, no. 4 (Winter 2018): 269–78.

160 **The full details of the drunken brawls:** Bessel van der Kolk, *The Body Keeps the Score: Brain, Mind, and Body in the Healing of Trauma* (New York: Penguin Books, 2015), 257–75.

160 **"As a child, she feared":** Pascale Gisquet-Verrier and David C. Riccio, "Proust and Involuntary Retrieval," *Frontiers in Psychology*, Feb. 12, 2024; "Fact Sheet III: Trauma Related Dissociation: An Introduction," International Society for the Study of Trauma and Dissociation, isst-d.org.

160 **would have dire implications:** Amy J. L. Baker, "Parental Alienation Syndrome—the Parent/Child Disconnect," *Social Work Today* 8, no. 6 (2008): 26, socialworktoday.com.

160 **And in some twisted attempt:** Bessel A. van der Kolk, "The Compulsion to Repeat the Trauma: Re-enactment, Revictimization, and Masochism," *Psychiatric Clinics of North America* 12, no. 2 (1998): 389–411.

160 **Larry was an unsafe savior:** "The Beginner's Guide to Trauma Responses," Healthline, healthline.com.

160 **An early proponent of this theory:** Maria Yellow Horse Brave Heart et al., "Historical Trauma Among Indigenous Peoples of the Americas: Con-

cepts, Research, and Clinical Considerations," *Journal of Psychoactive Drugs* 43, no. 4 (2011): 282–90.

161 **She and Lemyra DeBruyn:** Maria Yellow Horse Brave Heart and Lemyra M. DeBruyn, "The American Indian Holocaust: Healing Historical Unresolved Grief," *American Indian and Alaska Native Mental Health Research* 8, no. 2 (1998): 60–82.

161 **Supporters of this theory claim:** Krista Schafte and Sean Bruna, "The Influence of Intergenerational Trauma on Epigenetics and Obesity in Indigenous Populations—a Scoping Review," *Epigenetics* 18, no. 1 (2023).

161 **The American Academy of Pediatrics reports:** "Adverse Childhood Experiences and the Lifelong Consequences of Trauma," American Academy of Pediatrics, 2014, aap.org/traumaguide.

161 **study conducted:** Howard Pinderhughes, Rachel A. Davis, and Myesha Williams, "Adverse Community Experiences and Resilience," Prevention Institute, 2015, Oakland.

161 **ACE assesses associations:** Vincent J. Felitti et al., "Relationship of Childhood Abuse and Household Dysfunction to Many of the Leading Causes of Deaths in Adults: The Adverse Childhood Experiences (ACEs) Study," *American Journal of Preventive Medicine* 14, no. 4 (1998): 245–58.

162 **nearly three times greater:** U.S. Department of Health and Human Services Office of Minority Health, "Diabetes and American Indians/Alaska Natives," 2018, hhs.gov.

162 **Deaths from alcoholism:** Ibraheem M. Karaye, Nasim Maleki, and Ismaeel Yunusa, "Racial and Ethnic Disparities in Alcohol-Attributed Deaths in the United States, 1999–2020," *International Journal of Environmental Research and Public Health* 20, no. 8 (2023); Deborah Stone et al., "Suicides Among American Indian or Alaska Native Persons—National Violent Death Reporting System, United States, 2015–2020," Centers for Disease Control, Sept. 16, 2022, cdc.gov; Elizabeth Arias et al., "Mortality Profile of the Non-Hispanic American Indian or Alaska Native Population," *National Vital Statistic Reports* 70, no. 12 (2021), cdc.gov.

162 **Dr. Don Warne:** Johns Hopkins Center for Indigenous Health, cih.jhu .edu.

162 **Ursula Running Bear's research:** Ursula Running Bear et al., "Boarding School Attendance and Physical Health Status of Northern Plains Tribes," *Applied Research in Quality of Life* 13, no. 3 (2018).

162 **Her work is included:** *Federal Indian Boarding School Initiative Investigative Report*, Vol. 1, 89.

162 **"Traumatized people chronically feel":** Van der Kolk, *Body Keeps the Score*, 153.

163 **"We lost the bond":** Williams, phone interview by author, 2014.

163 **Denise Lajimodiere's parents both attended:** Lajimodiere, *Stringing Rosaries*.

164 **While he was intoxicated:** Lajimodiere, phone interviews by author, 2013, 2014, 2016, 2019, 2021, 2023.

164 **"I had to forgive my parents":** Ibid.

164 **"Before reconciling with the U.S. government":** Lajimodiere, phone interview by author, 2013.

164 **Chief Wilton Littlechild:** Speak Truth to Power Canada, sttpcanada .ctf-fce.ca.

164 **former hockey player:** "Wilton Littlechild-Building, Indigenous Peoples' Sports," Canada's Sports Hall of Fame, sportshall.ca.

164 **"Healing is an ongoing process":** Littlechild, interview by author, 2014, Ottawa.

165 **"It hit me pretty hard":** Littlechild, telephone interview by author, 2023.

165 **hearing about children's graves:** Shaun Griswold, "Indigenous Leaders Seek an Apology About the Mass Grave in Albuquerque," Source New Mexico, Sept. 3, 2021.

165 **He decided to help in the search:** Canadian Press staff, "Facts About the Former Alberta Residential School Site Pope Francis Plans to Visit," *Global News,* June 23, 2022, globalnews.ca.

165 **"Just being able to push":** Littlechild, phone interview by author, 2023.

166 **Gone had won the award:** "Award for Distinguished Professional Contributions to Applied Research: Joseph Patrick Gone," *American Psychologist* 76, no. 9 (2021): 1511–13.

167 **"These inequities didn't arise":** Ayurdi Dhar, "When Healing Looks Like Justice: An Interview with Harvard Psychologist Joseph Gone," Mad in America, Oct. 18, 2019.

167 **"Indian country needs a radical change":** Ibid.

167 **Funding for the Indian Health Service:** "Fact Sheet: The President's Budget Delivers on His Commitment to Tribal Nations and Native Communities," White House Briefing Room, March 11, 2024, whitehouse.gov.

167 **The historically underfunded agency:** Lindsay Whitehurst, "Supreme Court Sides with Native American Tribes in Health Care Funding Dispute with Government," Associated Press, June 6, 2024, apnews.com.

167 **Many essential services:** Felicia Fonseca, "Tribes Welcome Infusion of Money in Infrastructure Bill," Associated Press, Nov. 18, 2021, apnews.com.

167 **"You can never count on anything":** Gone, telephone interviews by author, 2014, 2023.

168 **Worse, pathologizing our high rates:** Joseph Gone and Laurence Kirmayer, "Advancing Indigenous Mental Health Research: Ethical, Conceptual, and Methodological Challenges," *Transcultural Psychiatry* 57, no. 2 (2020): 235–49.

168 **The popular polyvagal theory:** Stephen W. Porges, *Polyvagal Safety: Attachment, Communication, and Self-Regulation* (New York: W. W. Norton, 2021).

168 **Critics claim that polyvagal theory:** Caroline Giroux, Daniel Ahlers, and Alyssa Miawotoe, "Polyvagal Approaches: Scientifically Questionable but Useful in Practice," *Journal of Psychiatry Reform* 10, no. 11 (2021).

169 **Since the news in 2021:** Ian Mosby and Erin Millions, "Canada's Residential Schools Were a Horror," *Scientific American,* Aug. 1, 2021, scientific american.com.

169 **Most available mental health:** Victoria M. O'Keefe et al., "Increasing Culturally Responsive Care and Mental Health Equity with Indigenous Community Mental Health Workers," *Psychological Services* 18, no. 1 (2021): 84–92.

169 **EBP is a process:** "What Is Evidence Based Practice?," Process Recovery Center, theprocessrecoverycenter.com.

169 **The EBP model is the driver:** Vikas Gampa, Kenneth Bernard, and Michael Oldani, "Racialization as a Barrier to Achieving Health Equity for Native Americans," *Medicine and Society* 22, no. 10 (2020).

170 **There are more than fifty:** Mary Annette Pember, "A Fearless Fight Against Historical Trauma, the Yupik Way," ICT News, Sept. 13, 2018, ictnews.org.

170 **"Western interventions are built":** Ibid.

171 **the B. family home:** At the family's request, I will not name them in this story.

172 **"Our ancestors gave us tools":** Ibid.

173 **"I have prepared you":** Ibid.

174 **"My wife is Yup'ik":** Ibid.

174 **According to the FBI:** Federal Bureau of Investigation, Crime Data Explorer," cde.ucr.cjis.gov; John D. Sutter, "List: States Where Rape Is Common," CNN, Feb. 4, 2018, cnn.com.

174 **Alaska leads the nation:** Federal Bureau of Investigation, Crime Data Explorer, 2022, cde.ucr.cjis.gov.

174 **"a major health and social crisis":** Pember, "Fearless Fight Against Historical Trauma."

174 **the 1932 death rate for Alaska Natives:** "Medical Care in Early American Alaska Is Limited," Alaska's History and Cultural Studies, akhistory.lpsd .com.

175 **"Out of necessity":** Pember, "Fearless Fight Against Historical Trauma."

175 **"Authorities told most parents":** Ibid.

175 **Alaska Native communities grew:** LaBelle, interviews by author, 2014, 2023.

175 **"Chaos from unresolved trauma":** Pember, "Fearless Fight Against Historical Trauma."

175 **"Money has been spent":** Ibid.

176 **"The healing process is rooted":** Ibid.

176 **"The social framework within which":** Ayunerak, Alstrom, Moses, Charlie, and Rasmus, "Yup'ik Culture and Context in Southwest Alaska: Community Member Perspectives of Tradition, Social Change, and Prevention," Center for Alaska Native Health Research, University of Alaska Fairbanks, 2014.

177 **have begun to fund projects:** Pember, "Fearless Fight Against Historical Trauma."

177 **"Ironically, despite the holistic and balanced":** Margo Rowan et al., "Cultural Interventions to Treat Addictions in Indigenous Populations: Findings from a Scoping Study," *Substance Abuse, Treatment, Prevention, and Policy* 9 (2014): 23.

177 **"The leader explained":** Joseph P. Gone and Patrick E. Calf Looking, "The Blackfeet Indian Culture Camp: Auditioning an Alternative Indigenous Treatment for Substance Abuse Disorders," *American Psychological Association* 12, no. 2 (2015): 83–91; Gone, telephone interview by author, March 2022.

177 **"We have heard comments":** Pember, "Fearless Fight Against Historical Trauma."

178 **"Who we came to be today":** Ibid.

178 **"We saw the father's spirit":** Ibid.

178 **"The interventions that people need":** Gone, interviews by author, 2014, 2022, and 2023.

178 **"What we do have are thousands":** Gone, "Reframing Native Mental Health," Web presentation, Indian Extension for Community Healthcare Outcomes, October 2022, indiancountryecho.org.

179 **Echo-Hawk of the Pawnee Nation:** "Holly Echo-Hawk," Indian Country Echo, indiancountryecho.org.

179 **"It's a gigantic challenge":** Echo-Hawk, interview by author, 2023.

179 **"Psychologists also provided ideological support":** APA Council of Representatives, "Apology to People of Color for APA's Role in Promoting, Perpetuating, and Failing to Challenge Racism, Racial Discrimination, and Human Hierarchy in U.S.," American Psychological Association, October 29, 2021, apa.org.

179 **"the discipline was complicit in contributing":** "Report on an Offer of Apology on Behalf of the American Psychological Association to the First Peoples of the United States," American Psychological Association, 2013, apa.org.

Chapter 9: Accountability Before Reconciliation

181 **I traveled to Ottawa:** Indigenous Peoples Atlas of Canada, Indigenous Peoples of Canada, indigenouspeoplesatlasofcanada.ca.

181 **Indian Residential Schools Settlement Agreement:** "The Indian Residential Schools Settlement Has Been Approved," Residential Schools Settlement, residentialschoolsettlement.ca.

181 **"HEALTH: An acknowledgement that the current state":** "Truth and Reconciliation Commission Urges Canada to Confront Cultural Genocide of Residential Schools," *CBC News,* June 2, 2015, cbc.ca.

183 **"We heard survivors tell us":** Mary Annette Pember, "Truth and Reconciliation Closing Event," Indian Country Today Media Network, May 31, 2015, youtube.com.

183 **"Never in all my life":** Lorna Standingready, interview by author, 2015, Ottawa.

184 **"By the time we finished":** Littlechild, interview by author, June 2015, Ottawa.

184 **Littlechild earned a law degree:** Littlechild, phone interview by author, March 2023.

184 **"This is a commission":** Mary Annette Pember, "Cultural Genocide," Indian Country Today Media Network, June 3, 2015, mapember.com.

185 **"First Nation's people are as the fleur sauvage":** Mary Annette Pember, "Truth and Reconciliation: The Road to Healing Is Long and Arduous," ICT News, June 8, 2015, mapember.com.

185 **Harper made a statement of apology:** "Statement of Apology to Former Students of Indian Residential Schools," Government of Canada, June 11, 2008, rcaanc-cirnac.gc.ca.

185 **The government began processing claims:** "Indian Residential School Settlement Agreement," Anishinabek, anishinabek.ca.

185 **Ottawa is also investing $50 million:** "The Day Scholars Revitalization Fund," Justice for Day Scholars, justicefordayscholars.com.

185 **The government also promised:** Amanda Coletta, "What to Know About Canada's Residential Schools and the Unmarked Graves Found Nearby," *Washington Post,* July 25, 2022, washingtonpost.com.

186 **"At first, the project invoked hope":** Alessia Passafiume, "Yellowhead Institute to No Longer Report on TRC Calls to Action," *Canada's National Observer,* Dec. 21, 2023, nationalobserver.com.

186 **"I ask forgiveness":** Jason Horowitz and Ian Austen, "Pope Apologizes in Canada for Schools That Abused Indigenous Children," *New York Times,* July 25, 2022, nytimes.com.

186 **"It's something that is needed":** "Tribal Leaders, Members React to Pope's Apology on Schools," Associated Press, July 26, 2022, apnews.org.

187 **"Despite the historic apology":** Rachel Bergen, "Pope's Apology Doesn't Acknowledge Church's Role as Co-author of Dark Chapter: Murray Sinclair," *CBC News,* July 26, 2022, cbc.ca.

187 **Canadian Conference of Catholic Bishops:** Emelia Fournier, "Catholic Church Says It Will Take 4 More Years to Raise $30M for Survivors," *APTN News,* Oct. 1, 2022, aptnnews.ca.

187 **To date, the Catholic Church has paid:** Horowitz and Austen, "Pope Apologizes."

187 **A federal judge allowed the church:** Ian Austen, "How Catholics Avoided Paying Millions in Reparations for Residential Schools," *New York Times,* April 2, 2022, nytimes.com.

187 **the Catholic Church operated:** Ian Austen, "Canada's Residential Schools Were a System of Cultural Genocide, a Commission Found," *New York Times,* July 25, 2022, nytimes.com.

187 **This was especially disconcerting:** Geraldine Malone, "Pope Francis Tour Came with a Minimum $55 Million Price Tag," *Globe and Mail,* March 23, 2023, theglobeandmail.com.

187 **Details of the Catholic Church's vast wealth:** Jason Warick, "The Vatican Holds Billions in Assets. Residential School Survivors Say Pope Should Step Up on Compensation," *CBC News,* March 31, 2022, cbc.ca.

188 **a system both supported and orchestrated:** Nicole Winfield, "Pope Voices Willingness to Return Indigenous Loot, Artifacts," Associated Press, April 30, 2023, apnews.com.

188 **the doctrine helped form the basis:** Bill Chappell, "The Vatican Repudiates 'Doctrine of Discovery,' Which Was Used to Justify Colonialism," NPR, March 30, 2023, npr.org.

188 **139 residential schools:** Anderson Cooper, "Canada's Unmarked Graves: How Residential Schools Carried Out Cultural Genocide Against Indigenous Children," CBS News, Feb. 6, 2022, cbsnews.com.

188 **More than 500 boarding schools:** *Federal Indian Boarding School Initiative Investigative Report*, Bureau of Indian Affairs, May 2022, 87, bia.gov.

188 **669 day schools:** "Are You Part of the Federal Indian Day School Class Action," Crown-Indigenous Relations and Northern Affairs Canada, rcaanc-cirnac.gc.ca.

188 **Number of day schools unknown:** *Federal Indian Boarding School Initiative Investigative Report*, 87.

188 **64 Catholic-operated residential schools:** Pember, "Canada, US Differ on Boarding Schools."

188 **About 100 Catholic-operated boarding schools:** Ibid.

188 **2011 Indian population 1.4M:** "Aboriginal Peoples in Canada: First Nations People, Métis and Inuit," Statistics Canada, 2011, www12.statcan .gc.ca.

188 **2011 Indian population 2.8M:** Tina Norris, Paula L. Vines, and Elizabeth Hoeffel, "The American Indian Alaska Native Population: 2010," U.S. Census, Jan. 2012, uscensus.gov.

188 **2020 Indian population 5 percent of total:** 2021 Census of Canada, "Indigenous Peoples."

188 **2020 Indian population 2.9 percent of total:** "Native American Population by State," World Population Review, worldpopulationreview .com.

189 **In 1996, the Oglala Sioux tribe:** "Holy Rosary Mission–Red Cloud Indian School Records," Bureau of Catholic Indian Missions Archives.

189 **According to Amy Cary:** Cary, recorded interview by author, May 2022, Marquette University, Milwaukee.

189 **The bureau and other Catholic entities:** Code of Canon Law, Book 2, Title III, Can. 535, Holy See, vatican.va.

189 **The bureau was a lobbying organization:** "Bureau of Catholic Indian Missions," Bureau of Catholic Indian Missions Archives.

189 **The bureau still exists today:** Black and Indian Mission Office, blackand indianmission.org.

189 **"While the Vatican's decision":** Brad Angerman, "NABS Statement on Vatican Renouncing Doctrine of Discovery," National Native American Boarding School Healing Coalition, March 30, 2023, boardingschoolheal ing.org.

190 **Under the *Lemon* test:** Richard L. Pacelle, "Lemon Test," Free Speech Center, Oct. 17, 2023, firstamendment.mtsu.edu.

190 **The passage of the 1887 Dawes Act:** "Dawes Act, 1887," Milestone Documents, National Archives, archives.gov.

190 **"After 1887, the federal government":** Bureau of Catholic Indian Missions: Record Group 1 of Bureau of Catholic Indian Mission's Records, BCIM Historical Notes/Scope and Content, Marquette University, marquette.edu.

191 **In a shared investigation:** Mary Annette Pember, "Buried Secrets:

America's Indian Boarding Schools, Part 2," *Reveal* News, Oct. 22, 2022, revealnews.org.

191 **Mission work with Native Americans:** Prucha, *Great Father*, 51.

191 **Boarding schools began a partnership:** Francis Paul Prucha, *The Churches and the Indian Schools, 1888–1912* (Lincoln: University of Nebraska Press, 1979), 3–4.

191 **Catholics and other Christian missionaries:** Pember, "Buried Secrets."

191 **Catholic missionaries found themselves excluded:** Prucha, *Churches and the Indian Schools*, 8.

191 **They regained their status:** Mary Annette Pember, "The Catholic Church Siphoned Away $30 Million Paid to Native Peoples for Stolen Land," *In These Times*, July 7, 2020, inthesetimes.com.

191 **By the beginning of the twentieth century:** *Federal Indian Boarding School Initiative Investigative Report*, 82.

191 **Most of the Christian boarding:** Prucha, *Churches and the Indian Schools*, 4.

191 **According to the Court, allowing Indians:** *Reuben Quick Bear v. Leupp*, 210 U.S. 50 (1908).

192 **The majority of Native Americans:** "Act of June 2, 1924, Public Law 68-175, 43 Stat. 253, to Certificates of Citizenship to Indians," HR 6355, 68th Cong., 1st Sess., National Archives, catalog.archives.gov.

192 **Entrenched racism kept many Indian children:** "Federal Government Separates Native Children from Families in Efforts at Forced Assimilation," *A History of Racial Injustice*, Equal Justice Initiative, calendar.eji.org.

192 **Extreme poverty:** Child, *Boarding School Seasons*, 14, 15.

192 **Mission schools were often located:** Pember, "Catholic Church Siphoned Away $30 Million Paid to Native People for Stolen Land."

192 **Pressed on government forms:** Ibid.

193 **"One of the Indians":** "These Notes on Holy Rosary Mission, Pine Ridge, South Dakota, Have Been Translated from the German Diary of the Sisters of St. Francis, Who Have Been in Charge Since the Very Foundation," 28.

193 **Catholics operated about a hundred:** Bureau of Catholic Indian Missions Archives.

193 **Bureau archives at Marquette:** Charles Ewing to Casper H. Borgess, June 4, 1873, Bureau of Catholic Indian Missions Archives; Ewing to Rev. George Deshon, Oct. 7, 1874, Bureau of Catholic Indian Missions Archives.

193 **according to available records:** Pember, "Catholic Church Siphoned Away $30 Million Paid to Native Peoples for Stolen Land."

193 **According to a report:** "Catholic Indian Mission School Reports at Marquette University," Bureau of Catholic Indian Mission Records, Series 2-1 School Reports, 1877–1975, Bureau of Catholic Indian Missions Archives.

193 **Using the same sources:** Pember, "Buried Secrets."

193 **Beginning in 1900:** *Annual Report of the Commissioner of Indian Affairs, for the Year 1906*, Department of the Interior (Washington, D.C.: U.S. Government Printing Office, 1906), 60–61.

193 **According to a confidential memo:** "Report on United States Govern-

ment Support of Catholic Indian Mission Schools and Catholic Education in Government Schools During Biennium Ending April 1, 1925," Bureau of Catholic Indian Mission Records, Series 1-1, box 232, folder 11.

194 **"The political weight of the Catholics":** Prucha, *Churches and the Indian Schools,* 205.

194 **I found documents in the BCIM:** Rt. Rev. Msgr. William Hughes (director) to Sister Macaria, 1935, St. Mary's School, Odanah, Wis., Bureau of Catholic Indian Missions Archives.

194 **"I remember sleeping under the bed":** Mary Annette Pember, "St. Mary's Mission: 'This Place Is the Devil,'" ICT News, Oct. 13, 2021, ictnews.org.

194 **hundreds of lawsuits had been filed:** "Hundreds File Abuse Claims Against Oregon Jesuits," *Catholic Reporter,* Dec. 14, 2009, ncronline.org.

195 **In 2011, after the province:** Kevin Graman, "$166 Million Settlement Offered in Jesuit Bankruptcy," *Spokesman Review,* March 25, 2011, spokes man.com.

195 **Sixteen of those on the list:** "List of Jesuits from Jesuits West Province with Credible Claims of Sexual Abuse of a Minor or Vulnerable Adult," Jesuits West, July 2020, jesuitswest.org.

195 **"I was really angry when people":** Pember, "St. Mary's Mission."

195 **"Creator gave me this experience":** Sanchez, interview by author, Sept. 2021.

195 **Journalists began covering this story:** "Timeline of the Crisis," Bishop Accountability, bishopaccountability.org.

195 **I wrote about a database:** Mary Annette Pember, "Desolate Country: Abusive Priests Clustered at Mission Schools," ICT News, Oct. 20, 2022, ictnews.org.

196 **In 2010, the State of South Dakota:** Brad Brooks, "Native American Survivors of Alleged Boarding School Sex Abuse Want Justice," Reuters, July 27, 2022, reuters.com.

196 **This law was mostly aimed:** "Child Sexual Abuse: Time to Right a Wrong," *Lakota Times,* Feb. 4, 2021, lakotatimes.com.

196 **Eight of the thirty boarding schools:** Annie Todd, "30 Native American Boarding Schools Operated in South Dakota. Here's Where They Were Located," *Argus Leader,* May 12, 2011, argusleader.com.

196 **plaintiffs failed to follow:** Stephanie Woodard, "South Dakota Sex Abuse Scandal: A Peek Inside the Church's Drawers," *Huffington Post,* April 19, 2011, huffpost.com.

197 **Sister Henrietta describes the girl's story:** Sister M. Henrietta to Rt. Rev. Msgr. Wm H. Ketcham, Sept. 29, 1921, Washington, D.C., Bureau of Catholic Indian Mission Archives; Director to Sister M. Henrietta, Sept. 21, 1921, St. Agnes Mission School, Antlers, Okla., Bureau of Catholic Indian Mission Archives.

197 **The awareness was driven by the discovery:** Dickson and Watson, "Remains of 215 Children Found Buried at Former B.C. Residential School, First Nation Says."

197 **Like most Indians, Haaland's family:** Deb Haaland, "Deb Haaland: My Grandparents Were Stolen from Their Families as Children. We Must

Learn About This History," *Washington Post,* June 11, 2021, washington post.com.

197　**In June 2021, she announced:** "Secretary Haaland Announces Federal Indian Boarding School Initiative," Department of the Interior, June 22, 2021, doi.gov.

197　**The report includes information:** *Federal Indian Boarding School Initiative Investigative Report.*

197　**Haaland also launched:** Mary Annette Pember, "Road to Healing: Deb Haaland Pledges Boarding School Truths Will Be Uncovered," ICT News, July 9, 2022, ictnews.org.

198　**The National Native American Boarding School Healing Coalition:** "Funding to Support Oral Histories in Boarding School Era," Associated Press, April 26, 2023, apnews.com.

198　**It failed but was reintroduced:** "Indian Boarding School Bill Seeks to Create Accountability, Healing," *Native News Online,* Feb. 6, 2024, nativenewsonline.net.

198　**It seems unlikely that the United States:** Jeyan Jeganathan and Carla Lucchetta, " 'Felt Throughout Generations': A Timeline of Residential Schools in Canada," TVO Today, July 21, 2021, tvo.org.

199　**"What is important to me":** Pember, "St. Mary's Mission." Subsequent quotations from Grundy are from this article.

202　**"I hated picking up those windfall apples":** Ibid.

204　**Although approved in July 2023:** "USCCB Pulled Native American Pastoral Text over Language," *Pillar,* Dec. 7, 2023, pillarcatholic.com.

204　**"We apologize for the failure":** Mary Annette Pember, "US Boarding School Truth Inches Forward," ICT News, June 19, 2024, ictnews.org.

204　**Some Native people thought the apology:** Ibid.

204　**"If you're going to give an apology":** Rachel Nostrant, "U.S. Catholic Bishops Apologize for Traumas of Indian Boarding Schools," *New York Times,* June 14, 2024, nytimes.com.

204　**The language in the fifty-six-page document:** "Code of Canon Law," Holy See, vatican.va.

205　**"Fostering dialogue and engaging":** Pember, "US Boarding School Truth."

205　**"a portrait of pervasive sexual abuse":** Dana Hedgpeth and Sari Horwitz, "In the Name of God," *Washington Post,* May 29, 2024, washington post.com.

205　**"They're coming forward":** Pember, "US Boarding School Truth."

205　**have returned some cultural items:** Franciscan Sisters of Perpetual Adoration, fspa.org.

205　**they were still reeling:** Mary Annette Pember, "Death by Civilization," *Atlantic,* March 8, 2019, theatlantic.com.

205　**in the process of determining:** McKenzie, in-person recorded interview by author at St. Rose Convent, Franciscan Sisters of Perpetual Adoration motherhouse in La Crosse, Wisconsin, April 2022.

206　**"There was an effective erasure":** Dan Stockman, "US Congregations

Face Their Complicity in Trauma of Native Boarding Schools," Global Sisters Report, July 1, 2022, globalsistersreport.org.

206 **"one of Wisconsin's most lavish":** "Chapel Maria Angelorum, Viterbo University, Convent of St. Rose of Viterbo," Society of Architectural Historians, sah-archipedia.org.

206 **"The total cost of the church":** Sister Mary Ann Gschwind, interview by author, March 2022, Sisters of Perpetual Adoration Motherhouse, La Crosse, Wis.

207 **according to the order's history:** Carrie Kirsch, "My Perspective: Sharing the Ministry and Beauty of Adoration," Franciscan Sisters of Perpetual Adoration, fspa.org.

207 **The sisters offer a call-in prayer service:** Mary of Angels Chapel, Franciscan Sisters of Perpetual Adoration, fspa.org.

207 **For me, her apology:** Pember, "Our Ancestors Risked Their Lives and Freedom."

207 **But if the United States simply honored:** "Hundreds of Native American Treaties Digitized for First Time," *Smithsonian Magazine,* Oct. 15, 2020, smithsonianmag.com.

207 **"We'd like to have the resources":** LaBelle, telephone interview by author, Dec. 2023.

208 **"I'd cross the street to avoid her":** Ibid.

Chapter 10: Jingle Dress Healing

209 **posed like an Indian:** Shannon Vittoria, "End of the Trail, Then and Now," Metropolitan Museum of Art, Feb. 19, 2014, metmuseum.org; "Cyrus Dallin's 'Appeal to the Great Spirit,'" MFABoston, mfa.org.

212 **After the muggy heat of the day:** Daniel Hillel, "Marsh Gas: Soil in the Environment," ScienceDirect, 2008, sciencedirect.com.

213 **Joe fought in the Meuse-Argonne offensive:** "The Meuse-Argonne Offensive," Military Records, National Archives, archives.gov.

213 **Joe served in the infantry:** "Indians in the Army and Navy," WPA Indian Research Project, Chippewa Indian Historical Records, 1936–42, microfilm, envelope 16.

213 **the king of battle gases:** Gerard J. Fitzgerald, "Chemical Warfare and Medical Response During World War I," *American Journal of Public Health* 98, no. 4 (2008): 611–25.

214 **often killing days after exposure:** David Lakin, "Chemical Warfare in WWI: The Psychological Corrosion of Soldiers via Chemical Warfare and the 1925 Geneva Convention's Involvement in Eradicating Future Gaseous Afflictions," *West Virginia University Historical Review* 2, no. 1 (2021).

214 **"First wonder, then fear":** Ibid.

214 **"In more chronic cases":** Ibid.

214 **Soldiers were left to deal:** MaryCatherine McDonald, Marisa Brandt, and Robyn Bluhm, "From Shell-Shock to PTSD, a Century of Invisible War Trauma," *PBS News Hour,* Nov. 11, 2018, pbs.org.

214 **"They fought to demonstrate":** "Why We Serve: Native Americans in the

United States Armed Forces," National Museum of the American Indian, americanindian.si.edu.

214 **About 5 percent of Indian soldiers:** Ibid.

218 **He described his life:** Mark Anthony Rolo, *My Mother Is Now Earth* (St. Paul: Borealis Books, 2012).

219 **"Those sisters and priests":** Brewer, recorded interview by author, May 2022, Pine Ridge reservation.

219 **"You know, I think some of those sisters":** Deragon, recorded interview by author, March 2020, Bad River reservation.

220 **Sister Catherine remained at St. Mary's:** Franciscan Sisters of Perpetual Adoration archival document.

220 **"As a nun, I was taught":** Novitzke, interview by author, 2021, La Crosse, Wis., and phone interview by author, 2023.

225 *She most certainly did not:* Written notes, Sept. 2011, Cincinnati.

225 *My mother wasn't an easy person to love:* Written notes, Sept. 2011, Janesville, Wis.

227 **"And I rose / In rainy autumn":** Dylan Thomas, *The Collected Poems of Dylan Thomas* (New York: New Directions, 1953).

228 **"allowed me to blame":** Marylu Salawater, written interview by author, Oct. 2012, Odanah, Wis.

228 **"All of us were poor":** Written interview notes, Oct. 2012, Odanah, Wis.

228 **in 2013 all of the babies born:** Mary Annette Pember, "We Have to Know It to Heal It: Defining and Dealing with Historical Trauma," ICT News, Dec. 1, 2014, ictnews.org.

228 **eightfold higher rate:** "Neonatal Abstinence Syndrome," Minnesota Department of Health, health.state.mn.us.

228 **"What will become of our people":** Pember, "We Have to Know It to Heal It."

231 **"Mom wasn't one to dwell on the past":** Russell Spencer, written interview notes by author, June 2023, Lapwai, Idaho.

232 **"Don't take me back to Bad River":** Ibid.

232 **she'd appeased that windigo:** Uncle Russ, interview by author, June 2023, Nez Perce reservation, Wash.

232 **We all found out the hard way:** Divya Kumar, "Dear Brown Girl: Proximity-to-Whiteness Does Not Make You White," Embrace Race, embracerace.org.

233 **Indians were especially hard hit:** Leah Campbell, "Native Alaskan Villages, Once Devastated by Spanish Flu, Are Taking Action Against Covid-19," Direct Relief, May 6, 2020, directrelief.org.

234 **Scores of women in jingle dresses:** Tiffany Midge, "Thousands of Jingle Dress Dancers Appear at Standing Rock," ICT News, Sept. 7, 2016, ictnews.org.

INDEX

ABOUT THE AUTHOR

Mary Annette Pember is a citizen of the Red Cliff Band of Wisconsin Ojibwe. She is currently national correspondent for ICT News. She has also worked as an independent journalist focusing on Native American issues since 2000. Pember is the recipient of the Clarion Award, several Associated Press awards, and the Medill Milestone Achievement Award as well as Type Investigations' Ida B. Wells Fellowship, a Rosalynn Carter Fellowship for Mental Health Journalism, and the USC Annenberg National Health Journalism Fellowship. Her work has appeared in *Reveal* News, *The Atlantic*, *The New York Times*, and *The Guardian*, among other publications. Prior to beginning her writing career, she worked as a staff photojournalist and photo editor at the *Arizona Republic*, *The Oregonian*, and the *Green Bay Press-Gazette*. She currently lives with her husband and two children in Cincinnati. *Medicine River* is her first book.

A NOTE ON THE TYPE

This book was set in Sabon, a typeface designed by the well-known German typographer Jan Tschichold (1902–74). Sabon's design is based upon the original letter forms of sixteenth-century French type designer Claude Garamond and was created specifically to be used for three sources: foundry type for hand composition, Linotype, and Monotype. Tschichold named his typeface for the famous Frankfurt typefounder Jacques Sabon (c. 1520–80).

Composed by North Market Street Graphics

Designed by Jo Anne Metsch